Michael Fordham

Michael Fordham's immense contribution to analytical psychology has been marked by its combination of practical and theoretical genius. Before his retirement he ran a full clinical practice while concurrently developing the Society of Analytical Psychology and its child and adult training, co-editing the *Collected Works of C. G. Jung* and editing the *Journal of Analytical Psychology* for fifteen years. In his published work there has emerged a consistent and original contribution to Jungian thought, particularly in relation to the processes of individuation in childhood, and the links between analytical psychology and the work of the Kleinians.

In this important addition to the series *Makers of Modern Psychotherapy* James Astor takes a critical and informed look at Fordham's work and ideas. Using clinical examples to illustrate Fordham's theories, the author evaluates key developments in his work, from his first publication in 1937 right up to the present day, and shows the fundamental ways in which it develops Jung's theory in theory and practice.

Michael Fordham: Innovations in Analytical Psychology will provide a useful amplification of Fordham's own work for students of analytical psychology and a sound introduction to it for analysts interested in understanding the connections between post-Jungian and post-Kleinian thought.

James Astor is a training analyst at the Society of Analytical Psychology in London and a member of the Association of Child Psychotherapists.

The Makers of Modern Psychotherapy
Series editor: Laurence Spurling

This series of introductory, critical texts looks at the work and thought of key contributors to the development of psychodynamic psychotherapy. Each book shows how the theories examined affect clinical practice, and includes biographical material as well as a comprehensive bibliography of the contributor's work.

The field of psychodynamic psychotherapy is today more fertile but also more diverse than ever before. Competing schools have been set up, rival theories and clinical ideas circulate. These different and sometimes competing strains are held together by a canon of fundamental concepts, guiding assumptions and principles of practice.

This canon has a history, and the way we now understand and use the ideas that frame our thinking and practice is palpably marked by how they came down to us, by the temperament and experiences of their authors, the particular puzzles they wanted to solve and the contexts in which they worked. These are the makers of modern psychotherapy. Yet despite their influence, the work and life of some of these eminent figures is not well known. Others are more familiar, but their particular contribution is open to reassessment. In studying these figures and their work, this series will articulate those ideas and ways of thinking that practitioners and thinkers within the psychodynamic tradition continue to find persuasive.

Michael Fordham

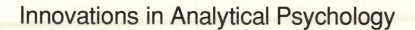

Innovations in Analytical Psychology

James Astor

London and New York

First published 1995
by Routledge
11 New Fetter Lane, London EC4P 4EE

Simultaneously published in the USA and Canada
by Routledge
29 West 35th Street, New York, NY 10001

© 1995 James Astor

Typeset in Times by LaserScript, Mitcham, Surrey
Printed and bound in Great Britain by
TJ Press (Padstow) Ltd, Padstow, Cornwall

British Library Cataloguing in Publication Data
A catalogue record for this book is available from the British Library

Library of Congress Cataloging in Publication Data
A catalogue record for this book has been requested

ISBN 0–415–09348–1 (hbk)
ISBN 0–415–09349–x (pbk)

Michael Fordham died on April 14th 1995. He read through what I wrote before he died and commented that it had the strange effect on him of my seeming to know more about him than he did himself. There is much in this book which he had forgotten about his life.

This book is dedicated to him with love and gratitude.

James Astor
23.4.95

Contents

Preface

I got to know Michael Fordham first through working with him as his course tutor when he had been the director of the child training during the last period of his active involvement in the Society of Analytical Psychology (SAP) in the 1980s. The friendship has deepened over the years, and has survived intense feelings of bewilderment, joy, anger, and love. As Fordham has grown older, and especially since his wife Frieda died (in 1988), I have become more involved in some of his writings and revisions particularly those involving his memoir (Fordham 1993e).

He has read early versions of this book but apart from correcting factual errors has not criticized the text. Others have criticized it in constructive ways, for which I am grateful and acknowledge elsewhere.

Acknowledgements

I wish to acknowledge with gratitude the permission given by the editors of the *Journal of Analytical Psychology* to quote from papers published in the *Journal*; Hodder & Stoughton for permission to quote from *Children as Individuals*; Free Association Books for permission to quote from Karl Figlio's interview with Dr Fordham in *Free Associations*, vol. 12, 1988, and from Dr Fordham's autobiographical memoir, *The Making of an Analyst*; Methuen for permission to quote from K. Lorenz, *King Solomon's Ring*; Princeton University Press for permission to quote from *C. G. Jung Speaking* and the *Collected Works of C. G. Jung*; Dr J. Marvin Spiegelman for permission to quote from *Jungian Analysts: Their Visions and Vulnerabilities*; Heinemann for permission to quote from *The Self and Autism*; Academic Press for permission to quote from *Explorations into the Self*; and *Chiron* for permission to quote from 'Abandonment in Infancy'.

Sonu Shamdasani drew my attention to correspondence and notes of Dr Fordham's which he had found in his files; in particular he suggested using the transcripts of the discussions on analysis and transference as an appendix. For the complete bibliography of Fordham's work I am indebted to Dr Roger Hobdell who generously made it available to me. To Karl Figlio who read the first two drafts and made many helpful suggestions and to Judith Hubback who read the penultimate draft I give special thanks. Laurence Spurling has made valuable suggestions, and given me a perspective on material that I sometimes could not see the significance of. Many others have helped too and if I have not named them it was because that was what they wanted; if it wasn't then please forgive me. Finally, I am especially grateful to Michael Fordham, for without his support I would not have had the enjoyment and interest I have had in doing this work.

Prologue

JUNG AND FREUD

For six intense years, between 1907 and 1913, Freud and Jung corresponded, shared ideas, discussed their clinical work, their dreams and interpretations, patients, theories and the evolution of their therapeutic methods. It was a true collaboration, in which each of these great men needed the other, but for different reasons. Jung was thrilled by psychoanalysis when he discovered it, and Freud was impatient for wider recognition and acceptance. His need for Jung was in part political. Freud's ideas were known in the psychiatric profession but they comprised only one of many competing theories. Jung had an international reputation as a psychiatrist. His researches into word associations had been well received. They gave empirical support to his theory of the complex, an unconscious constellation of factors contributing to the patient's psycho-neurosis. During this friendship and collaboration psychoanalysis took off in a way which, until recently, has made it the dominant theory for the dynamic treatment of psychological problems, such that when Freud died in 1939 W.H. Auden was to write, in his eulogy, that psychoanalysis was 'a whole climate of opinion'.

The history of Jung and Freud's relationship has been written about by numerous authors. In addition much of their correspondence has been published (*The Freud–Jung Letters* 1974). There are still many papers which have not been released by both families thereby ensuring that the history of their relationship will continue to be examined as more evidence comes to light. The usual way the story is told is that Freud had the insights; he attracted people, who came to him for a while but, finding they had reservations about his ideas, then went off to found their own schools. This view shows the continuing influence of the 'Freudian' interpretation of the history of the movement. In a recent book, however, based in part on the papers of Sabina Spielrein, John Kerr has cogently argued that 'Freud in effect presented himself to Jung and Bleuler as a scientific asset to be acquired' (Kerr 1994, p. 9). Kerr gives a detailed account of how Freud needed Jung and Bleuler and their prestige to move his psychoanalysis into an institutional framework. Kerr writes:

> At the time [the early 1900s] the people who mattered were Jung and his Zurich mentor, Eugen Bleuler, not Freud. Jung and Bleuler already possessed international reputations as pioneering psychiatrists. Moreover, they had the prestige of the Zurich medical school behind them and they commanded the Zurich Psychiatric Clinic with its attached psychological laboratory, where interested physicians could receive training. In short, it was Jung and Bleuler who possessed the institutional resources needed to turn psychoanalysis into a scientific movement. The rise of psychoanalysis directly reflected these institutional realities.
>
> (Kerr 1994, p. 9)

Kerr goes on to point out that the centre for the institutional development of psychoanalysis was Zurich, where the first congress was held, the journal was published, and the international association organized. When Freud and Jung went their separate ways both rewrote the early history of their collaboration, especially as it concerned the evolution of their ideas and the influences which gave rise to them.

> The story is both complex and disturbing. Of all its manifold dimensions, perhaps the most important has been the hardest to conceptualise: the relation between the personal factor and the theoretical struggle that arose out of it and ultimately supplanted it.
>
> (Ibid., p. 10)

What led to the break-up is not easily summarized. Essentially Freud and Jung disagreed about the nature of psychic energy: Freud considered that it was sexual, Jung that it was neutral. They differed in their attitude to dreams: Freud sought for a correct interpretation which was ultimately reductive; Jung thought their manifest and prospective meanings needed emphasis more often. Jung thought of the Oedipus complex as a symbol of a complicated internal process of development whereby the young man struggled to free himself of his mother. Freud saw the Oedipus complex as rooted in instinctual incestuous wishes. Freud thought of dementia praecox as originating from auto-erotism, Jung from introversion of libido. Jung was interested in hermeneutics, Freud in devising a manual showing how to interpret material and what symbols 'meant'. The differences between them were fundamental and characterlogical. Jung was introverted, from a Calvinist background; Freud was extroverted, from a Jewish background. Jung was more unstable than Freud. He was also better able to enter into the world of his psychotic patients. Freud was the founder of psychoanalysis; in Kerr's phrase, 'the artist who wanted to paint the picture after his own style', while insisting psychoanalysis was a science and that he was adhering to empirical truths. Jung was interested in alchemy as a precursor to psychology, in myths, religions and their symbols and the evidence for features within the personalities of all peoples across time which were archetypal. Every culture has religions, wise old men, prophets, witches, heroes, myths and rebirth stories. These impersonal features of the personality fascinated Jung and he wrote and thought about them in relation to the self and the lifelong task of becoming oneself which he called individuation. Reading his memoirs it is clear that it took him many years to understand how fundamental all of this was to his break with Freud (Jung 1963).

I could make a long list of their differences, many of which were present from the first. Ostensibly the break arose from Jung developing his own ideas which were not acceptable to Freud. Jung felt constrained by having to subscribe to all of Freud's ideas if he were to remain part of the psychoanalytic movement. Freud felt Jung's ideas were evidence of disloyalty. But perhaps just as important to our understanding of their break is that when Freud lost his trust in Jung he thought Jung would use his position as president of the international association to take over psychoanalysis and make his views the dominant ones. Freud as an extrovert was looking to the real world, Jung as an introvert turned to his dreams and visionary (hallucinatory) experiences. In fact Jung's response to the breakdown of their friendship was intensely introverted and he became very distressed, and for a period he felt he was needing all his resources to prevent himself from having a complete psychotic breakdown. Freud's response was to organize a secret committee whose 'sole purpose was to guard against future deviations from Freud's view' (Kerr 1994, p. 452). 'Whatever position Jung took would be drowned by a flood of counter publications' (ibid., p. 453). Tactically Freud's aim was to isolate the Zurich group and to get them to resign from the international association. This he succeeded in doing, the last straw being the publication of his *On the History of the Psychoanalytic Movement* (Freud, *SE* 14) which skilfully marginalized, omitted or diminished any contribution to psychoanalysis which was not part of

Freudian orthodoxy. That the Zurich group had to be marginalized remained a feature of the politics of psychoanalysis, wherever it was exported and wherever trainings were established. London, Freud's home in exile for his last years, was no exception. This was the professional climate in which Fordham began his work: a climate in which psychoanalysts, trained at the Institute of Psycho-Analysis, as a matter of loyalty to Freud did not read Jung.

FORDHAM, JUNG AND FREUD

Fordham in personality type is more like Jung. But his love of analysis and interest in the development of the mind has not been restricted by the disagreement of the pioneers. He has always been 'Jungian' in his immersion in and understanding of Jung's ideas. But if, as has been the case, psychoanalysts have concentrated on different areas of work from analytical psychologists, then he has studied their work as part of his education, especially if he has been wanting to work out a 'Jungian' contribution to the field. This has been so whether he has been writing about countertransference, which was a particular interest of Jung's, or infant development, which Jung largely ignored. It is important to be clear that Fordham has organized his theorizing within Jung's model of the psyche, modifying the model when the data did not fit. His borrowings from psychoanalysis have been initially Klein's method of child analysis (but not her theory), which in the 1930s was revolutionary, particularly in its understanding that a child's play was an expression of the child's unconscious phantasy. She gave him the courage to talk directly to children about their unconscious feelings. And he recognized very quickly that Klein's unconscious phantasy was equiva- lent to Jung's descriptions of archetypal experience. Similarly, his important work on transference and countertransference started from an overview of Jung's which he then worked on in more detail. His most recent work on unconscious communication between patient and analyst has concentrated on the 'Jungian' understanding of projective identification. This has involved comparing Freud's and Jung's views on the importance of identification in the growth of the personality, and the discussion of Jung's ideas about containment, empathy and *participation mystique*. His innovative researches into childhood have given a genetic basis to Jung's ideas about the importance of the self as both an organizing centre and the thing being organized within the personality. He has connected it both to Jung's work on the self in the second half of life and to emotional development as described by Kleinian psychoanalysts (the depressive position) while making clear what is distinctive about his 'Jungian model'.

To some Jungians in the early days of his work this was taken to mean that Fordham could seem to be putting 'Freudian' ideas into 'Jungian' psychology, where 'Freudian' meant psychosexual and 'Jungian' meant concentrating on the image in a more disembodied fashion. Carl Meier, a distinguished student of Jung's and a professor of psychology, has referred to Fordham as 'carrying the Jungian shadow', a phrase which gives archetypal significance to the resistance Fordham has encountered. The contemporary manner in which Fordham's work has been marginalized by some Jungians who find his embodied interpretative style difficult to apply is to refer to the child in the adult as just one of the archetypal images. This then allows them to offer alternative interpretations which include all the peripheral factors present while avoiding the infantile core of the transference. This problem of avoiding the core is not particular to Jungian psychology as, for instance, is revealed in contemporary psychoanalytic clinical studies such as Steiner's 'psychic retreats', which shows how patients can embroil their analysts in a subtle collusion in order to avoid painful truths (Steiner 1993).

FORDHAM'S SIGNIFICANCE

If, in our western industrialized society, we have modified the 'Rights of Man' from the right to the pursuit of happiness to the right to be happy, in so doing we have lost sight of, in my view, the curious paradox inherent in our society which accompanies this modification. Because of the emphasis on the right to be happy, supported as it is by the misuse of analytic knowledge, parents now feel that everything which goes wrong with their children is their fault. But the social perspective, as reflected in the attitude that it is a right to be happy, demands of the state, not the individual, a cure for all ills. It is as if we misunderstand psychoanalytic knowledge and blame our parents for everything that goes wrong while asking the state, like parents, to make everything right.

Michael Fordham, who has lived through these developments, has a distinctive voice which has always, following Jung, asserted the responsibility of the individual for their own destiny. Fordham's pioneering work has led to a conceptual and biologically based exposition of this fundamental truth that is biological but not biochemical. He has gradually worked out from his experience a revolutionary concept of the infant–parent relationship which has at its core the idea that it is not so much the parents who create the child as the interaction of parents and children which creates both. His work has been inspired by Jung but he has not been a 'Jungian', recognizing the truth of Jung's statement that he, Jung, was the only Jungian. What this has meant is that when Fordham has been studying Jung's work and has identified an ambiguity, he has relied on the clinical evidence to guide him and not, as so often happens, asserted that his view is the right one because it is what the master really meant, thereby introducing a moral element into the argument. The schismatic tendencies in the analytic world have been fostered by devoted pupils of the great masters claiming their interpretation is the right one. Fordham has eschewed this approach and in so doing stayed closer to the original spirit of his inspiration – Jung. He has avoided cabbalas and cults of personality. This book concentrates on his clinical contribution and not on his political and editorial achievements, which I shall briefly describe below.

In the first place, as well as being a clinician Fordham has played a leading part in the setting up of the Society of Analytical Psychology (SAP); and in this respect he has been quite different from Jung. He has been influential in devising the content and requirements of the trainings in child and adult analysis and has been director of both trainings. The Society was the first to offer a training in Jungian analysis; and Jung himself was its first president. And when in its later development the Society got into difficulties, with some members feeling that the direction it was taking was not in the mainstream of Jung's interests, Fordham returned to a prominent position and steered the Society out of what might have been a destructive impasse. It was resolved by a small group leaving it and founding an alternative Jungian association. In the 1930s there was a handful of clinicians in England influenced by Jung's ideas. Within nine years of starting the society it had grown to forty members trained in Jungian analysis, twenty-two of whom were doctors, and it had representatives in ten hospitals, three psychiatric clinics, and four child guidance clinics. Today the SAP has 140 members (40 trainees) and is a thriving teaching and training organization. Historically what has been significant about Fordham's influence has been his focus on trying to find out and understand what is happening when two people come together for analytical interviews, which was one of Jung's major contributions to the work. The early years of the Society involved him in frequent meetings during which he was actively trying to work out in discussion groups what was going on between patient and analyst. Some of these discussions might seem a little naive now, but were important then and reveal a playful and lively work-group atmosphere (see Appendix).

Secondly, while building up the Society in the post-war period, Fordham, through the forum of the British Psychological Society's Medical Section, was disseminating Jung's ideas, making them known to a wide group of clinicians, who for the most part were not familiar with Jung's work – or, when it became available in English, did not read it for political reasons (loyalty to Freud). In practice this has meant that he has, in return, been open to the work of other analysts in the British object-relations school. This forum was valuable in that the alternating Jungian and Freudian chairmen ensured that Jung's ideas were being given equal status. Fordham was always aware of the need for the smaller number of Jungians to have positions in hospitals so that their influence could extend to teaching and training within the National Health Service as it then was. The position in England for the Jungians was the reverse of the position in Europe in the early 1900s when Freud needed Jung in order to obtain an institutional base. Now the Jungians needed to get into the institutions in order to have a base to make known Jungian ideas.

His third major contribution to the dissemination of analytical thought has been editorial, as one of the editors of the *Collected Works* of C.G. Jung. He set out the shape of the *Collected Works*, proposing which papers should be grouped together to form which books and what the sequence of publication should be. He was involved in the first publications, later ceding this executive role to William McGuire. Reading through his correspondence with Jung, I was made aware not only of how thorough a grasp he had of Jung's work but also how much he set his seal on the detail of the editorial task, not just seeking clarification from Jung about content and meaning, translation and punctuation, but also as in, for instance, the synchronicity paper, seeking advice from statisticians. In consequence, with that particular paper he made detailed proposals to Jung as to how it could be revised to improve it – proposals which in the main were accepted by Jung. Jung's writing is difficult to read because he digresses frequently from his stated theme, almost as if he cannot resist his own associations. Fordham from my reading of the correspondence about editorial matters was consistently the editor who resisted attempts to tidy up Jung's work. This was because he felt to do so would violate the spirit of it. Fordham was also the inspiration behind the *Journal of Analytical Psychology* (*JAP*), and its first editor, a position he held for fifteen years, establishing a tradition of scientific rigour, which for most of its subsequent life it has maintained. In addition, he has written numerous books and articles on analytical psychology and a memoir (see bibliography).

He has been quite unlike Jung who did not want to establish trainings and societies and who said on one occasion while attending a meeting in Zurich of analysts interested in his ideas, 'Thank God I am not a Jungian!' Fordham's is a very strong personality, and he enjoys the emotionality of vigorous discussion. Part of the difficulty in untangling the significance of the influence he has had is that when he has disagreed with colleagues over the years it is not yet clear whether the issues were mainly theoretical or personal. The picture is also clouded by the fact that Fordham analysed some of those who later fell out with him. It is difficult to discern how much of the opposition he has stirred up has been to do with envy, or unanalysed transference arising from the special circumstances which ended the analysis, such as when a patient's physical illness led to the analysis stopping. Time will tell how significant Fordham's contribution has been to analytical psychology. What is abundantly clear now is that he has been the leader in establishing a high-quality Jungian organization for training analysts, that he has been creative and innovative as an analyst and is one of very few Jungian analysts to have an international reputation. His legacy is not just establishing two trainings, one for child analysis and one for adult analysis, and leaving a thriving society and many loyal and grateful colleagues and his own published work; there is also his impact on his patients' lives and his seeing into print Jung's *Collected Works*.

To many of us he has given us our work, shown us where to look and how to think about what we are looking at. Many tributes to him have been published. Some, like Donald Meltzer's (Meltzer 1986a), have compared him with Freud, Klein and Bion, but distinguished him from them in his capacity to combine pioneering clinical work with wearing the mantle of office, of running the Society, fostering the trainees and being neither inflated nor destroyed by the spoilers great men attract. Rosemary Gordon has written:

> It is Michael Fordham's particular, unique and important contribution that he has used his experience with children in order to underpin and to trace the roots of those processes that Jung had pointed to through his seminal concepts, the self and individuation. . . . Jung had been absorbed by the study of people who had arrived in the second half of life. The contribution that Michael Fordham, as a child psychiatrist and child analyst, has been able to make to analytical psychology has been an essential addition and an essential reinforcement of Jung's original formulations. . . . It has given strength, solidity, and authenticity to Jung's work.
>
> (Gordon 1986, p. 229)

For me the traditional Jungian style of analysis has treated mythology almost as metapsychology, looking to myths to illustrate behaviour. Fordham has reversed this tradition and used his clinical work with people to illuminate our contemporary myths. By turning it this way round, without renouncing altogether the use of myths to elucidate clinical material, he has not only done Jungian analysis a great service but he has also provided a clinical base for the myths themselves, grounded them and thereby stopped them floating away as if they were but fragments of an analysis drifting in a magical world.

Chapter 1

Thinking into feeling
The person

INTRODUCTION

The most remarkable characteristic of Michael Fordham is his capacity to think into feelings, to be affected by his experiences and gradually begin to find meaning in them, especially in the pain. Feelings represent our experience and to be able to think about the meaning of feelings is to take the first step on the road to conceptualizing experience, something which Fordham is particularly gifted at (see Hubback 1986a, b).

This quality of thinking into feeling has developed in him slowly over the years. As a child and adolescent he could use his thinking as an armour against loss and depression. To think, and struggle to know and understand, provided a structure which was reliable when the external world was unpredictable and unreliable. He was the youngest of three children and the naughtiest. He feared his naughtiness damaged his mother, who was delicate and suffered from asthma, and when he was fifteen she died from an asthma attack on a family holiday. This devastated him. He loved her deeply and from the account he gives in his memoir he did not truly mourn her. He became for a short while physically ill, somatizing his loss of his mother in an effort to internalize her and experiencing a feeling of her being there during the illness (Fordham 1993e), a feeling which was to return when he fell in love. He switched off his feelings of loss, and became a rather truculent schoolboy whose performance was uneven. Academically he was able to learn but was unteachable if he was not interested in the subject. His prowess at games made him something of a star, playing cricket, rugby and captaining the hockey team for the school. He also regularly acted in the school play. These activities gave him prominence and position in the school and helped him stabilize himself after his mother's death. He was a success but it felt unsatisfactory, and it lacked the authenticity for him to feel identified with the school ethos. He never became an 'old boy'.

Because of his forceful intelligence and ability to hold on to thoughts and to think while under pressure he could seem to the naive onlooker to be an unfeeling man. Nothing could be further from the truth. He feels deeply but does not deal in raw emotion, nor in confessional revelation. He has learnt from his experience to digest his feelings and the most important person in facilitating this process, after his mother, was Frieda, his wife for almost fifty years, who died in 1988. Judith Hubback, a senior training analyst of the Society of Analytical Psychology, wrote:

> Michael speaks of how Frieda's way of offering comments through-out the years has had a profound influence on him. He describes her as his 'supervisor' to whom he regularly entrusted clinical material; her responsive and wise judgement was evidently invaluable, given much less in the form of expounded theories or views or opinions, but rather – he stresses this – as stable comments.
>
> (Hubback 1986b, p. 245)

Her containing qualities provided the contemporary base from which he went out into the world. Her infirmity and gradual withdrawal from him towards the end of her life affected him profoundly in ways he has described in his memoir, some of which induced conflicts which brought him near to death (Fordham 1993e).

FAMILY

The Fordhams are a Hertfordshire family, landowners, and in the past they were active in local politics. Michael has a sense of himself, vested in part in a sense of place; he was told as he was growing up that his family owned all the land round their family house, as far as the eye could see. This, combined with the local importance of his relations – one of his uncles reached national and historical prominence inventing the science of cartobibliography, and being knighted for political services – gave him, he claims, a confidence which stems from knowing quality when he sees it. Almost as if this is innate to the breed, he's a Fordham 'bred in the bone'. There is a social (and snobbish) element to this: social in the sense of his deriving a sense of himself from an early experience of not having to 'prove' he was 'someone'. It was sufficient to be a Fordham, he felt, and in so feeling he identified himself with the family's arrogance.

Michael was born in 1905. He passionately loved his mother, and in the drawing he has of her she looks beautiful and serene. She was from a respected Manchester family, which was 'tainted' by an unconventional interest in the arts. She trained to become an opera singer. (At the end of the nineteenth century to allow one's daughter to train as a singer was a social risk bordering on the disreputable.) But she never had a career as a singer. In my view his wanting to understand what happened to his mother has been an important unconscious stimulus in his life. How could so much beauty have so much destructive asthmatic suffocation inside? In this book I do not emphasize the destructive aspects of the self because this has not been Fordham's special contribution, but that is not to say that this aspect of the self has not informed his work. It is noticeable in his writings on autism and psychosis and is an essential constituent of his understanding of his own life in his memoir. In fact his preference for Klein over Winnicott has been because Klein confronted the destructiveness of human beings and did not place too much optimistic reliance on the goodness of mothers, which is what Fordham feels Winnicott did. Nowadays the analytic landscape is often compared, since Klein's work, with the child's perception of the interior of the mother's body and much of Fordham's analytic work has involved the investigation of the internal chambers of the mother's body for the emotional significance of their contents (see Meltzer [1992] for a full description of the conceptualization of these projective states). This task has deepened his understanding of the self.

His father was active in local politics in Birmingham but sometime after he married he moved first to London then to the country for his wife's health. There he followed his interests in agriculture, about which he wrote books. He had other interests too and lived the life of a gentleman. He was particularly interested in the Arts and Craft Movement and writers were his friends. Galsworthy was Michael's godfather. But his father was not the eldest son, so did not inherit the properties, and towards the end of his life he ran out of money. It is possible that his death was suicide; he was killed by a train at a notoriously dangerous level crossing.

His father was devoted to his mother and her death was a great blow to him. Family life effectively came to an end after her death. From then on Michael had no real home until he married. And while his father was in the background if his son needed him, he mostly left him to get on with his life. Fordham's account of his good feelings for his father's reliability and the facts of his father being unable to sustain a family life for his sons and daughter when his wife died could seem to be a contradiction, if looked at from the point of view of thinking about how a father ought to be. But it seems, in talking to Fordham about this now, that what dominated this period of his and his father's lives were the feelings of devastation arising from his mother's death, devastation that had had as great an impact on his father as on him.

Michael became a doctor. His older brother suggested it to him because he thought it would be interesting to have one in the family, and Michael was good at biology, maths and, later, physiology. His ambition at school had been to go into the navy, but although he was short-listed to the last thirty for officer training, he failed the written exam. Medicine was an unusual choice, since in his family doctors were not shown to the front door: they had to come round to the side door, because it was regarded as shameful to be ill. He went to Cambridge and read natural sciences before qualifying in medicine at St Bartholomew's Hospital medical school.

In 1928 he married Molly Swabey (Fordham 1993e, p. 53). Molly was trying to establish herself as a journalist and Fordham was an impoverished medical student. They lived in a small flat in Bloomsbury and when Fordham eventually qualified in medicine they had a small house near his work in Epsom. Their son Max was born in 1933. During this period of his life Fordham was developing his interests in Jung and as soon as he could he moved back to London and a fellowship in child psychiatry at the London Child Guidance Clinic. The marriage to Molly was unsettled, both partners according to Fordham feeling restless. An additional symptomatic complication of this restlessness was that another woman fell in love with Fordham and he let the relationship develop. Baynes, his analyst, unfortunately treated this as an instance of Fordham needing to understand his anima, the female side of his personality, and encouraged the liaison (Fordham 1993e, p. 67). The marriage deteriorated, and both of them had affairs.

> Today it is quite usual for couples to marry when they are still students or for the wife to be the wage earner. This was the state of affairs in our marriage at first, and at this period we would both have needed to develop and deepen the meaning of the marriage for it to survive. Molly wanted to and went into analysis, but it was not enough, while my analysis had not helped me in that part of my development. As a result of that situation my identity as a man became disturbed and the attempt to correct it led to quarrels. I do not want to give the impression that my first marriage was not valuable;

indeed there was much in it that was rich and productive, Max being its culmination. It also led to each of us establishing ourselves professionally.

(Fordham 1993e, p. 75)

At this time (1934) Fordham met Frieda Hoyle with whom he fell in love. Out of guilt he tried to separate from her, although this did not work. Molly and he were divorced in 1940 and he married Frieda later that year. She had two sons from her first marriage. The war had begun so Molly took Max to stay with her brother in the Caribbean to avoid the bombs in London. He settled in well there and she decided to return to England to remarry. While crossing the Atlantic in 1942 her boat was sunk and she was drowned. Max today is married with children and is successful in his work as an engineer for which he was recently awarded an OBE. In addition he has a professorship at Bath University, and is an Honorary Fellow of the RIBA.

Michael Fordham never planned his life or career. Nor did he suffer from ambition. He turned down a consultant's post in the health service in the early years of his medical career, a post which in his words would have 'made' him (Fordham 1993e). But if he was asked to run some-thing and he liked the idea he'd do it. He thought there was more potential in analytical psychology than in running a clinic. The posts he refused nearly always involved too much time spent doing what he did not want to do. He wanted to lead a full good life, to be useful and creative. Both his father and Jung had a sense of social responsibility. Michael did too, but what frequently happened to him was that others had a high opinion of him, seeing in him qualities he was not confident of in himself. Part of his struggle therefore has been to discover his own talents, talents which felt authentic to him.

He had a driven quality once he found something to be interested in. It might have been scientific research but it turned out to be analytical psychology, almost fortuitously. He first met Jung when Baynes suggested he went to see Jung with a view to training in Zurich (ibid., p. 67). The aura surrounding this first meeting was in part created by the young doctor's awed feelings for this pioneer and apostate of psychoanalysis, who had developed his own system. Remembering it later Fordham mentioned in his memoir the setting by the lake of Jung's house and how this had a magic to it too, which contributed to the numinousness of the occasion. It was then that his anima fell in love with Jung (ibid., p. 69), a love which was similar to his love for his father (ibid., p. 113).

THE ANALYST

The connection between Fordham's thinking about and into feelings and his interest in the self began with his reaction to the loss of his mother, and flowered in the development of his scientific attitude to himself which was fostered in his first analysis, with Godwin Baynes (Fordham 1993e). This analysis was conducted without reference to the transference and while it was of limited value it did free up his unconscious and allow him to be more open in his attitudes to his own states of mind. At first this interest was predominantly intellectual, but gradually it became more integrated into his feeling. Jung's work on the self began to take its distinctive shape after his break from Freud, an event characterized by Satinover (1985) as the loss for Jung of a good object. In similar fashion Fordham's researches were stimulated by his interest in feelings of loss. Fordham's discovery of the importance of the self, which emerged out of a conscious decision to investigate childhood, took him by surprise. He did not expect to find symbols of the self in childhood. When he did, it was as if it was almost making retrospective sense of his own survival, which is how in his memoir he describes it. The ego may fragment, even disintegrate, but the self is indestructible, except by death. His subsequent championing of the self in childhood could be seen as a way of countering the deterministic, almost fatalistic bias which had crept into the popular consciousness with the arrival of psychoanalysis – namely, that if parents were at fault, as Jung originally thought, then without the self what chance did the individual have to free himself from the determinism of his childhood? Fordham's sustained investigation of this in his work began when he met Frieda Hoyle although his interest in the self began when sitting on his mother's knee when he had 'the first intimation that the self was important, as something greater than me, yet of whom I am a part' (Fordham 1993e, p. vi).

Just as the little boy's awareness needed the possession and relative safety of his mother's lap underneath him for the acknowledgement of the transcendent quality of his self, so too did Fordham's later work on the self have underpinning it his marriage to Frieda. This long, stable marriage (forty-eight years) was the most productive period of his life. When he felt safe emotionally this gave a greater depth and continuity of focus to his work. It was to her too that he took the rough drafts of his books and papers, and it was she who helped him turn them into readable English.

THE AUTHOR

Fordham's weakest subject at school was English and yet he has spent a lot of his professional life writing. Sometimes he has been consciously filling in the gaps left by Jung. His work on the biological basis of archetypes, on ego development, or on countertransference are examples of where Jung either had not filled in the picture, or had only sketched an outline which needed elaboration. Similarly he deliberately looked for an autistic child patient to analyse in order to test out certain ideas he had which derived from his study of Jung's work. This was in the context of his continuing investigations of childhood and his initially tentative revisions of Jung's view of individuation to include the beginnings of ego development in childhood. Being asked to write about abandonment for an American conference led to one of his most important papers (Fordham 1985b) which brought together his ideas about the self and his experience of infant observation. It further helped him to describe where he differed from Kleinian child analysts. Students asking him about Neumann detonated out of him the powerful paper he wrote on Neumann and childhood (Fordham 1981a). Often the analysis of a particular patient stimulated him to write about their work together, usually in an effort to make more sense for himself of what was happening, or had happened. His papers on transference and interaction and his much quoted paper on the defences of the self (Fordham 1974f) emerged in this way.

Another stimulus for his written work was the discussions within the Society of Analytical Psychology. For instance, when issues to do with training were being aired it often led to his setting out his views in a paper which might first have been given at one of the Society's scientific meetings. Papers on training analysis, supervision and transference come within this category. Retrospectively I have ordered this work to give the impression of a succession, one idea, thought or concept following on from the last. This does not correspond to Fordham's experience of his own life and work. When I wrote a preliminary paper on one aspect of his work entitled *The Emergence of Fordham's Model of Development* (Astor 1990), his response to it was that he did not realize that this was what he had done.

BEGINNINGS

In writing about Fordham's work I have not linked particular developments or changes in his ideas to his personal life, except in a general way. This is in part because he does not himself connect the evolution of his ideas to chronological time. What he was thinking or feeling at particular points in his life he has described in his memoir. There was the period before the Second World War when he was discovering Jung, working in psychiatry and beginning his interest in analysis. Then during the war years he was a consultant for evacuated children living in hostels in the Midlands. He was active among the Jungians in England during that time but they all felt very cut off from Jung himself. Meanwhile he was collecting the material which was to form his first book *The Life of Childhood* (1944). The rise of the Nazis, however, did bring refugees to the UK who had been trained by Jung, and some were later to gather round Fordham to form the Society of Analytical Psychology. After the war he came to live in London and worked in private practice and the child guidance clinic of the West End Hospital for Nervous Diseases, which was to become better known later as the Paddington Clinic. This period in London coincided with his being asked to help start the Society of Analytical Psychology. Prior to that, Jungians who were interested in Jung's ideas met at the Analytical Psychology Club, and those who were in practice met in a group organized by Godwin Baynes. The establishment of an organization for the training of analysts marked the beginning of the professionalization of analytical psychology (see Samuels 1994).

Fordham and others wished to create a training in London which was independent of Zurich where up to then those wanting to become Jungian analysts had to go for analysis and seminars. Jung was not particularly helpful about this training as he thought that becoming an analyst was a vocation, which had to be supported by a personal analysis and the study of mythology. (The Zurich Institute was started by his pupils, not by him.) Becoming an analyst was not something, he thought, you could be trained to do. From the beginning of the Society fundamental questions about group and personal identity formed part of the conflicts within it. Fordham was firmly against a cult of personality and stressed Jung's empiricism. He was director of training for many years and he also served as chairman of the professional committee and on two occasions he was chairman of the Society. Initially it was the adult training which he focused on and before long the Society was attracting good candidates from professional backgrounds in medicine, social work, religion and teaching. He saw himself as promoting the ideas of Jung and through the respect he earned from his colleagues he did much to counter the hostility and nastiness which was directed towards Jung by psychoanalysts (Fordham 1993e, p. 98). This hostility came from those who felt Jung had been sympathetic to the Nazis, as well as from those who still saw Jung as a heretic (Fordham 1993e, pp. 97–9; Gallard 1994). Loyalty was an important issue in these early days of the Society, especially in regard to identity, and he notes later on, when discussing whether members might go to psychoanalysts for supervision of cases of which psychoanalysts had had more experience than analytical psychologists, that this was a difficult and touchy point. He commented: 'Oh it's much easier to have a sense of identity if you have an opponent' (Figlio 1988). It is significant that when the Society started, very few of Jung's works were available in English and this state of affairs continued for some time. In addition, much of Jung's later work is less concerned with the applied aspects of analysis and the personal details of patient–analyst interaction and rather more with cultural and educational features of analytical psychology, so trainees found themselves of necessity reading psychoanalytic clinical studies.

Within the Society considerable tensions existed between those members who had trained in Zurich and those who came from a training in medicine and psychiatry in England. The Zurich members found themselves in conflict with the professional committee about the requirement that they should report on their candidates' analyses. This led the professional committee to interview potential trainees. Fordham wrote years later:

> These interviews showed up some alarming features: one candidate had no idea how to elicit a homosexual transference, another became offended when her patient showed signs of a negative transference. This investigation made me, but not others, feel that the Zurich analysts had acquired a quite unjustified prestige, and I was not at all sorry when they showed signs of such serious discontent that they might leave and form a new training on their own.
>
> (Fordham 1993e, p. 134)

This discontent, however, was contained for more than thirty years, by which time the Society was the largest Jungian training group in the world. One of the most prominent who did eventually leave to form his own group in the mid-1970s was Gerhard Adler. Although he retained his membership of the SAP, Fordham thought that the members of his group 'were in serious danger of forming a Jungian creed which Jung himself would have abhorred' (ibid., p. 135). There were other issues here as well in that Adler was overshadowed by Fordham and the two men were not friends (ibid., p. 110). More importantly, Adler had wanted in the early days of the SAP to make the professional committee into an oligarchy, which Fordham strongly resisted (ibid., p. 134). This issue of Adler wanting to have power came up again in the new small group he formed, the Association of Jungian Analysts, such that it, too, soon split into two, with half the members creating yet another small Jungian Institute (A. Casement, personal communication). Fordham was aware that he 'had defects as a Jungian' since he had not studied in Zurich and the nebulous accusation was made that he 'did not have the true Jungian spirit' (Fordham 1993e, pp. 94–5). This notwithstanding, he had been chosen by Jung to co-edit his *Collected Works*. Later Adler was added as another co-editor at Jung's request and his role as Jung explained in a letter to Fordham was principally to check the German translations, since Fordham did not speak German. The criticism made against Fordham has been that he has been 'too psychoanalytic' in his encouragement of the Jungian analytic community to pay attention to the childlike intensity of unconscious affects in the analysis of adults and the need to analyse their embodied quality. (Jung himself, however, valued this approach and praised Fordham's work on transference.) Fordham's answer to this criticism was, and is, that Jung employed different methods depending on the needs of his patients and that the essential constituents of transference feelings are infantile. As a leader Fordham had the task of establishing a Jungian training against a background of battles on all sides, within the Society against the Zurich group (who were reluctant to discuss the detail of patient–analyst interactions), and outside the Society in relation to the psychoanalysts who were denigrating Jung. Within the Society he also had to fight in support of those who wanted to make use of psychoanalytic knowledge without being tainted with disloyalty.

During this period, the 1950s and 1960s, Fordham was also busy editing the *Collected Works* and, from 1955, the *Journal of Analytical Psychology*. The *Collected Works* took much longer than he expected and while it was a labour of love which he said nearly 'drove me mad' (Figlio 1988) it ensured his place in the sun. His hospital work brought him into contact with psychoanalysts, as did his involvement with the Royal Medico-Psychological Society, the precursor of the Royal College of Psychiatrists. He was also active in the Medical Section of the British Psychological Society, an important forum for the exchange of ideas between psychoanalysts and analytical psychologists. Although there was interest in Fordham's ideas about children within the Society it took nearly thirty years before a training in child analysis was started there.

THE INFLUENCE OF KLEIN'S METHOD OF CHILD ANALYSIS

When first working with children Fordham found Klein's technique very helpful and her descriptions of unconscious phantasy close to Jung's description of archetypal images. Klein's work in the 1940s showed him a way to talk to children which would make their unconscious conflicts accessible to analysis. Fordham, reminiscing in his memoirs about the influence of Klein on his thinking in the 1940s, said:

> I read *The Psychoanalysis of Children* with amazement and emotional shock. What she described made sense of much of my material, although not the more dramatic archetypal dreams and pictures, which I find puzzling even today because I am not convinced by Jung's explanation. Be that as it may, I applied as much of Klein as I could digest and found that my relation to children improved, sometimes quite dramatically. What impressed me with Klein's work? First of all her daring in listening to, and taking seriously, what children said and her use of play as a means of communication. Then there was her acute perception as to the meaning of their activities in relation to herself. There was also her understanding of children's fantasies as basic in their development, which was a contention of Jung's, found particularly in his *Psychology of the Unconscious*. More specifically, I discovered analogies between what Jung found in myths and what Klein found in small children's fantasies about their mothers' bodies. Most impressive of all was the way in which she interpreted unconscious processes in the child in terms which were appropriate to childhood. She was also very clear that children developed a transference. In this early period of my development I was becoming increasingly impressed with the importance of transference and critical of my analyst's handling of it in my own case and in others. I had found that children formed one and I thought Klein was correct.
>
> (Fordham 1993e, pp. 65–6)

But he was not and never has been 'Kleinian' as some of his detractors have claimed. He said in an interview with Karl Figlio about the early influences on his work:

> I collected all the material I could, paintings and dreams and fantasies, and gradually developed a treatment technique. I was pursuing my own line of discovery all the time. I didn't go along with Melanie

Klein's more abstract statements and I did not make personal contact. It was her practice and her discoveries about children that impressed me.

(Figlio 1988, p. 18)

He did not go along with her dual-instinct theory because his biological training had led him to think of instincts being in the service of adaptation and survival, not death. Furthermore he was able to absorb only some of her work. This was because 'She was emotionally far too dangerous' to himself (Figlio 1988). He did not want to get pulled into her way of thinking. He wanted to make use of her direct way of talking to children. When he was asked years later why he did not go to Kleinians for supervision of his work when he was starting to analyse children, and Kleinians were in the forefront of analytic work with children, he replied:

> The answer is that it's a matter of loyalty. You see, this was a Jungian Society and if you are heading that society you cannot go over to someone else; you must not be tainted. If I'm doing all this for the Jungians, I stick to that and I think it is partly loyalty to Jung, but it's also the accumulation of work.

(Figlio 1988, p. 28)

THE SELF AND THE SCIENTIST

In his recently published memoir, he wrote that his life had a certain inevitability about the way it unfolded, which combined in him with a sense of contributing to a new science, initiated by Jung. For certain, his preoccupation with the self has led him to think of the events of his life, especially his failures – in examinations, for instance, throughout his early years at university and medical school – as not just preventing him going in the wrong direction, but pushing him in the right direction. In other words, that they were actions of the self. When he considered the combination of his early experiences with his mother, his meeting Baynes and then Jung, he realized that he wanted to become a Jungian analyst. His attitude to what this has entailed has remained humble in the face of the magnitude of the task of understanding human beings, despite his 'scientific' attitude to himself and his work. In his eighty-eighth year he described his discovery that he wanted to be a Jungian analyst as follows:

> I arrived there by a mixture of chance and good luck but I have a

strong sense that the pattern of my life was predetermined, however much I disbelieve in such exaggerated propositions as hocus-pocus.

(Fordham 1993e, p. vii)

But what of the impression his writings leave behind him? In 1986 the *Journal of Analytical Psychology* published an issue entitled 'Michael Fordham Re-Viewed'. In it Judith Hubback, a former editor of the Journal and a senior training analyst within the Society, wrote:

While Fordham the man has always seemed to me to have a quality of combined magnetism and idiosyncrasy, with at times some pure wickedness, his writing is invariably steady, it is consistent, calm, full of concepts and conceptions, it is attentive to theses and theories, problems, phenomena and processes. It is often very compressed. He defines his terms. He develops his arguments. He musters his evidence. He moves carefully from observation to hypothesis, to concept, to theory, to conclusion. In the Foreword to *New Developments in Analytical Psychology*, Jung wrote: 'Every single one of [these papers] is so carefully thought out that the reader can hardly avoid holding a conversation with it . . . in the desire to carry the objective discussion a stage further and collaborate on the solution of the problems involved.'

(Hubback 1986a, p. 235)

She continues to emphasize the scientific approach he brought to his analytic work and teaching, and pointed out that

he has shown himself to be very careful about his analysands' reaction to reading about themselves, which is perhaps why some of his pages sound detached from their human basis. My impression is rather that his capacity to extract or abstract from what is lived, and to formulate concepts is above average among analytical psychologists, parallel only to Jung's ability to do so.

(Hubback 1986a, p. 237)

As Hubback develops her exposition she discerns that behind every example she brings forward of Fordham the clinician are people with whom he is actively engaged. Without irony she comments:

He might appear to carry on as though thinking about them is the great thing – and to Fordham it obviously is – but it would be quite wrong to fail to see that there are patients behind the processes and phenomena. All through his career Fordham has stressed the need for careful analysis of concepts and for disciplined analytical thought, so that the results of research can be either validated, or falsified and then reconsidered. At the same time his writing is imbued with sensitive appreciation of the irrationality of human beings: he knows perfectly well that organised thought alone can never be adequate in a 'discipline which aims at expressing the wholeness of man' [Fordham 1958a]. So although he is evidently a thinker, he is much else besides.

(Hubback 1986a, p. 242)

This impression of the power of Fordham's intellect is the feature which is most often remarked on by those who know him. It is an intellect which he applies with a lack of preconception to the subject and the feelings which it gives rise to which have attracted his interest. This is what stands out about him and is an enduring feature of his personality. I can recall his giving a paper to the Applied Section of the Institute of Psychoanalysis in which he questioned the idea of the inner world as a necessary given when embarking on an analysis. He was drawing attention to the fact that some patients did not experience their world as inner to them at the beginning of an analysis. Sitting there I was amazed and thrilled that he should bring into that temple of inner-world phenomena a dangerous thought, challenging in its good sense, radical in its implications. As often with him, he expressed his idea in a very compressed form. Consequently it produced a protest of misunderstanding. But why should analysts assume all patients have inner worlds, when they might not? They may live in an impoverished world of stuck-on affects, where nothing is felt as inner to them at all. This presentation had an element of mischief in it too. Hubback has referred to his 'pure wickedness', meaning that he can be mischievous, at times malicious. But he is not judgemental, about either himself or others.

I do not wish to give the impression that he is without prejudice; he is not. What he is is rigorous. This quality brings an uncomfortable truth to relationships with him. He is not sparing, even if he likes you; but then nor is he sparing of himself. This wish to know, to understand and yet to be able to bear and be interested in what he does not understand, is a prominent characteristic of his.

The story begins in childhood, with Fordham working as a child psychiatrist interested in the ideas of Jung. He had come to Jung through his father who had writers, painters, musicians, analysts and craftsmen as friends. One of them, Godwin Baynes, an early follower of Jung, gave the young doctor an introduction to Jung. The effect of this first meeting was inspirational and kept alive in his heart a momentum he developed with his mind for the rest of his working life.

Chapter 2

Jung's psychological model

INTRODUCTION

Before further discussing Fordham's work I should like to outline Jung's ideas so as to give a point of reference to the subsequent discussion of the way in which Fordham has modified, diverged from, or remained close to Jung's thought and recommendations for clinical practice.

Jung's psychology is not easy to summarize. This is because in Jung's own words:

> my work consists of a series of different approaches, or one might call it, a circumambulation of unknown factors. . . . I always felt a particular responsibility not to overlook the fact that the psyche does not only reveal itself in the doctor's consulting room, but above all in the wide world, as well as in the depths of history. . . . I was always convinced that a fair picture of the psyche could only be obtained by a comparative method.
>
> (Jung, *CW* 18, para. 1165)

His work was based on his experience with people and his study of myth, legend, alchemy and anthropology. What he wrote he abstracted from these experiences. He described his studies as a new scientific psychology, which I understand to mean that he employed scientific methods which included empirical and comparative ones while being deeply influenced by the need to integrate the irrational into our understanding of human behaviour and motivation. To avoid 'scientific' sounding rhetorical, I am including in this use of the word the having and testing of assumptions and the making of models. Jung wrote out of his conviction of the reality of the existence of the inner world:

> All that I experience is psychic. Even physical pain is a psychic image which I experience; my sense impressions – for all that they

force upon me a world of impenetrable objects occupying space – are psychic images, and these alone constitute my immediate experience, for they alone are the immediate objects of my consciousness.

(*CW* 8, para. 680)

LIBIDO AND THE THEORY OF OPPOSITES

Jung's model of the psyche is of a dynamic self-regulating system with its own energy, which he called 'libido'. This energy is neutral – it is not a force – and it flows between two opposing poles rather like electricity. These poles Jung called the opposites. The more tension there is between them the more energy is generated. Some examples of opposites are consciousness and unconsciousness, progression and regression, extroversion and introversion. Opposites could also be between functions such as thinking and feeling, or within a function such as positive and negative feelings. The principle which governed Jung's conception of psychic energy was *enantiodromia*, which he described as 'sooner or later everything runs into its opposite' (*CW* 7, para. 111) or becomes its opposite. And Jung, being a psychologist, thought that:

> Everything is relative, because everything rests on an inner polarity; for everything is a phenomenon of energy.
>
> (*CW* 7, para. 115)

Part of the economics of this model of the psyche is compensation: for instance unconscious attitudes compensating for conscious ones, especially the idea that what is repressed from consciousness will find expression through the unconscious. Jung took the idea originally from Alfred Adler, who described in his work on the neuroses how feelings of inferiority were compensated for by the setting up of a 'guiding fiction' to balance these feelings. The purpose of this was to turn an inferiority into a superiority. Jung thought of compensation as the psychic equivalent of physiological self-regulation. He expanded the concept of compensation to refer to 'an inherent self regulation of the psychic apparatus' (Jung, *CW* 6, para. 694).

> The activity of consciousness is *selective*. Selection demands *direction*. But direction requires the *exclusion of everything irrelevant*. This is bound to make the conscious *orientation* one-sided. The contents that are excluded and inhibited by the chosen direction sink into the unconscious, where they form a counterweight to the conscious orientation. . . . The more one-sided the conscious attitude, the more

antagonistic are the contents arising from the unconscious, so that we may speak of a real opposition between the two.

(Jung, *CW* 6, para. 694)

Central to Jung's thinking about human development was the biological concept of adaptation. For Jung adaptation referred both to the external environmental conditions within which the person lived and also the inner state of his or her psyche.

THE ARCHETYPES AND THE COLLECTIVE UNCONSCIOUS

The most controversial aspect of Jung's psychology was his idea of the collective unconscious. He described a three-layered hypothetical internal structure consisting of consciousness, personal unconsciousness and a deeper level of impersonal unconsciousness. In a geographical image he described consciousness as the island in the ocean, the personal unconscious as the area just below the water level, consisting of repressed experiences of which we are only partly aware, such as forgotten memories or infantile impulses; while deep down connecting us to the earth and the millennia of human and animal experience lay the collective unconscious. Jung described the ego as the exponent in consciousness of the self. 'The ego stands to the self as the moved to the mover. . . . The self, like the unconscious, is an *a priori* existent out of which the ego evolves. It is an unconscious prefiguration of the ego. It is not I who create myself, rather I happen to myself' (*CW* 11, para. 391). This description of the ego works well enough until unconscious contents of the ego are considered, especially those which have never been conscious – that is, subject to repression – such as the ego defences (denial). This suggests that there must be unconscious features of the ego and these have come to be thought of as located in the shadow. A consequence of this is that the ego is now thought of as being near to an unconscious archetype, in other words near to the self of which it is a manifestation.

Employing a comparative method, Jung described the universality of certain uniform and regular unconscious behaviours across all peoples and races. These instinctual and spiritual behaviours had universal characteristics, implying that there was a strong pull within human beings to experience life along historical lines. The presence of a religious function, for instance, can be traced through the ages in its changing manifestations. So too can myths, which have impersonal as well as personal content.

In the deeper layers of the unconscious Jung imagined nodal points around which experience and emotion gathered, such that they acquired characteristics which he described in terms of the images that these nodal points gave rise to. He called those structures archetypes, and the images archetypal images. The images are not inherited but Jung postulated that there was an inherited predisposition to form images. A contemporary analogy which has some similar features would be to say that research into language acquisition indicates that, universally, up to puberty, human beings are 'hardwired' to produce syntactic structures, but each person learns their own language.

Some of the more easily recognized archetypes are the divine child, the wise old man, the hero, the animus and the anima. Jung regarded the archetypal image as the representative in consciousness both of instinct and of spirit. Thus an archetypal image has a bipolar quality, reflecting the way energy in the psyche travelled between opposite poles. According to Jung integration of the opposites was the task of the second half of life when the struggles to establish a strong enough ego had been achieved.

ARCHETYPAL IMAGES

An archetypal image such as Keats's 'La Belle Dame Sans Merci' is a good example of what Jung called the anima, embodying opposite qualities: she is alluring but destructive, sensuous but ethereal, inspirational but death-dealing. When these archetypal images appear in a person's life they combine aspects of the unconscious and momentary elements of their conscious situation. An archetypal image refers both to the inner world of unconsciousness and to that aspect of the inner world which is externally in consciousness, as if the person who experiences the image has one eye looking inwards and one eye looking outwards. This does not mean that the images themselves are innate or inherited.

Jung's theory of archetypes expresses his homeostatic view of the psyche. Originally he worked out his theory with psychotic patients; later he applied it to all psychopathology, and to the process of self-differentiation, which he called individuation. Jung thought of the psyche as self-regulating, producing images of an organismic kind, whose purpose was psychic homeostasis. Archetypal images arise from developmental processes which are impersonal, but which become increasingly personal. Archetypal images refer to relationships to significant objects. Far from being exclusively impersonal, archetypal images in their impact and intensity express what is more and more personal and primitive in the relationship referred to by the images. Their universality is in their form. In analysis it depends on the stage of the analysis and the maturity of the patient whether one emphasizes the impersonal elements of the image or the personal. The personal approach takes one down the road of reductive analysis, defined as reducing complex structures to their simplicity; the impersonal tends more towards the symbolic, or in some instances towards shoring up the feelings which create a distance from painful personal experience by emphasizing the collective constituents. In the early history of Jungian child therapy, practitioners focused more on the impersonal features of archetypal images in order to spare the child from the overwhelming effect of recognizing intense personal and very primitive feelings, impulses or thoughts, which it was thought might overwhelm the child's ego. It was Fordham who challenged this idea and in so doing discovered that Jung's concept of individuation was a lifelong task and not just a characteristic of the second half of life.

THE RELATION OF THE PERSONAL TO THE COLLECTIVE UNCONSCIOUS

When Jung was doing his research the Freudians were working mainly with patients under thirty-five and focusing on sexually related difficulties. Jung concentrated on those people in the second half of their lives who were ostensibly free of their parental transferences and were suffering from lack of meaning in their lives. He surmised that as they freed themselves from the personal unconscious, images would arise which would take on a prospective and healing function within the psyche. He was clear that this rarely could take place with young people and that first there had to be reductive analysis of the personal unconscious before the collective unconscious and the problem of the opposites could be tackled (*CW* 7, para. 113). Nowadays it is widely recognized among analysts working with Jung's ideas that reductive analysis is in fact a synthetic process, defined as bringing together in a healing way disparate elements in the psyche, and that the distinction as at first formulated owed more to Jung's need to separate from Freud than from experiences in the consulting room.

The relationship between the collective and the personal from a clinical perspective has been discussed by Mary Williams (Williams 1963). She noted that the separation of the collective from the personal unconscious historically formed part of the split between Jung and Freud. The book which did more than anything to polarize the differences between these two great men was Jung's 1912 edition of *The Psychology of the Unconscious*. In the Foreword to the fourth Swiss edition he referred to the book's coming upon him like a 'landslide' containing 'all those psychic contents which could find no room, no breathing space, in the constricting atmosphere of Freudian psychology' (Jung, *CW* 5, p. xxiii). Mary Williams pointed out, using clinical examples, that the personal and the collective could be separated for the purposes of exposition but that it was undesirable to separate them in practice. She encapsulated this in an influential formulation:

> (1) that nothing in the personal experience needs to be repressed unless the ego feels threatened by its archetypal power; and (2) that the archetypal activity which forms the individual's myth is dependent on material supplied by the personal unconscious.
>
> (Williams 1963, p. 49)

SYMBOLS

Combining Williams's formulations and Jung's assertions about the different tasks facing the individual, depending on the time of their life, we arrive at a balance which has at its core the Jungian approach to the symbol. Jung distinguished symbols from signs. Signs stand for known things; symbols, on the other hand, he defined as 'the best possible description or formulation of a relatively unknown fact, which is none the less known to exist or is postulated as existing' (Jung, *CW* 6, para 814). By examining a symbol fully what is revealed is that it 'is a living thing, it is an expression for something that cannot be characterized in any other or better way. The symbol is alive only so long as it is pregnant with meaning' (Jung, *CW* 6, para. 816). It combines personal and impersonal elements, rational and irrational, is essentially paradoxical and is not indicative of a symptom, as is sometimes the case in Freudian psychoanalytic theory. In psychoanalytic theory a symbol is often taken to mean representing in consciousness an unconscious idea, conflict or wish, which is a semiotic approach. Appreciation therefore of the symbolic attitude in Jungian psychology necessarily brings with it an understanding of the way in which opposing elements within the psyche co-exist creatively, which allows for a hermeneutic approach to interpretation. In any thorough-going analysis perhaps one of the most potent symbols which arises in some shape or form is that of the parental couple and the creativity of their intercourse, with all the concomitant conflicts that this gives rise to.

TYPES

Although he had mixed feelings about theories, Jung formulated a theory of types as well as his archetype theory. Habitual ways of responding denote personality types. Jung organized his delineation of the characteristics of types (a) by attitude – whether they were more introverted or extroverted; and (b) by function – whether they favoured thinking or sensation, feeling or intuition. The possible combinations of functions and types, which contain opposites, further elaborated his model of psychic functioning. Thinking, by which Jung meant the use of those processes which gave meaning and understanding to experience, is the opposite of feeling, which gives value to and weighs experience. These two are considered rational. Sensation consists of perceptions made through the senses, and intuition is the word Jung used to describe perception via the unconscious. These two are irrational. Combinations of these functions and attitude preferences give rise to personality types which have dominant and inferior functions and attitudes. Jung stressed the importance of paying attention to the inferior functions and attitude preferences within the psyche when related to the compensatory nature of intra-psychic regulation. If unattached to aspects of the personality, and pushed into unconsciousness, they can acquire great destructive potency.

INDIVIDUATION

Throughout Jung's psychology, however, ran his consistent attention to the need to find an individual solution to the problems of life. He gave a number of different descriptions of the individuation process and related it to his intra-psychic structure the self, which he sometimes described as an archetype, and sometimes distinguished from the archetypes. The definition of individuation Fordham has found especially helpful is:

> the process by which individual beings are formed and differentiated. In particular, it is the development of the psychological individual as being distinct from the general, collective psychology. Individuation therefore is a process of differentiation having as its goal the development of the individual personality.
>
> (Jung, *CW* 6, para. 757)

Jung's researches into the self, its actions, activities and purpose are one of his distinctive contributions to the study of psychology.

THE SELF

For present-day analytical psychologists the significance of the self in both theory and practice is one of the key concepts which separates analytical psychology from other dynamic psychologies. Recently, however, some psychoanalysts have been discovering the need for an intra-psychic superordinate structure to account for phenomena which transcend the ego. One of the better known is Heinz Kohut, who has written of the self as revealed in empathic understanding between patient and analyst (Kohut 1977). His descriptions are often close to Jung's when describing the impact of the self on his interactions with patients, but he is less concerned with the rich symbolism of the self which characterized Jung's special interest. Unlike other psychologies which have in the main linked the self to a feeling of being myself – i.e. locating it within the ego and thus part of consciousness – Jung, more influenced by Eastern religions (Taoist philosophy and Buddhism), described the self in terms which embraced consciousness and un-consciousness.

The self can bring together, within the person and in a spirit of reconciliation, all those aspects of the personality which oppose one another. This experience he called the transcendent function, and it transmutes these opposite experiences into something centred and free of the compulsion of either pole. This aspect of individuation deepened the individual's understanding of the paradoxical nature of his life. For the more introverted, perhaps, this could become the task for the second half of life. There were other ways in which he described the self too, linking it to the differentiation of the individual person from the collec-tive. It was this way of thinking about the self which in part guided Fordham's researches into infancy and childhood.

Chapter 3

Jung and Fordham

JUNG'S INSPIRATION

Jung was the inspiration behind all Fordham's work. Looked at through the ordered lens of retrospection his work shows him trying out Jung's ideas with patients and when the ideas needed modification struggling to assimilate the conflicts this gave rise to. Fordham has been exceptional within the Jungian community in his interest in the internal world of the child. The impact of this was to be felt not just in his studies of infancy but also in his understanding of transference phenomena in adult analysis. He thought that if Jung's ideas about individuation in the second half of life had their origins in infancy there would be evidence for actions of the self in childhood. Jung had written of the individuation process as the realization 'in all its aspects, of the personality originally hidden away in the embryonic germ-plasm' (Jung, *CW* 7, para. 186) but he did not follow this up. This was because he was more interested in the prospective functions of the unconscious and his patient's imaginative capacities, and less in their origins. This investigation has been Fordham's task. Jung had shown that there were two centres of integration in the personality, the ego and the self. But he nowhere demonstrated the significance of the self in childhood. He thought of the child as existing in a state of *participation mystique*, the phrase used by Lévy-Bruhl to describe the characteristic of primitive tribal people's relationship between themselves and an object, such that they were unable to distinguish themselves from the object. Jung thought of the child as unconscious, which in the context of his model of the psyche meant in need of protection by his mother from the dangerous contents of the collective unconscious. Much later, towards the end of his life, Jung became fascinated by children's dreams but was daunted by the prospect of researching this area. He wrote to Fordham:

I just cannot see my way to anything so ambitious as a book about children's dreams. This would really be your province and I should like to persuade you to try your hand on such material. . . . I'm now at an age when it becomes unwise to continue the great adventure of pioneering research. I must leave the joy and despair of it to younger forces.

(Jung to Fordham, 22 February 1952)

Fordham's relationship with Jung was personal as well as professional:

There was in my mind, a strong association between Jung and my father. . . . Thus it was easy for Jung to take on a paternal role for me.

(Fordham 1993e, p. 111)

Fordham felt real affection for Jung and the feelings were reciprocated:

He gave ample evidence of his good opinion of me and it was after all he who suggested I become editor of his *Collected Works*. He was always accessible when I wanted to see him, whilst his letters were, with one or two exceptions, perceptive and ended with 'cordially'.

(Ibid., p. 113)

He at times found Jung's outspokenness insensitive but it was a quality his father possessed and if it was apt he usually did not mind. He took his son Max to visit Jung, and Frieda would accompany him on some of his visits. Most of the work on the *Collected Works* was done by correspondence and was done in a spirit of co-operativeness and good feeling (ibid., p. 115). He noticed in his personal interviews with Jung, when they were alone together and he was telling Jung about a difficulty he was having, that if Jung 'got on the track of an archetype he tended to lose sight of the person in whom it was active' (ibid., p. 118). He enjoyed the informal meetings with Jung at his Bollingen house 'when', he said, 'one usually sat with him beside the lake on a stone bench with one of his stone carvings nearby' (ibid., p. 115). 'It was these meetings over the years that consolidated the goodness of the relationship' (ibid., p. 119). And he had a great respect for Mrs Jung, who supported his interest in children and whom he described as being 'perceptive' and 'penetrative' in conversation. 'She very much had a mind of her own which was appreciative of but not subservient to that of her husband' (ibid., p. 115). Apart from the war years he kept in contact with Jung right up until his death, seeing him for the last time just before he died in 1960. This last visit was especially poignant as Jung was feeling dejected and depressed. Fordham tried to reassure him that his work was significant and Jung looked at him bemusedly and then asked him to go.

Reflecting on the meeting afterwards Fordham has written that his reassurances were superficial and missed the point of Jung's preoccupations which he now thinks he would have conveyed by saying that 'it was the delusion of being a world saviour that made him feel a failure – I had not the stature to do that' (ibid., p. 120). Alongside the friendship and the mutual interest in transference, Fordham was finding that his own researches were challenging some of Jung's ideas.

PRELIMINARY WORK

Fordham was initially interested in the analysis of the personal unconscious (and its impersonal features) and emphasized the importance of analysing childhood. He was mindful of the gaps in Jung's researches and set about investigating them. In the 1930s he first began by drawing the attention of the psychotherapeutic community to the work of Jung and its relevance to our understanding of the psyche. He thought of Jung's work as being complementary to Freud's, not in opposition to it. He also had another motive:

> My personal relationship with him (Jung) made me aware of a trend amongst some of his followers, and his detractors as well, which he deplored. It hinted that analytical psychology was a sort of religion. It was an error that I also deplored, and so gave lectures and wrote papers to oppose the tendency.
>
> (Ibid., p. 117)

These articles also helped establish an interest in the application of Jung's ideas to clinical practice. Then in the 1940s he began to investigate the relationship of the self to the ego and out of this came his early descriptions of actions of the self and their relation to ego development. These papers arose out of his work with children and the development of his own ideas about the self and the need for a dynamic system to enable the self to come into relation to the environment. He described the original self as being integrated and coming into relation with the environment by a process he called deintegration (see Chapter 4).

SOME OF THE CHANGES FORDHAM HAS MADE TO JUNG'S MODEL

Fordham, when working as a psychiatrist, noticed that the children who had problems and who were brought for consultations by their parents exhibited features in their personality development which had similarities to Jung's observations of mandala symbolism. But his conclusions were radically different from Jung's. In Jung's examinations of mandala symbolism the centre, the contents which surrounded it, and the boundary circumference represent the self, which Jung differentiated from the ego (see *CW* 9, p. i). Fordham noticed with young children a relationship between the emergence of this boundary, often a circle, and the beginnings of ego development. The boundary could therefore represent, he thought, a circumference to the ego but also refer to the self because the ego was on a continuum with the self, being a representative in consciousness of part of the self. In Chapter 4 I give a fuller exposition of this discovery, which was a radical departure from Jungian thinking fifty years ago. Then a child's unconscious was invariably linked to the unconscious of the parents, implying an absence of this boundary. Fordham's investigations indicated that the child's ego emerged out of the self and that while the danger to the ego came from within the psyche (as Jung had suggested) the purpose of the boundary was to protect the ego from these dangers. These postulations of Fordham were brilliant in their insightfulness and now that modern scanning techniques have allowed babies to be observed *in utero*, what he described as being likely has been shown to be true. There is continuity between early states of the self and subsequent ego development. Piontelli's studies have revealed the relation between the 'character' of the foetus in a pre-ego state and the personality of the infant (Piontelli 1992). In Fordham's model this is equivalent to the importance of the self in individuation from the earliest beginnings of life to death.

At first Fordham was tentative in his formulations of the evidence from his clinical work, not daring to think that what he was observing in his investigations of small children were symbols of the self. Gradually, however, the empirical evidence was so forceful that he had to face up to the fact that these were symbols of the self in childhood and that this was going to have consequences for ego development. Subsequently his contributions to this concept have emphasized the lifelong nature of individuation as a dynamic process which begins in childhood. His ideas have been absorbed into the canon of Jungian theory without significant disagreement. He has managed not only to depart from and yet remain close to Jung but to be drawn creatively towards psychoanalysis.

In the British psychoanalytic object-relations school, evidence has been put forward for the child's wish cannibalistically to attack the breast, the hypothesized sequel to which is the child becoming anxious and concerned about the damage he has done (depressed but not clinically so) and his trying to make reparation. Ruthlessness and concern come together, and with this a considerable expansion of consciousness. This is a simplified description of what the Kleinians call the depressive position and Fordham calls individuation processes in childhood. It is an example of the way opposites can combine and is further elaborated in Chapter 4.

Fordham's contribution to analytical psychology has been focused on the actions of the self (a) in infancy and (b) in clinical practice. He has never thought of his work as 'developmental' in the sense of there being a distinction between 'developmental' and 'archetypal'. These distinctions have crept into the Jungian discourse following a book by Samuels in which, writing for a wider audience, he schematized the differences in emphasis of various Jungian organizations and their members (Samuels 1985). Fordham's objection to these categories is that they create confusion by claiming to make distinctions which Jung himself did not make (Fordham, personal communication, 21 August 1994). All Jung's work, in Fordham's view, is developmental, since this is the core of his concept of individuation, which concerns the growth of the personality.

Fordham, however, unlike Jung, has abstracted his experience less, and published more actual description of cases, so that it is easier to see from what he is deriving his argument. His work has always been clinically led. He started from the experience of the patient and then used theory to help organize his thoughts. If the theory has not helped he has changed the theory. This individual approach is within the tradition of analytical psychology as evolved by Jung. Although Fordham thinks of himself as a scientist, it could be said that since different theories could fit the same patient this individual method is not particularly scientific. (Objectively this statement could probably be established across all analytic work.) But if the nature of science is to evaluate the truth of propositions concerning the natural world, which includes the mind, then Fordham is scientific if not Popperian in his approach. His interest is in the individual solution rather than searching for causes and explanations in historical events. Looking back on this work now it seems as if he was trying to ground the analytical psychologists who were starting to work in England in a method which had a firm empirical base. He has tended to emphasize the scientific as an antidote to the cult of personality.

His most radical departure from Jung has been to describe the actions of the self in infancy and childhood such that the infant, far from being uncentred at birth, as Jung originally thought, is a person, with an individual identity even *in utero*. Almost unnoticed, remaining untouched by other researchers and practitioners, was the concept contained in this description of the workings of the self, which was that the self, present in the germ plasm, helped mould and create the environment in its interactions with it. This concept introduced the idea of the agency of individuals in their own development. The self as Fordham conceived it was the instigator as much as the receptor of infant experience. This biological idea, based on adaptation (almost a niche model of survival, where the niche adapts too), has become the most radical of all Fordham's discoveries. It has given rise to a theory of ego development which is particularly Jungian in which the interaction between mother and baby ensures the uniqueness of the situation, a uniqueness created as much by the infant as by the mother, without precluding the inclusion of the archetypal content of projections. (See Chapter 5.)

WORK WITH ADULTS

In parallel with his work on infancy and childhood, Fordham described in the 1950s interactions with adult patients and formulated them in the context of ideas he was having about the nature of the transference (alongside those being developed by psychoanalysts). In particular he described being able to make use of feelings projected into him by his patients in ways which were syntonic to the analytic process and the countertransference. Following on from this, he opened up the discussion among Jungians as to the ways in which the transference/countertransference could be used in analytic practice. This inevitably led to discussion of technique. In doing this he initially encountered opposition from those Jungians who felt that (a) technique was individual and to investigate it was to violate the individuality of the patient–analyst dyad; and (b) that detailed examination of the interactions occurring between patient and analyst would be an intrusion into the sacred space of the analysis. His focus was on the way archetypes and the perceptual system interact. The internal experiences of children and adults record not the event but the way the psyche experienced the event. This entailed examining the way the archetypal images were modified by experience as well as the converse. As part of these investigations he studied the journals of a Spanish mystic, St John of the Cross, and published his analysis of the initiation into the Dark Night of the Soul.

AUTISM AND CHILDHOOD PSYCHOSES

Fordham was especially interested in investigating psychoses in children. Jung had been interested in psychosis and had based his early views of psychopathology on his experience of schizophrenic patients. He had also discovered that schizophrenic patients could form transferences (contrary to Freud's theory of primary narcissism). Fordham made detailed studies of a number of children and published a very full account of the treatment of a boy patient he called Alan (Fordham 1976a) (see Chapter 7). This led him to examine current ideas about childhood psychosis and to describe how a theory of the self, based on Jung's model of the psyche but developed by himself, could make sense of the bewildering behaviour of these children. Some of Fordham's views on autism have recently been corroborated by colleagues from other theoretical orientations. For example Anne Alvarez, a gifted child psychotherapist, has described how she had to go beyond her psychoanalytic (Kleinian) training to understand and reach the children she treated (Alvarez 1992). When the book was reviewed by Elizabeth Urban, a Jungian child analyst, she commented that 'This model is identical to Fordham's model of deintegration and reintegration' (Urban 1994). Recently another leading clinician in the field of autism, Frances Tustin, has acknowledged the significance of Fordham's views and retracted the perpetuation of an error in her own work concerning the idea that there was an original primary state of autism (Tustin 1994).

CHILD ANALYSIS

Fordham's method of child analysis can be contrasted with that practised by those who have developed Jung's ideas in relation to children in other ways. For example the sand tray techniques of Dora Kalff and her followers involves the elaborate construction (often in a sand-pit using figures supplied by the therapist) of imaginary worlds, which are then interpreted in relation to a largely mythological world. From the arrangement of these figures and the story he told the analyst, inferences would be made about the state of the child's relationship to the archetypal figures in his unconscious. This approach emphasizes the collective features of the images and tends to support defensiveness against the integration of the personal relevance of the imagery. For Fordham this method shifted the focus too much away from the meaning of the child's fantasies as they were experienced in relation to him. His interactive method gave greater prominence to interpretation within the transference and subsequent close observation of the effects of the interpretation.

The rationale for not interpreting the archetypal features of the personal contents of the child's mind in child analysis was the feeling expressed by Jung that the contents of the collective unconscious once brought to consciousness would overwhelm the child's ego. But Fordham thought of the archetypal images of children as being bodily based and as such known to the child and therefore able to be integrated. If the problem was one of unintegrated oral sadism, for instance, he spoke to the child, not of the universality of images of devouring witch-like mothers as an archetypal image to be found in countless fairy stories, but, using the child's behaviour, drawings and talk, he described to the child the feeling he had in his mouth – that he wanted to bite. He would give him the reason for this feeling and describe the motive. By proceeding in this way he discovered that the children readily recognized what he was talking about and felt relief that it was now in the open. His application of this method arose from his study of Klein's work and his recognition of the common ground which existed between unconscious phantasy and archetypal images. The fear that these children would be overwhelmed by the intense affect within the archetype was not borne out. All of this seems obvious now but was new to Jungians then.

FORDHAM AND ARCHETYPES

Fordham was using Jung's term archetype, 'a dynamic structure closely related to instinct' (Fordham 1976, p. 5) to refer to the expression in children of impulses 'originating in neurophysiological structures and biochemical changes' (Fordham 1976, p. 6). What this meant was that Jung's description of the bi-polarity of the archetypes – that they comprised a spiritual and an instinctual pole – could now be thought of as bringing together in infancy and childhood the body and the psyche. The spiritual pole of the archetype would give rise to fantasies and the instinctual to impulses. On the one hand, Fordham was conceptualizing the archetype in a more creative way; on the other, he was stressing its bi-polarity in an embodied form. A consequence of this way of thinking was that in infancy and childhood Fordham expected to find that children had a predisposition to develop ideas, feelings and fantasies which arose from archaic layers of the psyche and were not derived from introjected experience. Naturally, as maturation progressed, the environment of the individual fed into this system, providing personal imagery for the expression of the unconscious archetypes.

In recognizing the need to place greater emphasis on the body than Jungians had traditionally done, Fordham was not opposing Jung so much as adding to and developing his often cryptic but significant asides. Jung, for instance, implicitly acknowledged, but nowhere developed, the connections between infantile sexuality and the subsequent emergence of particular values which guided the life of the individual. In the foreword to his paper 'Psychic Conflicts in a Child' he wrote:

> while perceiving in infantile sexuality the beginnings of a future sexual function, I also discern there the seeds of higher spiritual functions.
>
> (*CW* 17, p. 5)

Fordham took this to mean that Jung recognized that childhood sexuality was by its nature archetypal and not just personal (something Jung had disagreed with Freud about). Fordham expanded on Jung's view by including the knowledge derived from the psychoanalysis of children, concerning the importance of different parts of the body at different periods of development and of the perception of these body-parts as initially having an existence not related to a whole person. In this view the perception of the whole person would have to wait for the gradual construction of a body image. Thus he thought a child first experiences intense but imprecisely located feelings which, over time, coalesce to form a picture of 'Mummy', parts of 'Mummy', and of himself in relation to her.

This way of thinking about archetypal experience can easily be assimilated into analytical psychology since much of the child's thinking is mythopoeic in quality. In this way Fordham has been able to link Jung's discernment of 'higher spiritual functions' to development of character out of early object relations. It was, nevertheless, initially not well received (see Introduction to Fordham 1976a; Shamdasani 1995) when he started to write of the archetypal expressions of instinctual behaviour in children, almost as if the evidence for their conflicts denigrated the later manifestations of the archetypes, where spiritual was more often thought of as unconnected to the body rather than part of the whole person.

All of these activities have run parallel with his maintaining a firm clinical base to his work. He called his approach empirical but what, in my view, he meant by that was that he allowed himself to be affected by his patients, to think about what was happening to him and them and out of this mine new insights. It was an empiricism based on treating every person as an individual needing a personal solution to the problems of their life.

Chapter 4

The self in infancy and childhood
Pioneering discoveries

INTRODUCTION: HISTORY AND BACKGROUND

Fordham's pioneering work on the archetypes in childhood has spanned almost fifty years. It has been based on empirical foundations and derives its inspiration from Jung's formulations, necessarily modified by experience. Central to Jung's model of the mind is the idea that there is an individual self which is the totality of psyche and soma. The symbols of the self also function in an organizing way within archetypal forms. Like Jung, Fordham valued inferences and abstractions as instruments in the development of knowledge. Fordham's concept of the original self, which was a piece of inductive thinking, was just such an inference. It was later developed into a hypothesis, modified, and then found to be of value in organizing observations. His work on the psychic reality of the symbols of the self has led to his being able to trace the connections between individuation in childhood and its adult form when described by Jung as:

> the process by which individual beings are formed and differentiated. In particular, it is the development of the psychological individual as being distinct from the general, collective psychology. Individuation therefore is a process of differentiation having as its goal the development of the individual personality.
>
> (Jung, *CW* 6, para. 757)

Since Jung did not think that individuation characterized childhood, Fordham's initial investigations were against a backdrop which emphasized in the treatment of children the unconsciousness of parents rather than the individuality of children. Jung's view was that difficulties experienced by children could be understood from an investigation of their parents' unconscious and that individuation was a task for the second half of life. In the foreword to the first Jungian book on work with children, Frances Wickes's *The Inner World of Childhood*, Jung wrote:

> Parents should always be conscious of the fact that they themselves are the principal cause of neurosis in their children. . . . To put it bluntly, it is that part of life which they have always shirked, probably by means of a pious lie. That sows the most virulent germs.
>
> (*CW* 17, paras 84, 87)

About this attitude of Jung's Michael Fordham wrote:

> Jung's writings are at once a stumbling block to the study of children and an inspiration: a stumbling block because they emphasise one side only of the relation between parents and children, an inspiration because they provide a method of investigating the psychology of childhood which has not yet been applied.
>
> (Fordham 1944, p. 4)

The stumbling block in Jung's writings was his view that:

> the things which have the most powerful effect upon children do not come from the conscious state of the parents but from their unconscious background.
>
> (*CW* 17, para. 84)

Coupled with this forthright attribution of children's difficulties to their parents' unlived lives was Jung's assertion, based on the dreams of three- and four-year-old children, that:

> The unconscious psyche of the child is truly limitless in extent and of incalculable age.
>
> (*CW* 17, para. 95)

These two constituents were the main obstacles in the development of Jungian child analysis because they denied the existence of the child's individual life, especially the latter, which implied that the child lived in a mythological world with limitless access to the collective unconscious. It was almost as if Jung thought of the child's world as one of *participation mystique*. But as Fordham also pointed out, Jung's work was inspiring in that his psychology of archetypes provided a new instrument for investigating childhood. That was so, even if Jung thought that the powerfulness of archetypal images would overwhelm the child's mind. Later, after the Second World War when he was able to resume contact with Jung, Fordham read Jung's seminars on children's dreams and 'to my astonishment and pleasure found archetypal images in them and even a symbol of the self' (Fordham 1993, pp. 64–5). At the time of this research, however, he was very much a lone Jungian separated from the umbrella of Jung's protection, out on a limb in his researches into childhood and the potentially 'heretical' evidence of the presence of symbols of the self in children's material.

EARLY RESEARCHES INTO THE SELF IN CHILDHOOD

In the early therapeutic encounters with children which Fordham recorded in *The Life of Childhood* (1944), and later in *Children as Individuals* (1969), he described how the children referred to him in a child guidance clinic revealed in their play the difficulties which were obstructing their development.

Joyce was six when she was referred because of fears of the dark and school phobia. Her mother had recently had a baby boy. In her initial play Joyce smacked the bottom of a 'bad' black doll and lavished love on a 'good' white doll. This white doll was 'the baby'. The play continued with Joyce being a little mummy to her babies, who were not always entirely good or bad. Sometimes the good doll 'could not go to sleep' and the bad doll was given nice presents. The main feature of the play was directed towards punishing the bad behaviour violently. She was quite ruthless and behaved as if the doll's mother was extremely fierce and punitive, quite unlike how her actual mother was with her. As her therapy continued, the baby, the 'good doll', began to become less good, in particular in wetting her knickers and anal activities, while the bad doll was removed altogether.

Joyce became a little less ruthless although she was intolerant of frustration. She used the reality of the sand she was playing with to control her anger at the baby. It was sand, not 'busy' (her word for faeces) which had got on to the baby's knickers. In the next session she chewed the teat of the bottle and talked about the baby spitting out the milk, for which she was spanked. She found chalks and broke them up and investigated her baby who wetted her when she was fed. She threw into the rubbish-bin the toy soldiers who had guns. Water got spilt over the floor, and she smacked the baby and bit the baby's bottle.

Joyce showed through her play how she struggled with her wishes to be a baby and her ruthless attempts to keep these wishes under control by punishment. As all of this came more into the open, then her feelings about sexual differences started to emerge and she threw away soldiers with guns and broke up pieces of chalk more often, making clear what she felt about her little brother's penis. Her play also revealed how her attempt to solve these problems herself, by identifying with the baby, did not work because she could not conceive of the baby being both good and bad, only good or bad. She also knew that this was not the case – the bad baby did have redeeming features and the good one was naughty too. She had projected on to the schoolmistress the punitive figure and this prevented her going to school. Her therapy helped her resolve this, such that, far from experiencing the archetypal images as overwhelming, by confronting them she obtained relief.

The way the good baby could turn into the bad and vice versa was an example of Jung's description of the behaviour of the opposites and their tendency to converge, which he had called 'enantiodromia'. Fordham commented on this, that 'the most organized expression of enantio-dromia is found in Chinese philosophy':

> The Great Monad is a standard 'diagram' used probably for medi-tation. It depicts two fishes, one representing Yang, the other Yin, each being the same size as the other and containing within it a germ of its opposite. The monad infers a phasic relation of the two; when Yang predominates Yin is recessive, and vice versa. This principle has been applied to the whole of nature and to the history of nations. The cultural significance of Joyce's play is thus that she is expressing in a direct, simple, flexible form the pattern of a dynamic system which has been abstracted, refined, meditated upon and developed into a complex philosophical idea.
>
> (Fordham 1969a, p. 40)

This case, and there were others like it, demonstrated the usefulness of Jung's theory of archetypes and their cultural significance. But it also raised questions about Jung's ideas about development. For while Fordham was being a conscientious Jungian, making connections of this kind, he was also noticing that the children he was seeing were getting better without any significant changes occurring in the unconscious of their parents. Further, he was beginning to find evidence for the activity of the self in childhood.

THE DISCOVERY OF 'I'

The significant data he began to think about started with the obser-vations of a one-year-old boy who was allowed by his parents to scribble on the walls of his nursery. Fordham noticed that the scribbles became more and more circle-like and as they did the boy discovered 'as if by revelation' the word 'I'. The circles then stopped.

The relation in time between the discovery of the circle and the discovery of 'I' suggests that the circle represented the matrix of the self out of which the ego arose. The self seemed to prepare the ground for its emergence, to create a temenos in which the event could occur.

(Fordham 1957a, p. 134)

The circle seemed both to express the feeling of 'I' of completeness, of momentary recognition of his individual status, and a feeling of a boundary between himself and others. Its particular significance to Fordham was that the presence of the boundary to the self suggested that Jung was wrong to think of the infant and young child's world as one of *participation mystique*, in which the environment and psyche were one, and the child's unconscious was of limitless extent.

THE SIGNIFICANCE OF MANDALA SYMBOLISM

Jung discovered that mandalas were 'cryptograms concerning the state of the self'. The discovery was gradual. It began with him sketching in a notebook. He noticed the form of his drawings, which were circles, with a centre, framed by a square and with the whole area loosely divided into four. He saw that the variations in these drawings corresponded to the state of his self: 'In them I saw the self – that is my whole being actively at work' (Jung 1963, p. 187). At first Jung did not know what to make of that and felt isolated. Then he was sent Richard Wilhelm's manuscript of *The Secret of the Golden Flower* and saw that the mandala was an important Taoist symbol of wholeness. Combining these experiences with his work with patients, who in dreams produced a series of mandalas, he began to work out their significance, not just as a symbol of the self, but also as a way of understanding how his fragmented patients sought and found containment (*CW* 9, i).

What then was the purpose of the boundary to the circle? Jung had implied that the function of the mandala was protective. Fordham had noticed in his work with children that they used the circles they drew, both as containers which could include even bad experiences, and as protective barriers against intra-psychic dangers. In Jung's examinations of mandala symbolism the centre, the contents which surrounded it, and the boundary circumference represented the self, which Jung differentiated from the ego. Fordham noticed that with young children there was a relationship between this boundary, often a circle, and the beginnings of ego development. The boundary could therefore represent, he thought, a circumference to the ego (not the self) but also refer to the self, because of having emerged from it. This was because his investigations indicated that the danger to the child's ego came from within the psyche (for instance nightmares) and the purpose of the boundary was to protect the ego from these dangers. But the self had to have a boundary too, for without it differentiation of consciousness from unconsciousness could not occur, since the ego emerged from and existed outside of the self.

A TWO-YEAR-OLD WITH 'FITS'

A case which made a deep impression on Fordham was one in which a two-year-old girl was brought to him suffering from fits during which she became completely unconscious. She was clingy and would hardly let go of her mother. Separating from her to come into the consulting room was at first too difficult. Gradually this changed. Then one day she drew a circle and said 'me'.

> Almost at once her whole manner changed and she got down off her chair and played with some toys for several minutes.
>
> (Fordham 1957a, p. 149)

She became more confident, and Fordham started making mothers and babies, under her direction, in Plasticine, which she tore up and then ran out of the room to see if her actual mother was all right. Her mother reported to Fordham at this time that her daughter had a tremendous curiosity about babies. Whenever she saw a pram she had to investigate it. More and more she wanted to repair the mummies and babies and with this came greater independence from her mother. The fits stopped.

Fordham understood this experience of anxiety, followed by the emergence of 'me' and the subsequent working through of the destruction and then reparation of mummy, as being her way of working out the difficulty which had arisen from her not being able to separate her attacks on her internal mummy from herself (expressed in her fits which indicated the absence of the protective function of the boundary to the self and her consequent regression into unconsciousness). Checking on her mother during sessions and on babies in prams was part of the process of separating fantasy from reality. For Fordham here, in the gradual psychotherapeutic resolution guided by him but resolved by her, was an instance of an ego development arising from actions of the self: the scribble became a circle, and she integrated the realization that there was a boundary between fantasy and reality.

IMAGES OF WHOLENESS

Further evidence for the importance of the self in childhood came from his elucidation of a series of drawings done by an eight-year-old girl. Fordham carefully related these drawings to the alchemical pictures in Jung's essay on the psychology of the transference, and demonstrated that the conjunction of opposites led to an image of wholeness with the consequence that she 'changed from a miserable woebegone person almost completely absorbed in crying into an independent personality quite able to fend for herself' (Fordham 1957a, p. 144).

In his essay on transference (*CW* 16) Jung examined a series of pictures from an alchemical text and described how in his view they represented the equivalent of the individuation process in that realization of the self occurred through the conjunction of opposites (*CW* 16). When Fordham first studied the child's drawings 'the whole meaning of the series was thoroughly obscure until I started to look at the alchemical pictures and read Jung's text with its full quotations' (Fordham 1957a, p. 138). He then re-examined the child's drawings. He was able to make sense of the phallus in the sky (which was also a cloud). It filled a boat with rain and standing in the boat was a man. The first alchemical drawing in Jung's series also had a female container into which a male spout flowed. By systematic comparisons of this kind Fordham could discern the same unconscious process in the alchemical drawings as was exhibited by the child. Both led to images of wholeness. That this was accompanied by a remarkable change in the child indicated to him that out of these activities of the self had occurred a development of her ego.

At about this time Kellogg, in San Francisco, published some of her research into the scribbles and drawings of nursery-age children, later gathered into a book entitled *Analysing Children's Art* (Kellogg 1969). She noted that the children's pictures seemed to begin with rhythmic activities producing scribbles. Out of these could be abstracted definite shapes which were then combined to form pictures. Fordham thought of the three stages of the development of these pictures as evidence of archetypal activity of the self in childhood leading to ego development. The rhythmic scribbling arose from activities of the self, which led to a process of abstraction, followed by the combination of the images into a definite picture.

Whereas the work of the ethologists, for example Tinbergen and Lorenz with their studies of innate release mechanisms, and psychologists, such as Piaget with his studies of intellectual development in children, confirmed the presence of internal organizers, Kellogg's work gave evidence for the way images built up and were separated out by the child from his own activity. Out of basic scribbles emerged definite shapes and forms as if out of the self emerged the ego.

THE SELF

The self is a central Jungian concept. There were broadly two ways in which Jung described the self. On the one hand he wrote about it in a manner similar to that found in Eastern mysticism. This self was the whole personality outside time, space and desire. Its characteristics were reflected in symbols. This self clearly could not be experienced; nor could it be observed, since it contained the ego, which would be doing the observing. This idea of the self on its own is not compatible with the idea expressed earlier, that individuation is a process of self-differentiation. But combining this view of the self with the other way in which Jung mainly, but not exclusively, wrote about the self, as an archetypal idea, it is possible to arrive at a self which is both ultimately mysterious and yet manifests itself in the life of the individual in ways which form the basis for personal identity. Its particular archetypal quality, he suggested, was that it 'is the real organising principle of the unconscious' (*CW* 9, ii, para. 318). The self, in my view, cannot be an archetype because the symbols of the self include the ego, the centre of consciousness, as part of the totality, and Jung specifically differentiated the ego from the archetypes – although there are times when both Jung and Fordham write of the self as an archetype. But it does give rise to experiences which are archetypal in quality. (It will be clear, I hope, that the self eludes precise definition, being both abstract and metaphorical.)

In the light of the material he was uncovering Fordham was beginning to think a primary self must exist which combined the totality of conscious and unconscious systems. There must be, he thought, an original state of integration. If there was evidence for actions of the self in childhood it would imply that individuation processes were active in childhood. But Jung had described individuation as a process occurring in the second half of life. He contrasted the tasks of the first half of life with the tasks of the second. In the first half of life the child had to adapt to the collective values of the society in which he lived. He wrote:

> before individuation can be taken for a goal, the educational aim of adaptation to the necessary minimum of collective standards must first be attained.

> (*CW* 6, para. 760)

Jung thought of the child as leaving parts of the psyche projected into the world. Later he saw the second half of life as being a gradual process of withdrawing these projections, when individuation became a sort of intense introversion.

Jung's psychology is a purposeful one with aims and goals. The aims of childhood therefore were seen as different from the aims of the mature adult. Fordham summarized the difference for Jung as follows:

> Individuation is conceived to involve a goal opposite to that of childhood, when strengthening the ego is all important; the goal of individuation appears, on the contrary, only when 'a suspension of the will results'.
>
> (Fordham 1969a, pp. 24–5)

For Jung individuation was a process of the self whereby the individual gradually became free from the opposites by a symbolical solution ('a suspension of the will') which allowed them to have complete equality. The opposites in this instance were the self and the ego.

> When there is full parity of the opposites, attested by the ego's absolute participation in both, this necessarily leads to a suspension of the will, for the will can no longer operate when every motive has an equally strong counter motive. Since life cannot tolerate a standstill, a damming up of vital energy results, and this would lead to an insupportable condition did not the tension of the opposites produce a new, uniting function that transcends them.
>
> (CW 6, para. 824)

But Jung had also written of individuation in a way which had highlighted the self-differentiation inherent in the process:

> Individuation is practically the same as the development of consciousness out of the original state of identity.
>
> (CW 6, para. 762)

This statement encouraged Fordham in his researches, although he did not dare to think at this stage that individuation occurred in childhood. But he was discovering that there were processes active in childhood which were not describable in terms of ego development exclusively and seemed to originate from the self.

Studying the evolution of Fordham's work, what is noticeable is how he began by demonstrating the impact of archetypal images on child development. Later he emphasized more the affective state of the child in the consulting room, in relation to him. Gradually he began to piece together a theory of development which, while derived from Jung's work, was very different from it. He did try to interest Jung in it but without much success. In his memoir he remarks that:

> Jung had the germ of such a theory but he lacked the necessary experience, which I had. From time to time I tried to interest him, but my efforts never had much success even though he gave a seminar on children's dreams. One day when we were having lunch I made a renewed effort, but he would only concede that the dreams of children were scientifically interesting, but as for child psychotherapy, if a child was brought to him he 'got the mother by the ears'. He went on in this vein until Emma broke in: 'You know very well you are not interested in anybody unless they exhibit archetypes!' and that was the end of the matter for quite a time. Emma [Mrs Emma Jung, Jung's wife] was a good ally of mine in this work.
>
> (Fordham 1993e, p. 117)

The particular nature of the work Fordham was working on was a theory of the self which extended Jung's use of the concept to include eventually a primary or original state of integration, somewhat analogous to the potential in DNA but probably without its hereditary constituents. This primal self, he thought, gave rise to structures from interaction with the environment which it in part created. It existed outside of time and space, and was similar to a mystical (or contemporary scientific) concept (see Chapter 11 for a discussion of the value of mysticism), whose manifestations had archetypal form. This primary self was integrated, and in Jung's sense it was an agency of the psyche which transcended opposites. His theory required the self to have some sort of dynamic, a potential energy, so that its actions could in time contribute to ego development.

DEINTEGRATION AND REINTEGRATION

By deductive reasoning Fordham called this dynamic deintegration and reintegration since the self was an integrate. Deintegration was the term used when referring to the energy going outwards towards objects and reintegration when the energy was returning to the self. Parts of the self which deintegrated, Fordham called deintegrates. A deintegrate of the self would retain characteristics of wholeness. A deintegrate could be an instinctual act, such as the hungry baby's cry – i.e. it would be contributing to the organism's biological adaptation – or it could be the creation of an image with potentially symbolic meaning. In the former example the deintegrate is manifesting itself objectively, in the latter it is subjective.

In terms of this model the most significant deintegrate of the self is the ego. Part of the difficulty of conceptualizing this is that it sounds as if Fordham is describing the ego as being like the self, when previously I have emphasized that Jung described the ego as the centre of consciousness and that this was what made it distinct from the self. In his later writings Jung was, however, to describe the ego as having unconscious features, which it has mainly been the task of psychoanalysts to reveal in their work on ego defences, such as projection, identification, rationalization and so on. In Jungian terms therefore, if the ego has unconscious features then this would mean that it has a shadow, and that would make it more like an archetype. So what Fordham's discovery revealed is that the features of the ego which make it near at times to the self is further evidence for his proposition that the relation of the ego to the self is a dynamic one in which the ego is a deintegrate of the self, and maintains a continuity with it.

Occasionally Fordham, like Jung, wrote of the self as if it were an archetype. Thus when bringing together the subjective and objective experiences and the different ways of thinking about the self Fordham wrote that the main body of the ego 'has a special relation to the archetype of the self: that the central archetype can be thought of as an organiser of the unconscious' (Fordham 1985a, p. 32). He is muddled here in his use of the term archetype to describe the self, since he is not differentiating the two, which he does elsewhere. This is similar to Jung who was not consistent in his descriptions of the self. What Fordham now thinks is that the self is *not* an archetype and that its main characteristic is its dynamic function (Fordham 1985a).

In imagining how the infant self would come into relation to the environment Fordham has described the process as follows:

> In essence, deintegration and reintegration describe a fluctuating state of learning in which the infant opens itself to new experiences and then withdraws in order to reintegrate and consolidate those experiences. During a deintegrative activity, the infant maintains continuity with the main body of the self (or its centre), while venturing into the external world to accumulate experience in motor action and sensory stimulation. . . . Such a concept of the self brings a new dimension to both depth psychology and developmental psy-

chology, for it is now conceived to be a dynamic structure through whose activity the infant's emotional and ego growth takes place.

(Fordham 1988f, p. 64)

What is contained in this statement, and was later to be confirmed by infant observation, was that the self in infancy actively created the environment within which it would grow. If the baby adapted to 'the niche' then 'the niche' most certainly adapted to the baby. Returning now to Kellogg's work it can be seen that out of random activity came shapes which by abstraction began to have a deintegrative form. These forms were then combined, which was the reintegrative process, into images which were recognizable. Later the child, with intention, employing memory, perception and other developing ego qualities, would be able to attempt to draw the image he had in his mind.

To understand the relationship between the self in infancy and childhood, and maturational processes, it is necessary to consider ego development with particular attention to these early states of mind.

Chapter 5

Ego development in infancy and childhood
The integration of observational research

EGO AND PRIMARY SELF

The features which characterize Fordham's theory of ego development are that the self is active in infancy and that the dynamic of the self called deintegration/reintegration, which probably begins *in utero*, continues throughout life. It is both a dynamic and a structural theory. The source for his discoveries was his own clinical work, combined with his perspicacity when reading Jung, Klein and contemporary research in paediatrics and ethology. From Klein he acquired a method for eliciting children's phantasies, recognizing the while that her descriptions of unconscious phantasy were close to Jung's descriptions of archetypal images, especially those centring on the dual aspect of the mother. Contemporary paediatric research, ethology and Piaget's studies also influenced his thinking since in their different ways they all gave evidence of innate capacities for discrimination, and of structures within the unconscious.

Jung had described the self and the ego as centres of integration within the person. He thought the self acquired greater prominence in the second half of life. Fordham suggested that before there was an ego there was a primary self. This primary self he thought of as integrated, a psychosomatic potential waiting to unfold in interaction with the environment. The primary self expressed itself through actions which brought it into contact with the environment. This is the form his model eventually took; arriving at this point was a gradual process, combining observation, study and clinical practice. The evolution of his thinking took place over many years.

The earliest observations of what could be thought of as the deintegrative process have been made of infants' behaviour *in utero*: drinking, thumb-sucking, moving about and reacting to noises. Fordham recently suggested (Fordham 1993a) that birth could be understood as a massive deintegrative experience. If as usually happens nowadays the baby is immediately given to the mother after the birth, reintegration would probably occur. Later experiences of falling for ever or of catastrophic chaos probably derive from that first deintegration. Soon after birth mother and infant start getting to know one another. These actions, deintegration and reintegration, give rise to deintegrates. A consequence of these early interactions is that the ego begins to form. The ego is a deintegrate of the self. Fordham would say therefore that the self is known through its deintegrates.

As the self meets the environment, objects are formed. At first there is not much distinction between subject and object:

> mouth and nipple are one total experience. Soon total experiences are separated into those that satisfy and are blissful, and those that are frustrating and rejected – the first equivalents of later good and bad objects have been experienced.
>
> (Fordham 1976a, p. 38)

The separating out of subject and object frequently begins when the infant encounters aspects of the environment which it finds difficult to adapt to; for instance the shape of the nipple or teat. The discomfort which arises from these experiences Fordham called constructive anxiety, since the infant's pain is in the service of its own development. Originally, when Fordham first published his theory, he thought that the fit between mother and baby had to be perfect (Fordham 1957a, pp. 127–8). Later he realized that by not being perfect it set in motion actions of the self, which stimulated ego development. The self provided the underlying potential structure for the individual baby's response to the world. Later, further structuring of the personality occurred with the development of the ego. As development proceeded subject and object became more distinct. A boundary began to be formed. This process of separating out 'me' and 'not me' Fordham thought of as the beginning of the individuation process. This led to the infant's self helping to create the environment in which it developed, whether by evocative actions which elicited an empathic response from its mother or by its own sensitivity to what its mother could bear.

Historically Jungians had thought of the self as an integrator of experience. Fordham's work has the self actively creating a dynamic system in which it then has to participate for its own development. He thought of the self as throwing itself into the experiences of the individual from birth onwards and in this way being involved in the creation of an inner world whereas Jung had emphasized more its containing, integrating and symbolic aspects. Both men, however, recognized the awesome power of the self, which could destructively overwhelm the ego, such as happens in the schizophrenias.

Babies do not react passively to their mothers, they engage in numerous actions of the self, eliciting from them what they need. Fordham further understood the mother's function of containment as something the infant also in part created. Through these interactions the baby can know in a primitive way about the capacities of the mother and in this way too the mother becomes partly the creation of the infant's self. The expectation the baby has is archetypal, just as the mother's is, but the realization of these potentials comes about through the response each has to the other.

In Chapter 4 I described some of Fordham's researches; now I want to consider the developments occasioned by observational studies.

THE IMPACT OF INFANT OBSERVATION

A significant part of the confirmation of this model occurred when infant observation became part of the training of child analysts in 1976. Then what had previously been speculation became in Fordham's language fact. For two years the trainee analyst spends an hour a week with a baby and its mother. What occurs during that time, including the recording of the observer's own responses to the situation, is then written up and presented to a group of other students also observing infants. The seminars are moderated by an experienced observer and child analyst. A very detailed record of the infant's first two years is built up from this sampling process, which focuses mainly on the emotional quality of the interactions between mother and child, child and siblings, father, grandparents and other significant caretakers. Fordham joined these seminars in the child training programme at the Society and was surprised to find that the model he had postulated did in fact seem to be an accurate description, in outline, of what actually happened in development. But some modifications were required. The first modification was to Jung's ideas of primitive identity. Originally Fordham had followed Jung in proposing an initial state of primitive identity (*participation mystique*). He had thought that the infant and mother were in a fused state. The observational studies revealed these states as being periodic. Jung's idea was that the infant was mainly in touch with the collective unconscious, and prior to the infant-observation seminars Fordham followed this idea, but then experience showed him that the infant was engaged in a dynamic interaction with another person. The consequence was that he rejected the idea of primitive identity as the earliest stage of development, with the infant being immersed in some sort of primal relationship (via *participation mystique*) which had characteristics of mother and infant being indivisible. Instead he acknowledged that there were, on occasions, states of mind which infants could go into (as did their mothers), which had qualities of feeling fused with another person, but that this was not the dominant characteristic of infancy. What was more important was the mother's capacity to receive and make sense of the baby's communications such that the baby took in from its mother's attention an experience of the world, usually of safety and of being understood. He noticed also that his hypothesis of the primary self helped the observers make sense of what they were observing, and realized that it provided the core for Jungian studies of infancy.

> But more than that the postulate of the infant self changed to something like a description of the facts of an infant's life; what started as a speculative hypothesis acquired characteristics of a fact: the baby shows he is a person whose nature is consistently recognisable (continuity of being), having an individuality of his own (no baby is the same as any other).
>
> (Fordham 1985a, p. 51)

One of the babies in Fordham's study group, Baby N, was thought of by them as a 'sparing' baby:

> his mother had a very low tolerance for aggression and her inner resources were limited. Baby N seemed to know just that and how, at a very early age, to get the best out of her by sparing her any aggressive attacks on the breast or undue screaming. Baby N was not unique and I would like to mention another baby whose mother was very uncertain as to her capacities as a mother. Her baby gave her such clear signs of what he needed that by following them she discovered what was in her and so she literally became 'a good enough mother'.
>
> (Fordham 1985a, p. 53)

There are two points here. The first is that the baby is not passive but is active in the way it engages the mother's interest. The second is that its expectation that it will be met with an appropriate response after birth contributes to that happening. So the mother as container of her child's anxiety is not a given, so much as part of a dynamic system based on the interaction between her and her baby. Naturally she is also drawing on her own experience of being mothered. Here is a description of Baby N at two weeks old:

> Baby N was lying in his bassinet on his right side with his right arm tucked under his body and his left arm bent up so his hand was near his face. His head with its soft covering of jet black hair was touching the top of the bassinet and F, his mother, said he had wriggled his way right up to the top of this bassinet. His eyes were open and he was moving the whole of his body slightly as if a little restless (he seemed neither awake nor asleep), F said he was probably hungry as it was near feeding time. N then suddenly quietened and for several minutes he lay absolutely still with his black eyes staring at the bassinet.
>
> (Fordham 1985a, p. 51)

Baby N pushing his head against the bassinet in his half awake, half asleep state seems to be behaving as if he's coming out of being *in utero*. F, the mother, then picked up N, the baby, and gave him to the observer. The account now continues in the first person:

> I continued to hold N while F drank her coffee. She talked to N gently and lovingly, smiling a great deal at him, and saying she couldn't believe he was really there. Then she took the baby and put him to her right breast to feed. It took a few attempts for N to get the nipple properly in his mouth but he then sucked loudly and greedily and hiccoughed. . . . N sucked vigorously, occasionally stopping for a rest. At first his eyes were wide open but after a couple of minutes they shut while he continued to suck. . . . F put him to her left breast and he sucked vigorously with lots of little grunts looking intently upwards. I thought he was trying to see her face, but F said he was looking at her red jumper. He then fell asleep and stopped sucking.
>
> (Fordham 1985a, pp. 51–2)

Looked at from the perspective of Fordham's theory this is a description of a deintegrative/reintegrative sequence and of a baby bringing out of his mother at that moment what he needed from her: an experience of the breast as the whole world. N is completely engrossed in the feed. The feeling that is conveyed to me by this sequence is not only of a mother responding to her child as a person, but also of the infant evoking this response. In truth this baby is borne in mind by his mother, she thinks about him, makes efforts to anticipate his needs, relieve his discomfort and in so doing helps him distinguish between what is inside him and what outside, what is bad, what is good. She is helping him develop rudimentary thoughts about the breast in a way which is not split off and inaccessible to him. In the context of Jung's theory of the opposites, maternal care of this kind can facilitate the development of psychic structures based on opposites and this is in the service of adaptation.

Fordham's theory helped the observer recognize the quality of this exchange from the vertex of the infant's actions of the self. This is what Fordham has emphasized, rather than the activities of the ego which, for instance, Kleinians describe as significant in this period. They have focused more on the emotional function of the part-object and its relation to omnipotence of thought. Fordham has stressed the way the infant brings the response out of the mother. Initially the baby treats the breast as his whole world (which may episodically feel to the baby similar to *participation mystique*), then gradually through deintegrative/reintegrative sequences the baby begins to reconstruct the breast out of an assortment of complicated interactions with the maternal environment, of which feeding is but one of them. The difference therefore between Fordham's theory and Jung's is in the emphasis Fordham puts on the activity of the baby's self. Fordham has compared the impact of the early feeds on the baby's mind to mandala symbolism:

> The whole object might then be compared with a mandala that has a nipple at the centre and various objects placed within the magic circle.
>
> (Fordham 1988f, p. 65)

For Fordham to liken the breast to a mandala was to root his investigations of infancy in the symbolism of the self and the way it unfolded through interaction. Jung had written of the significance of mandalas for his theory of the self:

> they [mandala symbols] signify nothing less than a psychic centre of the personality not to be identified with the ego.
>
> (*CW* 12, para. 126)

This conceptual leap from mandala to breast opened the way to further elaboration of Fordham's theory of infant development. The maturational processes of development are here being conceived as beginning with an archetypal relationship to what is felt to be a whole object. The gradual differentiation which follows this initial state is what links maturation to individuation. Thus 'individuation becomes realization of his condition through the development of self representations' (Fordham 1985a, p. 54). A self-representation here is a product of the deintegrating self combining with the environment, for instance the breast (Fordham, personal communication). A self-representation is different in quality from a self-object. 'A self representation is that which gives rise to a preconscious sense of self and other' (Fordham, letter to the author, 4 October 1994). The nature of self-objects, which I discuss later, is that they are understood by Fordham to be 'heavily loaded with libido and give rise to fantastic parent and other imagos. One might include here unconscious fantasy, archetypal matter etc' (ibid.).

Fordham's concept of the primary self emphasized the unity of the body and the emotional state in infancy; just as Jung's monistic attitude treated psyche and soma as one. In his writings on the primary self Fordham has stated that there is no difference in these first few weeks between behaviour and mental events (Fordham 1993a, p. 6). The primary self precedes consciousness and unconsciousness and out of the early deintegrative and reintegrative activity the ego begins to form. At the centre of Fordham's model is the biological idea of adaptation. Infant observation studies exemplify this, showing babies behaving in ways which promote their survival. Consequently this suggested to Fordham that the babies' first object relations were adapted to reality. From Fordham's perspective the evidence from infant observation supported the datum of the self in infancy. For Fordham the self 'integrates the ego fragments and so produces the ego centre' (Fordham 1957a, p. 126).

> Why did I invent, or rather infer, the idea of the primary self in childhood? It was at first a speculation, but over the years it has proved useful in counteracting the tendency to deny an infant a personality of its own.
>
> (Fordham 1985b, p. 18)

To summarize: Fordham discovered there was an original self in infancy, that there was a centre, an original integrate to the child. He studied this through children's pictures, through analyses and finally through infant observations. The result of his study was that he found evidence for the self's creating the environment in which the infant's emotional development took place. An example of this would be:

> A mother was starting on feeding with her second baby. She did so with trepidation because her attempt with her first baby had been difficult. The second baby, however, gave such clear indications of what his needs were that the mother could read them and so a good feeding couple was established. It was as if the baby showed his mother how to behave.
>
> (Fordham, letter to the author, 4 October 1994)

This is the most radical aspect of Fordham's theory and where it departs from other theories about infancy. He also emphasized the infant's first relationship with the breast as an experience characterized by feelings of wholeness, and only episodically with feelings of fusion.

FURTHER ELABORATIONS OF FORDHAM'S MODEL OF DEVELOPMENT

In an infant observation we are observing principally physical acts, but they are perceived as having psychic content. Jung, when lecturing at the Tavistock in 1935, was asked by Bion (not then a psychoanalyst) about this vexatious problem of the apparent dualism of the baby's world. He replied:

> You touch again on the controversial problem of psycho-physical parallelism for which I know no answer, because it is beyond the reach of man's cognition. As I tried to explain yesterday, the two things – the psychic fact and the physiological fact – come together in a peculiar way. They happen together and are, so I assume simply two different aspects to our mind, but not in reality. We see them as two on account of the utter incapacity of our mind to think of them together.
>
> (*CW* 18, para. 136)

Fordham's work attempts to penetrate into this area of psycho-physical parallelism by imaginative speculation combined with astute observation and reflection. He implicitly rejected Jung's idea that ego development consists of the coalescence of *islets of consciousness*, for this suggested there was no centre to the infant. Jung thought there was no centre to the infant until the ego developed. He described the emergence of consciousness and linked it to the gradual development of 'I-ness', distinguishing early perceptions from later ones which were linked by memory (*CW* 8, para. 755). Fordham, however, thought of the infant as having a centre and of his experience as being on a continuum, with a sliding scale for the degree to which a perception was suffused with real qualities as distinct from having primarily a self-object quality. Fordham described a self-object as follows:

> When the object is mainly a record of reality, it may be called a reality object; when it is mainly constructed by the self and so records states of the self, made out of exteroceptive and introceptive sense data, then it may be called a self object. . . . It appears that self objects

increase in affectively charged states, whilst in quiet contemplative exploring activities real objects predominate.

(Fordham 1985a, p. 56)

Experiences that are suffused with qualities of the infant's self are initially those that Jung referred to when describing 'identity'. 'Identity' is the precursor to states of identification and 'on it also depends the possibility of projection and introjection' (Jung *CW* 6, para. 741). Fordham's thinking is based on observation of the infant's emerging capacity to refine its discriminations:

According to self theory the self has boundaries by the time birth takes place as infant observations indicate, it also has potential for developing structures, but I assume they would require self objects finding representation in the ego. These objects would develop through deintegrative/integrative sequences. According to Jung's early formulations there was no self and only ego fragments not developed enough to form definable boundaries let alone structural forms. Only in later years did he recognise that individuation was a life-long process which presupposes that the self is active in childhood, but he never worked out the consequences of his conclusion which it has been my attempt to do. I shall argue that at first an infant has not sufficient structure for projective identification to occur without an earlier period in which identity between subject and object predominates, out of that state enough structures form to make the theory of projective identification useful.

(Letter to the author, 30 April 1992, enclosing a revision, not incorporated in the text, to 'Identification', in Fordham 1994b)

So out of 'identity' come states where self-objects find representation in the ego. These self-representations herald a 'preconscious sense of self and other'. Structures begin to form gradually out of deintegrative/ reintegrative sequences, and states of normal projective identification begin to occur. Bion described normal projective identification as 'the link between patient and analyst, or infant and breast' (Bion 1959, p. 105). (This is distinct from the original descriptions of projective identification which concentrated on its omnipotent features and the way in which it destroyed awareness rather than in this instance enhancing it. These later projective and identificatory states either can be used as a means of gaining knowledge about an object or can be a way of eliminating it by taking possession of it and controlling it in fantasy.)

Here is part of an observation of Baby G taken from Fordham's book *Explorations into the Self.*

> Baby G was an active aggressive baby who could make his wishes known in no uncertain manner especially over nappy changes during which he made loud and noisy protests. One day a health visitor arrived during a breast feed and demanded information immediately. Mother interrupted the feed lying her baby down for a short period. He made protesting cries which escalated into screaming and drowned all conversation; in addition he soaked and dirtied himself. At first he was not to be calmed down and mother became worried though in an appropriate way; she initiated and persisted in efforts to relieve her baby's distress. Finally she was successful so that the feed could be continued and was followed by sleep. Thus a potential disaster was well and adequately dealt with – integration took place.
>
> (Fordham 1985a, p. 57)

The process of integration in this example is facilitated by the mother's actions and by her thinking about her baby's pain. She had been filled with his distress and by metabolizing these experiences was able to feed back to him her empathic understanding which he took back into himself (reintegration). This is an example of an action of the self, of the deintegrative/reintegrative sequence and of normal projective identification. But suppose the mother had not persisted and had not been able to retrieve this situation? Suppose too that this had been repeated over a number of occasions? Then the experience would not have been reintegrated.

The baby above who is screaming, defecating and protesting loudly is trying to get rid of the experience of badness. These qualities of badness are, in adult language, subsumed under the heading of rage and frustration. Baby G has not, however, split off the badness: he is still vigorously engaged in trying to put it somewhere where it can be made sense of for him. This his mother helps him achieve. It is a deintegrate possessed of badness. In psychoanalysis this is called splitting and idealization, because the objects are split into their wholly good and wholly bad aspects, so that the one does not contaminate the other. While there are different versions of splitting in the psychoanalytic model, for the sake of comparison I am here referring to the fairly coherent splitting of the object, as distinct from, for instance, the fragmenting of the ego, to which this term can also refer. The reason the good object is described as idealized when this happens is that the feeling of goodness about it is precarious and can quickly turn into its opposite. In analytical psychology we reserve the term splitting for those occasions when we think that what has happened is pathological, i.e. wholeness has been violated, the ego split. For what is split is not integrated, it is held in projection or denied and in this way can become fixed. Fordham has compared splitting and deintegration:

> Klein spoke of splitting, whereby she suggested that a baby in the course of development splits up in such a way that wholeness is violated. Deintegration, by contrast, means that the quality of wholeness permeates the baby's actions. The difference between these two hypotheses may be thought about as follows. Early on in extrauterine life, a baby experiences one breast as good and another one as bad, depending on the degree of satisfaction or frustration experienced in feeding. It is believed that the baby does not know that both breasts are the same: that awareness comes later as cognitive and emotional development proceed. One can say that the two breasts are the consequence of splitting, or that deintegrates become classed as good or bad because emotional development has not reached the stage of being able to grasp that the two experiences emanate from the same source. Whether one or the other of the hypotheses be correct, the distinction becomes important in emotional development.
>
> (Fordham 1985b, p. 4)

Fordham is emphasizing developments within infancy which have characteristics which he thinks of as having more to do with the totality of the infant and therefore coming from its self, rather than theorizing in terms of defences of the ego. His description of the distinction between deintegration and Klein's splitting is not wholly accurate in its representation of Klein's point of view. It refers to splitting of the ego. But Klein, prior to 1946, also described splitting and idealization as a necessary process for separating good and bad experiences without the ego splitting. This does not necessarily lead to pathological development where characterological change occurs. Fordham's language keeps pathology and development separate. He perceives the deintegrate's continuity with the wholeness of the self as serving the emotional development of the individual, without splitting being necessary, unless something goes wrong. He is also reluctant to attribute to the infant ego what he feels is better described as a quality of the self.

A common example of the way the quality of an object becomes fixed, of a splitting, is when it becomes persecutory. Fordham has published a detailed description of the events leading up to an infant's developing a split in its personality. Observations of Baby N, the boy referred to earlier, gave evidence that the impact of being left by his mother with Grandfather, whom he knew, had, to everyone's surprise, been catastrophic. Gradually the seminar was able to piece together a picture of the world in which N lived and how it had changed.

He was initially an affectionate baby who had a sensuous and loving relationship with his mother. It was noticed that he seemed sensitive to what she could bear, but following being left, 'N became increasingly clinging, and this alternated with violent screaming, yelling, growling, and fierce attacks both on his mother and on the furniture in the house' (Fordham 1985b, p. 11). It seemed as if his trust in his good object had been broken. Frequently after this he became anxious when his mother went out of the room. At five months he was weaned, and following this he became aggressive, demanding and omnipotent, stuffing food in his mouth until he made himself choke.

> His scavenging increased and almost anything he could lay his hands on would go into his mouth, including his thumb. But central in that was the fluff he collected from any soft and vulnerable object. It seemed as though he was seeking the softness and sensuousness of the lost breast. But his behaviour was also attacking and so was his way of working out his attack on the breast that he had spared. This seemed expressed in the ways he would burrow into his mother's neck or push up between her legs as if he wanted to get inside her. . . .
> At around six months, N began to use expulsive ways of getting rid of his bad feelings; he would start hissing, blowing and snorting through his nostrils, while looking challengingly and aggressively at his mother or the observer. . . . While this was going on it began to look as if N was increasingly afraid of his own violence.
>
> (Fordham 1985b, p. 16)

Baby N split off the bad experience and became more and more clingy, seductive with his mother and jealous of his older sibling. N's mother was often at a loss and the observer began to feel that she was looking to Baby N to contain her distress and relieve her of the pain she was going through. Gradually a theory began to emerge as to why N's development had taken a pathological turn.

> If it be assumed that N experienced his mother's absence as the result of his actions – for on more than one occasion he had told her 'Go!' – and that he had discovered that his mother could be either a good or a bad mother, and if we add that these mothers had now coalesced,

then if in his violence he had wished the bad mother dead (to go), he would know that he had destroyed the good mother as well.

(Fordham 1985b, p. 15)

What happened to this child later is not known; efforts to provide help for him and his mother were refused at the time and as Fordham points out:

One feature of this kind of work is the great difficulty one finds in making predictions, which is in marked contrast to what might be expected from that kind of analysis of childhood that relies on finding causes for mental disorders. . . . I have not made mention of archetypes, but I regard N's experience as archetypal but without much mental imagery. One is reminded of Jung's metaphor [*CW* 8, para. 414] of the spectrum, in which archetypal experience took on many forms. At the infra red end, the experiences merged into physical action. It is to this end that we have to look in order to understand what happened.

(Fordham 1985b, p. 19)

Fordham found in Bion's language a suitably abstract expression for what he imagined could be happening and he has linked his model to Bion's theory of thinking. He thought of what Bion called beta elements, particles of as yet undigested sense data, as equivalent to the first deintegrates, and successful reintegration as equivalent to the effect of maternal reverie and alpha function, which is the process of generating meaning out of sensations (Bion 1967, p. 115). Early reintegrated experiences, therefore, might carry with them a potential thought, but not thinking. Fordham shares with Bion the view that the mother's capacity to contain in her mind the infant's pain contributes to the infant's capacity to bear this pain. He thinks of the mind structuring itself through the digestion of experience, at first through the activity of the self, then the archetypes, later through the activity of the ego. Additionally what Fordham proposed is that the baby in its sensuous and physical being has the potential to generate the mental equivalent of physical experiences, rudimentary thoughts which can later be used for thinking as the ego develops.

Thus when N, at 10 weeks, was seen 'watching his mother with a look of serious concentration on his face', that can be thought of as the operation of alpha function; something like a thought may be going to happen or may occur, but we cannot say that it does. . . .

These formulations attempt to penetrate into, to use Jung's metaphor, the infra red end of the spectrum of archetypal action.

(Fordham 1985b, p. 19)

Having a thought is the precursor to thinking. Thinking here becomes the equivalent of digestion. Out of this interaction of baby and environment the baby's potential is realized. This is a route full of pain, not least because of the baby's struggle to make use of the anxiety to which those experiences give rise. This pain is full of meaning, which is contained in the emotion. This process recognizes that thoughts and feelings originate in the unconscious, that what we feel (and I'm here including the unconscious aspects of emotion) contains the meaning of our experience. Our creative activities can be understood as the representation of these meanings. Baby N's experiences began well but then deteriorated. Splitting and the mobilization of total defences occurred, called by Fordham defences of the self, 'because it involves more than the ego'. The feeling of badness had a reality for Baby N and Baby G, which was subjective and infused with violence and rage. While we may know the baby's mother is going to do her best to make it better, the baby does not. He is not able to distinguish the thing in itself, the absent breast, from his feeling of its absence. In that sense the absent breast is a true archetypal image combining personal and impersonal elements. When the breast is removed only its badness has remained; good feelings and memories of it are lost to his mind. He is inside the badness. The good breast has now gone. The infant has identified with a bad internal object.

These observation experiences revealed that the idea that infants are part of their parent's unconscious – i.e. that there is a primary state of fusion between mother and infant – is incompatible with the infant's having an original self. This does not mean that experiences of fusion do not occur. There is an early stage when subject and object are less distinct (called here states of identity), when the experience of the baby is mainly pleasurable, which can be thought of as a blissful fused state. This state is, according to Fordham, transitory and probably connected partly to the absence of a developed perceptual apparatus and partly to the avoidance of the pain of consciousness. It is also often described as the blissful goal of regression.

FORDHAM AND NEUMANN

Fordham's empirical approach and his expansion of Jung's concept of the self revealed that fusion was not the initial primary state of mother and infant, such as is meant by the phrase *participation mystique* or 'primary relationship'. Following on from this it ceased to be tenable that mother and infant were in a state of primary identity. If the infant was an integrate then the infant's self could not be carried by the mother. Fordham rejected therefore the idea that the infant lived in a mythological world, from which he gradually freed himself and to which he longed to return. This idea was described by a prominent Jungian, E. Neumann. He was an early follower of Jung, and wrote an account of child development from a genetic point of view. This followed Fordham's earlier publication (Fordham 1944) in which he had pointed to the need for a genetic theory of development in analytical psychology.

In his book *The Child*, Neumann (1973) described mother and child immersed in an archetypal relationship which controlled them and out of which the stages in the child's development emerged. Fordham was very critical of this (Fordham 1981a). He argued that it read as if development was predetermined. Furthermore he took issue with Neumann for suggesting that ontogeny recapitulated phylogeny. Neumann's approach asserted the primacy of collective influences in infancy, leaving little room for the individual capacities of the mother and the child. I will summarize Neumann's thesis and Fordham's response, omitting the numerous neologisms which Neumann coined.

At the core of Neumann's theory is the controversial statement that development is determined by the structure of the archetype. This is in contrast to the empirically based view of students of development, who universally describe an interaction between inner states of mind, external reality and phases of development. At the centre of his model is 'the primary relationship' between mother and child, in which mother and child live 'in an archetypally conditioned unitary relationship' (Neumann 1973, p. 17). In this unitary world 'there is universal relatedness; everything is connected to everything else and one thing can and must stand for everything else' (ibid., p. 153). 'The mother not only plays the role of the child's self, but actually is that self' (ibid., p. 13). Neumann characterized this state as similar to intra-uterine life. This is an idealized and unreal account of mothers and babies, drawing its inspiration from myths of paradisiacal states and fantasies that intra-uterine life is blissful. He also assumes there is a universal wish to return to this state of imagined fusion of mother and child. The book elaborates the stages of ego development the author imagines occur. These too are full of conceptual confusions – for instance that the ego is an archetype – and lack of awareness of the empirical studies of children's cognitive development. This model is not based in the observation of children but is derived from applying a theory about the development of culture to the development of a child.

By contrast, Fordham's work was based on studies of real babies, where the mother in relation to her infant is acting as a mediator of archetypal experience. Fordham's work on infancy and childhood is congruent not only with the experience of the ordinary devoted mother but also with our experience of adult life.

I have scarcely mentioned consciousness or unconsciousness since these concepts do not, in Fordham's view, help us think about what is happening when observing infants. Rather he is approaching development from the point of view of realization of the self. This keeps the focus on adaptation. This is not passive acquiescence to environmental pressures but rather the biological meaning of learning to live in a particular environment. There may be observable and intense affects which are exaggerated but most of the infant's experiences seem, on the evidence of observational studies, to be adapted to reality.

SYMBOLIZATION AND DEINTEGRATION

Why do we need a theory like this, and what does it add to our existing conceptions of infancy? Theories are mainly of value if they help us think about observations. First, the theory focuses attention on the infant and what it does. The investigator starts his scientific inquiries from the same position as the ordinary mother, thinking of the baby as a separate person. This leaves room for the baby's capacity for discrimination. Next, a theory of deintegration focuses our thoughts on the observed behaviour of the infant as being continuous with the self. What this means is that the development of the individual baby is in effect an early form of individuation, as experiences are being reintegrated within a continuum. So this theory lets us proceed on the basis that the infant is a separate person but it also takes into account the fit between the infant and its mother and how actively the infant contributes to this.

Why is it useful to think of experience as being on a continuum? Because it takes us away from linear thinking where one stage replaces another, and puts in its place a model which allows previous experience to coexist with contemporary experience such that each may modify the other. Historically this has been very important since it has provided a grounding for the analyses of children and for investigations of technique based on transference analysis.

The implication for symbolization is that when the baby can hold in his mind the experience of a breast which is sometimes blissful and sometimes hateful, then it can become a symbol and in a sense the paradigm for all his future good objects. The breast is fantasized to have been destroyed because it is a bad breast that frustrates, but the experience of the good breast survives this attack. And in this way the symbol arises. Why symbol formation is important is that without this capacity intellectual development is impaired, in such a way that the progression from concrete representation, via ideographic representation, to verbal thought does not occur. How does the baby achieve this state of being able to symbolize? Fordham writes:

> In order to create a symbol the self object must be destroyed, otherwise the urgent need for a creative act is not brought into being: since the breast (as self object) is destroyed, while the real breast is still in existence, the constructive act can take place only in another way, by abstraction from the object – the abstraction being the symbol.
>
> (Fordham 1976a, p. 21)

A significant attribute of symbol formation is that experiences in order to become symbolized must have a life over time; they must have occurred sufficiently often for them to have continuity of existence in the infant's mind. For something to become a symbol it has to have entered consciousness. The implication of this view is that symbolization is associated with ego development and the depressive position since this is when the infant realizes he has lost his good-breast object (when he was weaned) but can retain in his mind the good experience of this breast which he can build on. Fordham does not hold with fixed positions in development (Fordham 1988f, pp. 64–5). He prefers a more flexible approach such as expressed by Bion's double arrow between the sign for the depressive position and that for the paranoid-schizoid position, indicating that these are states of mind which the baby can go in and out of. This suggests that symbol formation is a gradual process, which to begin with comes and goes. Only with experience does it consolidate into something which reliably exists over time. If this is the case then we must be careful not to confuse symbol formation with symbolic thought. Symbolic thought characterizes infancy and only later does directed thinking take over. I understand the difference between symbolic thought and the developed capacity to symbolize, such as, for instance, you see in children's play, to be similar to the difference between thoughts which are free from the realism of fact and thoughts which acknowledge the realism of fact and concretism but transcend them. Symbol formation requires a level of abstraction absent in symbolic thought.

THE FUNDAMENTAL FEATURES OF FORDHAM'S THEORY

Fordham begins with the primary self, which has no features. It cannot be experienced. This is the first tier; then, secondly, it acquires characteristics. When parts of it are brought into relation to the environment it initiates a process which leads to the structuring of the mind. The first contacts between mother and baby are suffused with states of identity, giving rise to self-objects, which gradually lead to self-representations with the consequence that there now develops a rudimentary awareness of self and other. By now there is sufficient structure for projective identification to occur, and a rudimentary ego begins to form as deintegrative/reintegrative activity is organized by the self. The dynamic of this self – its way of acting – Fordham called deintegration/reintegration, to preserve the idea that the self did not disintegrate in action. Each deintegrate would have a physical and a psychic dimension; and, most significantly of all, he has suggested that the infant self helps create the environment in which it will develop. The most significant deintegrate of the self is the ego. From the observation of this process the self's features can be inferred. It is a psychosomatic entity, having the potential to form a body and a psyche. The exteroceptive skin experiences are important in infancy as they help define the boundary of the infant and the feeling of its body being a container. Inside this container an inner world can develop. In response to environmental conditions the self responds in preformed ways.

Fordham has also indicated that for disturbed children the early relationship to the breast could be understood in terms of failures in the deintegrative and reintegrative process with particular reference to the defensive boundary of the self. This idea he later expanded, following his investigations into childhood psychoses. It has implications for the idea that all babies necessarily have inner worlds from the beginning, rather than that the capacity to experience an inner world is related to deintegrative/reintegrative activity.

Chapter 6

Archetypes
Their biological basis and actions of the self

One of the difficulties in separating the actions of the self from the activities of the ego in infancy is that phenomenologically they are the same. In later life they are not and Gordon's work on 'big' and 'little' self has helped to conceptualize the differences (Gordon 1985). For Jung the ego was the centre of consciousness, a centre he thought took up to five years to develop and which he poetically evoked in his image of 'the conscious rises out of the unconscious like an island newly risen from the sea' (*CW* 17, para. 103). Jung asserted from his study of very different sources, from patients to primitive societies, from alchemical texts to religions – God (the self) made man (the ego) in his own image – that the self in its observable manifestations was objective whereas the ego was personal. What this meant was that the manifestations of the self were archetypal and so of the collective unconscious. The organs of the unconscious are the archetypes and these are present before birth. Fordham explained this in the following way:

> The theory of the collective unconscious and so of its organs, the archetypes, is based upon the notion that the fundamental structure of the psyche is uniform and that in the last resort, if we could eliminate the conscious, there would be little or no difference between one human being and another. There is therefore an 'X', psychic* but unconscious in its nature, out of which consciousness grows. This 'X' is the precursor of dream and fantasy. When it appears in imagery, it seems to be the expression in consciousness of instinct; but it always adds something else which is not, and never has been, exactly defined, and which is, and always has been referred to in such terms as 'spirit', 'pneuma', or 'numinosum'.
>
> (Fordham 1957a, p. 2)

---

* Jung later questioned its psychic nature and referred to the 'psychoid archetype'.

Now, in the late twentieth century, psychoanalysts too have joined in the investigation and description of phenomena which are not ego, for instance Jacobson, Federn, Hartmann, Klein, Winnicott, Sandler and Kohut. I do not propose to discuss those authors' different emphases (nor to discuss whether Fairbairn's central ego is really the self by another name) but rather to try to describe what constitutes an action of the self and how this relates to the biological basis of archetypes. In discussing actions of the self I am discussing the self which realizes itself in the maturational and interactional experiences of the first few years of life, and continues from infancy to old age. For this is one of the significant contributions Fordham has made to analytical psychology: to show how the self has a biological origin and a conceptual framework rooted in adaptation. In this sense adaptation refers to the biological concept of the organism changing actively in response to the environment so as to better its chances of survival.

BIOLOGICAL BASIS

Jung's researches led him to describe archetypal images as the representations in consciousness of spirit and instinct. Studies of instinctual behaviour in animals were therefore a relevant source for Fordham's inquiries into the biology of archetypes. He investigated the contemporary research being done by the ethologists who demonstrated the presence of a perceptual system within animals which could be consistently elicited. They studied the stimuli (equivalent to the instinctual aspect of the archetype) which elicit specific behaviours in animals, called by them innate release mechanisms. They showed that by producing the stimulus at the right time in the life of the animal a response arose which determined a pattern of behaviour, which was instinctual. Fordham called this almost an example of 'the environment fitting the deintegrate' (Fordham 1957a, p. 121) as if the environment were adapted to the self-realizing psyche. The value for psychologists of experimental animal work, not only of the ethologists, but also of those working on the endocrine and neural systems, had been to show there is a hierarchy of neural patterns for instinctive behaviour. Fordham studied this work and linked it to advances in neurophysiology. He recognized that these neurological studies which through the introduction of electronic concepts showed purposive activity, for instance, feedback, oscillation and reverberating circuits, could be linked to:

the unconscious as a dynamic unit which functions as a whole and is yet made up of operative centres (perceived, in consciousness, as archetypal images). The parallel has greater force if the concept of relative localisation be compared with that of the archetypes, for in each case the functions are relatively transferable and yet have an apparent specificity. When it comes to the nature of the nuclei, the psychic and neurophysiological concepts diverge in that the one is finalistic and purposive and the other mechanistic.

(Fordham 1957a, p. 17)

Piaget's studies on how children learn, and on innate schemata which mature, provided further evidence for there being a hierarchy of innate predispositions which respond in particular ways. Piaget conceptualized experience in infancy as being assimilable through schemata. He identified a schema, for instance, which co-ordinated eye, hand, mouth and object for the purpose of sucking. He suggested that these schemata incorporate objects which become part of the schema and are not initially differentiated. This is a cognitive psychological description for what Fordham has called a self-object (not the same as Kohut's self-object). Further, it implied a biological basis for the origin of later perceptual experiences since Piaget went on to say that this action of assimilation 'foretells later and much more important generalisations' (Piaget 1953). To Fordham this meant that the early undifferentiated archetypal activity gave way to focused, directed and now more consciously purposive actions, with the gradual development of ego functions such as memory and perception. R.D. Scott, with whose work Fordham was familiar, studied the localization of sensory stimuli in relation to consciousness of the body image. Scott argued also that Kant's categories were the same as the archetypal potentials, that Piaget's schema existed as a 'third thing' between a concept and an object, and that he agreed with Kant that 'not images of objects, but schemata, lie at the basis of our sensuous conceptions' (Kant 1934, p. 119). He quoted approvingly Professor Head's work on 'the sensory integration of the nervous system' which led Scott to propose that the body image as such was not an encoded specific image but a 'schema' which, as a physiological process, is between an image and an action and is 'a constantly changing "plastic model" of the individual's own body in space and time' (Scott 1956, p. 146). Why this was important for analytical psychologists and Fordham's work in particular was that it demonstrated that localization of sensory stimuli did not require consciousness, i.e. the ego. The parallel to analytic concepts which Fordham noted was that the neurologists', ethologists' and cognitive psychologists' work all provided evidence for the unconscious being a dynamic unit 'which functions as a whole and is yet made up of operative centres (perceived in consciousness as archetypal images)' (Fordham 1957a, p. 17). Operative centres, schemata and archetypes seem therefore to be different terms for the same sort of dynamic structures. The neurologists' work especially interested Fordham since he could make parallels between their electronic concepts and Jung's suggestion that rhythmic energies were significant in development and evolution (*CW* 5, para. 204).

The voluminous work on object constancy from the Gestalt psychologists, to the perceptual studies made popular by Gregory (1963) also provided evidence for perception consisting of the formation of schemata in order to maintain the invariance of the object when looked at from different angles. This experimental scientific work and the philosophical arguments of Kant supported the idea that there were structures outside of consciousness which had regularities and patterns. At the time Fordham made his study of biological theory and archetypes, he used the concept of adaptation to bridge the gap between patterns and purpose. Today I think he would have been studying evolutionary epistemology, in particular the idea of a Darwinian model of the mind developing by natural selection, at the level of neuronal networks (Edelman 1987) as this work, in my view, is attempting to bridge the gap between patterns of behaviour and aims and purposes. Edelman's work post-dates Fordham's. If, as is likely, the primal self is biologically rooted, would it be more brain than mind? This question loses its relevance if we accept the teleological actions of all living things. It is self-evident that organisms act to stay alive and this is Jung and Fordham's position. The comparison Scott made when writing of children's inability to perceive object constancy was to say of the children that:

> they have not got the relativity of other objects sufficiently differentiated and are so to speak, stimulus bound. . . . If we transfer this relatively psychological level to a more perceptual level, the primitive undifferentiated state would correspond to the perception of stimulus intensities, as such, with little object constancy.
>
> (Scott 1956, p. 158)

Since we cannot think physiologically we have to add a third element, the idea of the schema, or the archetype, in order to create the perceptual world for ourselves. Following on from this, Fordham argued that the purposiveness of the psychic concepts is integrated by the activities of the self. These activities are extroverted in their deintegrative aspect and introverted in their reintegrative aspect. So, at a basic level of functioning, the meeting of instinctual needs could be understood as the action of the self directed towards adaptation. This psychological fact recognizes the purposive activity of nuclei as having the potential to be represented within the psyche, which is implicit in archetype theory.

When working out his position Fordham made use of the work of Call (1964) who studied the anticipatory approach behaviour of infants. In these studies he described how the instinct to root for the breast in new-borns was present from the first feed. Each baby showed a remarkable capacity to adapt to the mother's specific feeding style, taking as a cue kinaesthetic sensations derived from the mother's holding position. This finding surprised Call and his fellow researchers: 'for the two day old infant's capacity for anticipation and adaptation to the specific mother's feeding style we were not prepared' (Call 1964, p. 289). In Call's discussion of his findings, mainly organized from the point of view of traditional Freudian psychoanalysis and the American ego psycholo- gists' developments of it, he is impressed by the infant's capacity to discriminate:

> It would seem an error to designate the first six months of life as a period during which the infant remains in a symbiotic relation to the mother. This is so only relatively. Beginnings of the differentiation of self from other are coming about, albeit in a very restricted fashion, right from the beginning.
>
> (Ibid., p. 292)

He demonstrated the interactional nature of this early period of mutual adaptation. To Fordham this showed that it was as much an action of the self that the mother responded to the infant's needs by picking it up and by her milk letting down and by her holding it in a particular way, as it was an action of the self that the baby rooted when held in a particular position. The mother's response, therefore, could be a further example of what Fordham called, when discussing the ethologists' research, 'the environment fitting the deintegrate'. But its essential relevance, in my view, is that he is drawing attention to an inter-psychic, interactional root to psychic development, expressed in terms of an action of the self, which is irreducible. Call's work on discrimination based on observational studies has echoes of the ethologists' work, the equivalent of the releasing stimulus being the kinaesthetic sensations. Call's work has been built on by Stern (1985), and many others, whose later research has provided detailed evidence for the infant's capacity to discriminate.

Each researcher has a preferred model for organizing their findings, and Stern's is different from Fordham's. This makes comparisons difficult because each has different assumptions about what cannot be observed. But Stern and Fordham do share a wariness about ascribing to the infant ego capacities for fusing with objects and for splitting of the ego during infancy. Stern described this as coming later and being dependent on the establishment of boundaries, literal and symbolic between oneself and another.

EVOLUTION

In locating the self in the biology of the individual, Fordham, on the one hand, was necessarily raising the question as to the origin of archetypes and, on the other, whether there had been a change in them over time which could be perceived. Jung side-stepped the biological argument as to whether experience could be inherited. His suggestion that for archetypes 'their origin can only be explained by assuming them to be deposits of the constantly repeated experiences of humanity' (*CW* 7, para. 109) implies that early human beings, just like contemporary human beings, could be said to experience archetypal images arising from the activity of the archetypes in the unconscious. This statement does not violate biological theory, which is opposed to the inheritance of acquired characteristics. But it could seem to imply that experiences modify archetypes, such as Professor Plotkin has recently pointed out:

> A priori ordering of brain function relative to an ordering of the world can be explained as an instance of instruction in somatic time due to a posteriori selection in evolutionary time, without detracting at all from the potential power of a selectional theory of brain function operating in somatic time.
>
> (Plotkin 1991, p. 489)

Fordham, as part of his evaluation of the biological relationship between archetype and behaviour, examined an alternative explanation, diffusionist theory. This is an anthropological theory which proposes that specialized knowledge diffuses outwards from a centre to the rest of the world. He concluded that diffusionist theory:

> takes no account of how the assimilation of a new concept of whatever kind takes place, and it is just here that psychological studies are necessary. If we identify the development of culture with the emergence of consciousness, then a new and revealing line of approach is opened

up. It redefines the whole problem as follows: the conscious origin-
ates in the unconscious, its first expression is in the form of images,
inspirations, dreams, etc. Amongst these the archetypal images take
the main place; only later do they become systematized as
knowledge. Science is not only the most recent but also the best
example to take for the illumination of the problem, since never
before the 'scientific age' has consciousness increased so rapidly.

(Fordham 1957a, p. 22)

Fordham considered that some support too came from a paper written by
the scientist W. Pauli in which he linked Kepler's scientific discoveries
to ancient religious doctrines. He wrote:

The process of understanding nature . . . seems to be based on a
correspondence, a 'matching' of inner images pre-existent in the
human psyche with external objects and their behaviour.

(Pauli 1955, p. 152)

Although an archetypal image is not pre-existent, Pauli was making the
important point that scientific discovery was not dependent on rational
processes. He pointed out that the archetype *per se* did not evolve in a
discernible way but what did evolve and change was the form we give it.

Fordham has addressed the link between biological theory and the
formation of images from the perspective of the growth of the personality, and I will summarize his argument – so far not disputed. Jung, it
will be recalled, felt it was sufficient to demonstrate that if it could be
shown that an archetypal theme could not have first been in the consciousness of the patient – i.e. that it originated in the unconscious – then
it could not be due to learning. Fordham noted the scientific inadequacy
of this assumption and of Jung's methodology and examined contemporary research into biological theory. To the analytical psychologist
with a teleological approach, the archetypal potential was in the germ
plasm and the archetypal image arose from the interaction of this
potential with environmental pressure, whether conceptualized as
internal to the person or external. Fordham, familiar with Mendel's laws
and Weismann's theory of the continuity of germ plasm, stated: 'the
only factors which are inherited are those contained within the fertilized
ovum; everything else is a product of the inherited factors and the
environment' (Fordham 1957a, p. 11). The problem this left him with
was the nature of the images which the archetypes give rise to. In
Chapter 4 I described how Fordham linked the circular scribblings of a
little boy patient of his to the discovery of 'I' and the beginnings of a

sense of his own identity. Fordham combined all the sources of knowledge we have so far discussed: (a) the experience of children in analysis; (b) Kellogg's researches showing how children combine rhythm, random activity (deintegration) and abstraction (reintegration) to create images; (c) Piaget's researches; (d) Call's observational studies; (e) studies of instinct in animals; and (f) physiological and neurological studies. And in so doing he traced the innate predisposition to respond to images and its connection to theories about the formation and organization of them – the dynamic of which he characterized as actions of the self.

Finally, to show the common features of an instinct across centuries and species, Fordham compared an account from a medieval mystic, Mechthild of Magdeburg, in which he described a devil losing his power over a woman when she withdrew from the conflict and left it 'to the interaction of the devil and God upon her person' (Fordham 1957a, p. 25) – in effect almost turning the other cheek – and the account by Lorenz of the submissive behaviour of timber wolves (Lorenz 1952). Comparing the two experiences he noted that the common features of the two accounts were as follows: in each case the conflict was one of possession; for the mystic it was possession of the soul, for the wolf of territory. There was a struggle, a crisis, the weaker submitted and emerged unscathed and intact. In both cases the attacker wanted to attack but just could not. In the mystic's account the devil lost his power, acknowledging that 'because thou givest thy soul meekly to torment, I lose all my power' – i.e. submits (to the devil's power). With the wolf-fight the weaker offered his neck to the stronger, and Lorenz commented: 'the victor will not close on his less fortunate rival. You can see that he would like to, but he just cannot! A dog or wolf that offers its neck to its adversary in this way will never be bitten seriously' (ibid., p. 186). The differences between the two experiences are very great but there is a dynamism which links the two accounts, which cannot be attributed to nurture and seems to have a common instinctual feature. Fordham accounted for the dynamism of the two events and the common link between them in their form as being derived from 'instinct and spirit combined in a single unconscious unity which we call an archetype' (Fordham 1957a, p. 28). In both instances we have an example of an adaptive response arising from the unconscious which takes precedence over other conscious factors. My understanding is that this occurs when what Jung calls a preconscious state of mind is dominant, in which images emanating from the unconscious are felt to be highly charged and the functions of the ego are correspondingly weak.

ACTIONS OF THE SELF AND EGO DEVELOPMENT

Fordham's revolutionary definition of the self as both an integrator and also a system which could deintegrate gave a new vitality to the description of actions of the self. First, where infancy is concerned, it gave a conceptual framework for thinking about observations. This built on Jung's work on the interrelation between the physiological, rhythmical and non-sexual activities of children and the part they played in bringing the child into an adaptive relation to the environment. Unless one conceptualizes these early experiences as being organized by an unconscious aspect of the ego, without the self and its dynamic of deintegration and reintegration, one is left without a way of thinking about how these experiences are integrated.

Additionally the actions of the self include the powerfully disruptive experiences of breakdown which, while awful when happening, can lead to significant developments. But, more importantly, Fordham's dynamic of deintegration corresponded to the observed experiences of mothers and babies where the baby's behaviour matches what the mother can tolerate. Fordham called this the baby's self creating the environment in which it was interacting. He was not primarily concerned when describing actions of the self in infancy with consciousness or unconsciousness. This was because actions of the self are theoretically prior to the development of consciousness out of unconsciousness. Babies discriminate *in utero*, mainly it seems on a hedonic principle. He thought of the deintegrative/reintegrative process as rhythmic, with deintegrates being new experiences which were affectively or cognitively digested.

Using the psychoanalyst Bion's abstract language of mental process, Fordham's deintegrates have the potential to change from being beta elements, via alpha function, into experience which can be thought about. Beta elements can be raw sense data or other accumulations of experience which are not, and cannot be, thought about, but which have to be evacuated. Alpha function is the term used for the process of making meaning out of sensations; it refers to the conversion of sensations or sense data into mental contents (Hinshelwood 1991). If there was no primary self, as some of Fordham's critics have asserted, but only a sense of self in the ego, where would these beta elements be integrated? One would have to postulate that they form part of unconscious areas in the ego or, if as Jung thought, the ego was the centre of consciousness, then in the unconscious, where their content may be personal but where their form is impersonal. An additional argument in support of the idea that the self in its unconsciousness is the source of beta elements is the evidence Fordham collected from children, and Jung from adults, that self symbols compensate the ego and lead to a growth of consciousness and greater internal harmony. These experiences imply that what is happening is more than the making conscious of what was unconscious. Further, since the evidence we have so far examined indicates that the unconscious is structured, infant observations then become studies of the unfolding of individual archetypal potentials with the self integrating the opposites. This is a description of how a baby builds up a mental life.

Mary Williams recognized that there was a tendency among analysts to separate the personal from the archetypal. She pointed to the interdependence of the personal and the collective in 'image and pattern making activities' and wrote:

> first: Nothing in the personal experience needs to be repressed unless the ego feels threatened by its archetypal power, and second: the archetypal activity which forms the individual's myth is dependent on material supplied by the personal unconscious.
>
> (Williams 1963, p. 47)

Fordham agreed with this and has suggested that deintegration lies behind the differentiation of the functions of thinking, feeling, sensing and intuiting (Fordham 1987b). Within the self is what Jung called 'an unconscious prefiguration of the ego' (*CW* 11, para. 391) which can then be looked at from the point of view that the mind matures like the body as a consequence of the interaction between heredity and environment.

THE SELF AND THE EGO

Jung's early interest in the self was focused by his work with patients whose egos were less available to them, but whose self provided some compensation for this absence. The regression within the schizophrenic, he noted, was away from the ego towards the early indestructible core self. We also know from Jung that the shadow is an aspect of the self which cannot integrate opposites. Implicitly the recognition, therefore, that an object can be both good and bad is an action of the self. In the neurotic patient this understanding leads to a strengthening of the ego.

> So long as the self is unconscious, it corresponds to Freud's superego and is a source of perpetual moral conflict. If, however, it is withdrawn from projection and is no longer identical with public opinion then one is truly one's own yea and nay. The self then functions as a

union of opposites and thus constitutes the most immediate experience of the Divine which it is psychologically possible to imagine.

(Jung, *CW* 11, para. 396)

Psychosomatic illnesses are a source for the understanding of the relationship between self and ego in clinical practice. In an example, for instance, where a patient feels that his or her body is behaving like their mind (somatic delusion), that the hurt, soreness and distortions of the mind are being expressed in a physical illness (felt as actual pain but understood as a deintegration of the self), then in the examination of the illness, by means of imagining with the patient the fantasy of the body's illness (by trying, in Bion's terms, to turn a beta element, the somatic pain, into an alpha element, a thought about the illness), a productive conflict can be set up between the ego and the self. This has the effect of enabling the split-off feelings, expressed as physical soreness, to be integrated. At the same time it strengthens the ego's boundaries. To Jungians this is an example of the self assisting the ego to become more conscious, and in Fordham's view it could be said to be an instance of where individuation is a 'special case of ego development' (Fordham 1985a, p. 45). This is congruent with Jung's idea that individuation can be understood as

the revelation of something which existed before the ego and is in fact its father or creator and also its totality. Up to a point we create the self by making ourselves conscious of our unconscious contents, and to that extent it is our son.

(Jung, *CW* 11, para. 400)

Jung defined individuation as

the process by which individual beings are formed and differentiated. In particular, it is the development of the psychological individual as being distinct from the general, collective psychology. Individuation, therefore, is a process of differentiation having for its goal the development of the individual personality.

(*CW* 6, para. 757)

And this definition inspired Fordham to extend the concept from something which referred to an introverted process going on between ego and self to being something which gave more prominence developmentally to the ego:

My thesis of self postulates, besides an unchanging self, a stable representation in consciousness, the ego. The ego grows out of the interaction between deintegrates and the environmental mother, and her extensions. The interaction produces many self representations, the most stable and prominent of which is the ego.

(Fordham 1987b, p. 363)

THE SELF AND SELF-HEALING

If actions of the self are so important for the individuation process then it is likely that for both Jung and Fordham their work on the self would connect to their own personal experiences. Jung's interest in the self began in his childhood and developed in his work with psychotic patients and from his personal confrontation with the unconscious, following the breakdown of his collaboration with Freud. With neurotic patients, at the beginning of an analysis one is mainly presented with problems within areas of ego functioning. Later issues concerning the self come more to the fore as the progress of the analysis initiates the move from the concrete to the symbolic. With psychotic patients, where it is harder to address an ego since the ego is often less accessible, the self can become more of a focus of the clinical work right from the start. This issue preoccupied Jung in a way that it did not preoccupy Freud. Winnicott reviewing Jung's autobiography wrote:

> The search for the self and a way of feeling real, and of living from the true rather than the false self, is a task that belongs not only to schizophrenics, it belongs to a large portion of the human race. Nonetheless, it must also be recognised that for many, this problem is not the main one.
>
> (Winnicott 1964, pp. 454–5)

Jung in his autobiography described how, after the loss of his relationship with Freud and following the turmoil of his breakdown, he found in the drawing of mandalas a new peacefulness. A state of inner calm came over him which he felt was especially significant. He described the non-linear approach to the self (for him playing and drawing) as a circumambulation with an overall directional aim towards a centre (Jung 1963, p. 196). The centre for him was in the mandala. For Jung this mandala imagery gave him stability, he wrote: 'I knew that in finding the mandala as an experience of the self I had attained what for me was the ultimate' (ibid.). It was this that Fordham imaginatively took hold of and postulated could be the core in infancy out of which, by deintegration and reintegration, the infant came into relation with the environment.

Jung's experience of the self transcended the limitations of the ego's consciousness and took him forward out of the impasse he felt stuck in. Since all actions of the self potentially contribute to individuation another way of describing what happened to Jung might be as the realization of the self. Retrospectively this could look like the development of one's self after one's own image.

Jeffrey Satinover has argued that after the upset and turmoil of breaking with Freud, Jung gradually recovered his sense of himself out of his own experience and also by creating a theory. In other words, Jung's statement that he reached the ultimate is not only a statement of his recognition that he had a mystical experience and recovered his equilibrium but that, instrumental in this, after the event, was the creation of a theory to explain what had happened to him (Satinover 1985). Jung's emphasis on introversion in the search for meaning led to a theory of the self which had the central idea that becoming one's self was a process of differentiating one's self from one's social identity. This theory was to help many others, since it recognized that the psychoses of his patients were their way of trying to heal themselves. Consequently psychotic patients' transferences, language and behaviour were to be approached from the point of view of the interested inquirer searching for meaning. Creating the theory formed part of his self-healing. Using his mind and formulating his experience was in its directed thinking more of an ego activity; in its undirected thinking it included his experiences of the self.

Jung's recovery and subsequent work were partly an assimilation of his psychosis. After he had recovered from his psychotic experiences he could think about psychoses in others. These actions of the self were gathered by him into a model where psychic equilibrium was maintained by compensation. Shakespeare knew that 'great wit next to great madness lies', or, to refer it to the analytic profession, analysts who have acquired great insight and the capacity to tolerate their own madness have done so often at great cost to themselves. Satinover pointed out there was a fairly strong defensive element in Jung's account of his experience, centring around the way he treated the lost good object – in this instance Freud (Satinover 1985).

Fordham's development of Jung's ideas about the self reflect an inner emotional resonance with Jung. In Fordham's memoir he wrote of how at different times in his life his career in the eyes of the world seemed to be failing: he failed important exams, did not accept advancement when it was offered and yet in a circumambulatory fashion has in his long life expressed the meaning of being himself.

He was clear also that the loss of his mother had had a powerful impact on his emotional development.

To think of actions of the self over time is to imply a perspective which can be examined from the point of view of the overall meaning of the life of the person. These experiences can be thought of as evidence of the self presiding over the process of individuation, almost as if the self is the enveloping arms of a mother's love and approval. While this is only partly true, I agree with Satinover that more weight needs to be given to the significance of real object loss – in Fordham's case of his mother when he was fifteen years old.

> She came into my room in her dressing gown and sat down and I lay there enjoying her. The next day she was dead and the family went to see her corpse – she looked so tranquil. . . . Contrary to what might be expected I am deeply grateful for that last memory of her visit to my bedside – it meant that my 'naughtiness' had not harmed or damaged her. But it did leave me with a ghost, an enduring memory and as I later realised also a terrible one. . . . From that point on [when his mother died] the family fell to pieces. We were all shattered. [Fordham became ill.] My illness was never diagnosed but I am rather sure I was depressed and dissociated. . . . My patchy work performance was, I learned from analysis, a symptom of a profound splitting. . . . School life began well but, after my mother's death and the disintegration of family life, it changed. I did not realise why at the time but I knew later I had split and my emotional life went underground so that much of the pleasure in achievements was lost and my self esteem became precarious.
>
> (Fordham 1993e, pp. 17, 39, 48)

Much later, in his seventies, Fordham was to become severely ill again. On this occasion it coincided with the deterioration into invalidism of his much-loved wife Frieda. He was still working in London and spending quite a lot of time away from Frieda who lived quietly on her own in the country during the week. I'll let Fordham take up the story.

> I fell violently in love with a younger woman. I was determined that this love would not interfere with my love for Frieda but the conflict was altogether too much for me. I tried talking to Frieda about my feelings – that was a mistake because, understandably, Frieda became alarmed and feared I would abandon her. She could not understand I would never do so. Eros is, however, a mighty daemon and eventually I became ill, gaining the impression the doctors did not know

what was wrong with me. It was clear that I had a virus infection giving rise to herpes of the fifth cranial nerve but it was more than that, and I consulted Dr Bayliss in London, who said the main trouble was my heart and I should go into hospital at once, which I did. . . . But the puzzle remained. . . . I . . . thought I was dying. There was about a week when I had no consciousness except for a sense of drifting away and a knowledge that it was an experience of death – very agreeable I thought.

(Ibid., p. 141)

The theory of the self, as originated by Jung after his separation from Freud, relied in part on the significance of profound disappointments being gathered up into a pattern which gave retrospective meaning to them from a compensatory point of view. Fordham's personality, like Jung's, is schizoid in its architecture. Working on his theory of the self helped Jung recover from the loss of Freud, a recovery which was to enable him to continue his distinctive work. Writing his memoir (a therapeutic task suggested to him by Donald Meltzer) helped Fordham recover from this breakdown. Retrospectively both Jung and Fordham, in their autobiographies, viewed their lives from underneath the panoply of their self theories. Not that Fordham's experience of falling in love was retrospective in its impact; he was aware of the destructiveness of these actions as they were happening. They were part of his ego psychology, especially the splitting of his love object. It was another powerful instance in his life of an action of the self, but this time a destructive action. In that sense the emotional meaning was not retrospective, but what came later, in the digestion of the experience, was its significance, and it is here that the self, with its representations in consciousness, becomes important. For there is good evidence that Fordham's interest in the self has been, in part, an effort to make sense of what happened to his life, in relation to his mother and his family following the impact of her death. In part this has been approached as a research task, in part a search for insight into personal conflicts, and in part a therapeutic task. Its interest was not least that despite his failures and disappointments he came through the pain and loss, surviving in a manner which was mysterious to him at times. The writing of his memoir contributed to his recovery as well as being partly an endeavour to get insight about the loss of Frieda and the violence of the erotic compensation for that loss. Although Frieda had already withdrawn from him a lot before she died, her anticipated death was very frightening, almost like his mother's all over again in its revival of intense feelings of loss. Frieda had nearly died and recovered many times during this period, but was helped back to life each time by Fordham, from what they came to call together her 'death trips'. When eventually she died it was because she did not want to go on living. It felt to both of them that she wanted to be relieved of life.

Returning to Fordham's model it is, in my view, a two-tiered model. The first tier is the primary self, which is an inference. The second tier consists of all those actions of the self which I have summarized above, and more. For Fordham this tier has emotional conviction much as it did for Jung, who did not have to believe in God, because as he said in his television interview with John Freeman, 'He knew'. What I think this meant was that what 'he knew' was the expression of God through his own experience. In that sense God was a self-representation. If the concept of the self is felt to be confusing it is, in my view, because the term describes both the totality of the psyche, conscious and unconscious, and the ordinary feelings of identity, self-awareness and self-esteem, which are part of our everyday experiences. It also has mystical other-worldly transcendent features which gain conviction in the life of the individual over time.

Chapter 7

Autism

A disorder of the self

The study of autism and childhood psychoses has become more extensive over the years, with significant contributions being made by Kanner (1948), Bettelheim (1967), Tustin (1972), Meltzer *et al.* (1975) and (Alvarez 1992). Numerous other researchers and clinicians have been drawn to the locked-in worlds of these children. It was natural for Fordham to venture here since Jung had studied schizophrenia in adults and had evolved a theory of the self which described psychosis as an extreme form of a disorder of the self. He elaborated this in his descriptions of the compensatory and homeostatic nature of the psyche whereby he thought of his patients' psychotic symptoms as the psyche's way of restoring itself to health; correctly channelled, therefore, psychosis could, according to Jung, be a step on the road to self-differentiation or individuation.

Later, when Jung was working mainly privately, many of his patients consulted him because they felt the meaning had gone out of their lives. He recognized in these people the depressive and schizoid aspects of their personalities and he would encourage them to become more introverted and to study the self-symbols in their dreams and spontaneous play as manifestations of the archetypal constituents of their personalities, which needed attending to. This was the method he discovered for himself and wrote about in his autobiography (Jung 1963, p. 168). He described how he was able to effect a reconciliation of two parts of his own personality by allowing his unconscious spontaneous expression in his play with stones and water. Jung's understanding of these unconscious processes was that they were objective in the sense that they were manifestations neither of an inner world nor of an outer world, although containing something of both. It was a symbolic world. There were two main features to this activity which Jung identified: first, the actions (play) themselves were therapeutic, in that they promoted wholeness within the personality, by allowing him to integrate important childhood memories; and secondly, their symbolic content contained not only impersonal features, but also split off, repressed and defended against personal conflicts from both the inner and outer world, the study of which enhanced the individual's adaptation to the world.

Many of the researchers into childhood psychosis presumed that the children they were studying had an inner world which they were defending from impingement. If this was so, access to this inner world might be possible by employing Jung's methods. Alternatively if the disorder was arising from the self as Jung supposed, might it not be that the self was failing to engage with the world, failing to deintegrate, in Fordham's language (for fear of the ego disintegrating), and therefore creating a different sort of barrier to development? This was a novel hypothesis arising from Fordham's discovery of the importance of the self in infancy and childhood. The implication of this latter hypothesis was that there would be not so much an inner world of objects which was being protected, as a world of self-objects, acting to annihilate anything which was not a self-object (see Chapter 6).

Fordham's work with ordinary neurotic children was indicating that the individuation process began in childhood. He now began to study children, who were more schizoid than neurotic, whose difficulties were similar to those of the adults Jung had worked with. These children had a profoundly disturbed body image and had not been able to adapt to living with others. They also had not been able to identify with any group during the usual socialization processes of education. Would allowing them to have an experience of the self, such as Jung described in his autobiography, heal the splits in their personalities too? Jung's method was to focus on the meaning of the images and experiences as they emerged. Would these children produce images and facilitate the process through play? And, more importantly, would this touch the core of their psychosis? When Fordham began his research during the war he was in charge of evacuee children in the Nottingham area and opportunities for intensive work had to wait. Later, over a period of eight years, he was to work with five cases intensively. This work with one child, Alan, taught him much about the self, analysis and the development of the mind.

ALAN

In the 1950s, when Fordham was working at the Paddington Child Guidance Clinic, he let it be known that he was interested in working analytically with a young psychotic child. Quite soon a potentially suitable referral was made. Alan was a pale, dark-haired six-year-old, with a diagnosis of infantile schizophrenia. Fordham's initial interview with Alan was intended to establish whether he could form a transference. This involved Fordham in monitoring closely the effect on Alan of the things he said to him. He found that, although Alan often pushed away what he said, he did not treat his words as irrelevant. Of especial interest was the way Alan was so emphatic, as he seemed also dreamy and remote. This made Fordham wonder whether there was not something quite organized in him. As the first interview developed Alan's interest in the room and its contents increased to such an extent that it seemed as if he was communicating with Fordham. He began to play, and in his responses there were transference manifestations. Fordham referred Alan's dreamy look in the session to 'Mummy being miles away', and noticed Alan linked it to hospital (where Mummy went to have another baby). This was the beginning of a transference to a 'mummy' he was suspicious of. Therapy had begun; potentially he was accessible and this encouraged Fordham to take him on.

> He evoked in me the feelings of care, interest and belief in himself, which were his own qualities in a very primitive stage of development.
>
> (Fordham 1976a, p. 200)

There were five stages to Alan's therapy. In the first he was active and restless and behaviourally very manic. In the second stage 'he developed a ritual framework to his activities'. There then followed a brief homosexual transference as part of the oedipal configuration, then fantasies of a sadistic primal scene; the final part consisted of his supervising the imagined good intercourse of the parents. Alan taught Fordham much about how to analyse children and not least how to speak to a child who used his mind for his own affective ends and not for reality-testing. Alan, for instance, would prepare broadcasts. Fordham listened. To begin with he did not interpret the defensive aspects of the broadcast, since this would not have respected the form of the communication. What he did do was stay close to his countertransference feelings and speak out of them; what this often meant was that he was closely following Alan's ideas and clarifying them, making links based on Alan's analogous way of thinking.

The essential feature of Fordham's interpretative method was to refer to Alan's world as he experienced it, namely outside of himself. He spoke of it as if it was in projection only and not inner to him. To have referred to his 'mad world', that is, his world of projective identifications, as part of his inner world, which had a relevance to his unconscious fantasies, would have made no sense. I do not mean that Fordham avoided the way Alan defended against his depression; rather he treated it interpretatively as not existing inside him. In other words he analysed the projective identificatory content, in projection. There is a feature here which is characteristic of Fordham's work and reveals his deep understanding of Jung's clinical legacy. It would be possible to interpret the part-object nature of Alan's play when it was occurring, but to do so would not have taken account of the wholeness of his feeling in the moment. Implicitly this attitude recognizes that defences are of value to the individual and it is their irreversibility and rigidity which give rise to the difficulties.

Alan's play, described in detail in *The Self and Autism* (Fordham 1976a), had manifestly archetypal themes in it. Retrospectively these were examined by Fordham in relation to mythological themes. Most of those described by Jung as characteristic of the child archetype – themes of abandonment, of heroic deeds and of invincible action – were present in Alan's play. Fordham did not, however, interpret along those lines. He did not amplify or refer the material to known archetypal themes, such as the hero's struggle with the mother. Nevertheless he relied on Jung's approach, which was that the psyche contained its own healing powers. At the same time, while he recognized that, by studying the symbols of the collective unconscious, therapy could be set in motion, he would have to stay close to the personal unconscious initially, since he did not feel with Alan that there was sufficient separation between the personal and the collective. The distinction between what is personal and what is collective in a psychotic child is often difficult to identify since in image-making the collective and the personal are thought to be interdependent. In staying close to the personal in his interpretative comments Fordham was proceeding as if personal experience had fed into Alan's archetypal world and that it was the personal experiences which were giving rise to the unconscious conflicts, which were being amplified by the archetypal. In doing this he was diverging from Jung's method of working mainly within the impersonal archetypal themes. Instead he was allowing Alan's deintegrative activities to be accepted and reintegrated in his own way without imposing knowledge on them which was not relevant to the immediate transference/countertransference climate of the session. Essentially this approach evolved from Alan's literalness and concreteness which prevented the interpretation of his material 'as if' it referred to the way his mind worked rather than to 'things' themselves.

Alan's thinking was largely based on analogy, on finding sameness in difference. Jung's injunction 'to remain within the framework of traditional mythology' (*CW* 16, p. 268) when analysing psychotic patients was helpful to Fordham in its orientating function when speaking out of his countertransference. 'Traditional mythology' as it applied to children was translated by Fordham as infantile fantasy. Take, for instance, the way water featured in Alan's play:

> Thus water represented babies' urine felt by babies to make floods; this was like rain, which was God urinating, so babies were good like God. Rain-urine was dangerous and in crises it would be released as urinary incontinence, which once or twice happened in the interview. God flooded the world to drown people, just as babies imagined they could drown parents and especially mummy. But urine could be good and be drunk like milk; on the other hand it could be evil and full of poisonous germs, which bring death. So God could be good or bad. He used water to make the biggest sea in the world – 'bigger than the Thames or the Atlantic ocean'. Numerous fantasies were enacted upon it: prominent amongst them were storms and floodings; in contrast water was also soft and plastic, so it became mother whom he caressed and stroked. It was mother's milk and became an ocean inside babies; he sucked in the water breast so he came to possess a 'minnick' breast, which could feed an unlimited number of babies and restore damaged parents. It was also father's milk which was in his genital and which was sucked or ejected into his mother to feed and give pleasure. When he felt that his destructiveness had created a desert, then water would redeem the situation as rain or as a river (of tears).
>
> (Fordham 1976a, p. 206)

The above examples of the uses Alan made of water also reveal his inability to cope with frustration and his insistence on the power of God, rather than parents, to make babies. Fordham's account contains, as part of the working through of Alan's conflicts, some of the links and clarifications which brought the unconscious into relation with the conscious, especially where aggressive, destructive and anally sadistic material was concerned. The evidence of the symbols suggested that Alan was unconsciously compensating for his conscious attitudes, in particular the separation of them from their instinctual sources. The symbol in Jungian analysis is treated hermeneutically – i.e. investigated interpretatively for its significance but felt to be ultimately irreducible – whereas historically in classical Freudian analysis it is treated semiotically

– i.e. standing for something, as if it were a conscious sign pointing towards an unconscious meaning. Fordham's understanding of this fact was that it left room for the patient in Jungian analysis to be understood without always being interpreted to.

Alan's play was characterized by what Jung called undirected thinking (*CW* 5), his way of describing what Freud had called primary-process thinking but which included some logical operations. Fordham thought of Alan's undirected thinking as being similar to a play area in the mind, perhaps a transitional space where Alan could live in his 'mad world' but sufficiently in contact with Fordham to recognize that, while it was his world, it was also not his, since it was external to him and part of the therapy room. This is sometimes referred to as a third area (see Winnicott 1965) not internal to the person, nor external to them entirely but existing between them and a significant other – in this instance, Fordham as therapist. Doing things with feeling to the objects in the room, where Fordham was paying attention, was the therapy. And this, with the help of his clarifications and interpretations, became a way for Alan to use his mind to understand his feelings, which, as his use of water revealed, were poorly located in his body. Thus when the babies' urine was linked to the huge storms in the sea there began a process of conceptualization of his infantile omnipotence. In effect, therefore, this analysis was a process over which Fordham presided. In doing this he was closely following the material and clarifying it when Alan himself had lost the thread. If he failed to do this Alan would become anxious and more violent in his play. He was contained by Fordham's thoughtful attention, and within this environment, under the direction of the self, Alan began to bring back into his body/mind what he had split off from it. Specifically the characteristic which distinguished this approach from that of Kleinian child analysts was (a) the absence of analysis of the defensive structures in the early period of the analysis, and (b) the understanding of the material which was ego-dystonic as deintegrations from the self, which only required commenting on if they were accompanied by so much anxiety that they could not be reintegrated without interpretation.

> The theoretical consideration behind this idea is that the archetypes are the functions, which, if allowed to work, will, through their own activity, heal the child, i.e. they act as compensatory functions just as in adult life.
>
> (Fordham 1957a, p. 169)

According to Fordham's self theory, the numerous forms in which Alan's conflicts expressed themselves gave evidence of deintegrative processes of the self. Was Fordham departing from Jung's views of the self in understanding Alan's material as manifestations of the self? In considering this he found there were many similarities in the ways the alchemists used water, a symbol of the *prima materia*, with the meanings water had for Alan. The significance of this was that according to Jung's theory alchemy was 'a precursor of individuation initiated by the self' (Fordham 1976a, p. 212), so Alan's behaviour exemplified both Jung's and Fordham's theories: Jung's that certain symbols would appear during the individuation process, Fordham's that the original self deintegrated in ways which revealed the continuity of the dynamic of the self throughout the life of the person as part of the individuation process.

In *The Psychology of the Child Archetype* the discussion of the imagery of myths which centre round the child as divine or as hero, and which characterize them as precursors of the individuation process, also reveals similarities to Alan's material (Jung, *CW* 9, i). In both myth and Alan's fantasies the child's origin was miraculous; he was then abandoned, performed heroic tasks, felt both vulnerable and invincible. All these feelings were expressed by Alan in his play and fantasy, especially the feelings of being abandoned. For Alan, therefore, the archetypal features of his fantasy world needed to be elucidated from his personal experience since it was these personal experiences which had precipitated his difficulties. Where Fordham differed from Jung was in his understanding of the self-symbols which had archetypal qualities in the material. Jung saw the child as foreshadowing individuation processes and these symbols referring to origins, but not emanating from an integrated core. Fordham saw these symbols as evidence of the primary state of the child's self.

In relating Alan's experience to deintegration/reintegration it can be seen that the deintegrating parts of the self were being held in a split-off and projected world in the service of defence. Alan exteriorized his conflicts and treated them as not part of himself. He did not acknowledge interpretations which referred these experiences to his inner world. His difficulty was arising from failures in reintegration rather than failures in deintegration. How he used objects such as the water in his play depended on his feeling. Sometimes he seemed to be reflecting in a creative way such as when he stroked the water and called it 'Mummy's soft breast', at other times his play with water contained a revelation of the dangerous quality of the babies' urine, when it was linked to his infantile omnipotence and wish to drown her babies inside her. The purpose of the splitting was to protect himself from feeling guilt and depressive pain as the consequences of his aggression. Underlying this split, however, were the continuing activities of the self, which held together personal, repressed and archetypal contents of the unconscious and in so doing were fostering the drive to maturation. It was, however, an integral part of Fordham's conceptualization of the work that the archetype is bi-polar: at one end, the physical (Alan's acts); at the other, mental (his words – the way he represented these acts). His behaviour was dominated by omnipotence much of the time, which meant that he treated objects, including his therapist, in ways which related, not to reality, but to an imaginative representation of his own needs. His defences could be linked to specific periods, or failures, of ego development.

> According to the theory of the self that I was working on, de-integration leads to the formation of ego-nuclei round the oral, anal and genital zones especially. In the course of maturation they become linked to form a body image by a complex of processes. Though anatomically the zones are separated and serve distinct and different functions, this is not how a baby experiences them; the knowledge has to be acquired. At first it may be assumed experiences are registered in terms of pleasure and pain, very little located in space or time, and so similar experiences are treated as identical. Because of this, states of excitement in the zones are very much mixed up with each other; this was reflected in Alan's play activities and in the fantasies that went with them. The distinguishing of different kinds of excitement no doubt grows by repeated experience but they cannot be completely located and differentiated until a body image is formed; this involves perception and cathexis of the skin surface. In Alan's case it is likely that this was disturbed.
>
> (Fordham 1976a, p. 218)

A significant part of the analysis concerned the gradual development of his body image. Alan seemed quite unaware of his body. He behaved as if he did not have one. Even when he had a bad fall getting off the bus 'he treated it as if it had never happened'. It was not until Fordham had worked on this for some time that Alan acknowledged that he was angry with the bus conductor for starting the bus before he had got off. Alan then could say that his head hurt from the pain occasioned by the fall. Similarly in his play he never connected the stories and their fairly obvious references to his own bodily experience to his own body. It was always someone else who had the feeling. Fordham details in his account of this therapy how this changed and he even formulates an aetiological explanation from his piecing together of his experience of Alan in therapy and what he discovered of his history. This is difficult to summarize in a way which carries conviction, but what Fordham gives as a reconstructive interpretation based on his experience of Alan, and from his history, is that Alan learnt early on that violent screaming elicited Father's support against Mother; and that when his mother went into hospital following the birth of his brother, John, who was suffering from pyloric stenosis, Alan became depressed, a depression he had not recovered from by the time he came to therapy four years later. During the therapy the oedipal situation reversed: Alan started therapy loving his father and hating his mother. Quite soon he developed a strong hatred for his father and love of his mother. Retrospectively Fordham wondered whether by taking up his pre-oedipal conflicts in the transference when he was six he had enabled a development to be worked through, which he had begun when he had a significant regression at the age of three and a half.

Alan's analysis was successful. He later went on to university and a professional life. What the work with him revealed in detail was that, by paying attention to the actions of the self in childhood, and by the analyst thinking about their symbolic meaning but only interpreting them when necessary, severe splits in the personality could be healed, much as Jung had demonstrated with patients in the second half of life. This also gave evidence for Fordham's theory of there being a primary self which deintegrated when it came into relation with the environment. This primary self could have problems of a deintegrative or reintegrative kind and was a prime mover in the maturational process. It was also continuous with the self Jung had described in his older patients.

> It is only through maturation and good mothering that the infant gradually recognises the difference between self and not self and the primary self converted into symbolic representations. This had taken place in Alan but the representations were mental – it was as if the unity of the self were perpetuated in his mind, which treated objects as self or not-self. If they did not fit his omnipotent self feeling, they were treated as alien – hence the predominance of violence in an attempt to destroy or triumph over them.
>
> (Fordham 1976a, p. 223)

If, as Fordham and Jung contended, psychoses in children were disorders of the self, then severely withdrawn children who, for instance, did not even speak would exhibit a failure of the deintegrative process. With this in mind he took on James.

JAMES

James was referred at eight years old. Five days before he was born his father had been killed in action and his mother had been reported as seeming not to mourn his loss at all; rather she behaved like someone warding off a depression. She was very controlling, direct, capable and persistent in bringing James to his therapy, which lasted eight years. During the time James was being seen by Dr Fordham she was seen by a psychiatric social worker, who reported that she never showed any feeling, never said anything intimate or personal. She had one idea about the clinic's involvement with James and that was that they wanted James physically to destroy her home, which was important to her. Fordham commented, 'This was what she felt would happen if she relaxed control of James and perhaps of herself also'(Fordham 1976a, p. 261). James's stepfather, whom his mother married within two years of the death of her husband, was a retiring man who could, however, be driven to a frenzy by James. The impression these parents gave was of being uncommunicative, obsessional and rather isolated. This obsessionality was expressed also in the structure imposed on the therapy by the family's rigid time-keeping. In trying to imagine how a baby would have experienced this mother Fordham reconstructed:

> her baby would be made to fit into her competence, in which there is, however, no room for it to develop a self-representation, since his mother does not see him as a person; through her own affective depletion, she sees him like an animal, to be trained.
>
> (Fordham 1976a, p. 264)

Although the prognosis was poor, Fordham wrote:

> I wanted to test my ideas about autism, which I thought might be a disorder of integration and might represent the persistence of the primary self that had prevented the infant relating to his mother at the start. That there were no bouts of screaming, crying or other signs of distress during the breast feeding period suggested that the integration was unusually complete and that the baby did not feel the effect of inevitable frustrations, nor did he give evidence of passing through the crisis periods in early development.
>
> (Fordham 1976a, p. 257)

James's initial symptoms were backwardness: he did not walk until he was two, and showed no interest in crawling. He was an only child, had a normal birth, and had been a good feeder. He was gradually weaned from the breast at eight months and had been toilet trained by two years. Talking never developed although he silently mouthed words like 'wee' and 'lav'. He was passive and unassertive and did not play with other children. Fordham tried different approaches to James, from being very passive himself to interacting in hide-and-seek games or playing chasing games. For long periods he sat quietly behind him; then there was a period when James sat on his knee and moved Fordham's arms as if they were mechanical aids. He occupied himself entirely with objects which were inanimate or which he treated as if they were inanimate. He avoided eye contact, eventually settling into a pattern of walking backwards into the room so as not to look at Fordham, and much of his activity was similar to that of a 'normal child who might be mentally defective' (Fordham 1976a, p. 268).

There were many hours when James played repetitive games, threw the toys out of the window, or filled and let out the water from the basin while waiting excitedly for the gurgling sounds. Interpretation of this play in terms of the noises in his body, of faeces and flatus and the way they might come to life, seemed meaningful to him; and efforts to help him accept his noisy, dirty, smelly inside feelings seemed to be getting through. He would look pleased. Later Fordham was able to develop this and link the feeling of one session to the next. His visual avoidance stopped and he seemed much relieved to be understood. His behaviour changed and he spent less time in the lavatory and in the secretary's office. These developments occurred just before a holiday break after eighteen months of work. During the holiday James regressed and became unmanageable at home, such that he repeatedly upset his mother. On his return that brief contact, previously made with Fordham, was absent and he reverted to his old ways.

Not all days were the same; sometimes there were messy days of painting and tidy days of keeping toys in rows. He persistently chewed his hand, occasionally was ill and consistently showed great interest in looking underneath and inside any object. His play showed evidence of memory, tenacity and elementary problem solving. On IQ tests he scored well for non-verbal tasks. There were moments throughout the therapy when Fordham began to wonder whether he was beginning to suffer, to allow himself to know what he was feeling. But this did not last and he would switch into some new activity which, like the previous one, would be continued until it became ritualized and meaningless. Interpretations about his interest in the inside of Fordham's body followed a long period of exploratory play during which he examined Fordham's face, opened his mouth, twisted his nose and pulled his hair. He frequently became aggressive and would then run outside to see if anyone was there. Simple interventions which attempted to delineate where the good people were and what made them turn bad helped to alleviate his anxiety, but not in a way which led on to further developments. Fordham had hoped that he would be able to allow this boy to have an experience of his self without impinging, but this did not happen. There was no feeling of deintegrative and reintegrative experiences contributing to the sense of the continuity of his existence over time. Instead his defences remained as obsessional as ever with great importance being attached to the room, which he divided into safe and unsafe parts. There seemed to be an internal obstacle with a pattern of conflict centring on the splitting of good objects from bad objects.

The treatment was a failure and when James reached the age when he was no longer a child, according to the legal definition used in child guidance clinics, Fordham stopped it. The barrier between James, the environment, his family and surrogates was too intense and the effect of this was to induce depression in those closest to James. The question remains as to what might have set off this pattern, and other workers in the field – notably Tustin (1972) and Meltzer et al. (1975) – have strongly suggested that depression in the mother may be a significant contributing factor. This depression in the mother, it is thought, is split off by her and projected into the baby when its ego is too fragile to cope with it. Fordham felt that James and his mother co-operated in their use of obsessional defences and for her this was a way of warding off her depression. Fordham too felt that:

> the barrier systems that James showed were not so much defence-systems of the ego but the primary defence systems of the self, which had persisted from his infancy and become organised into obsessional structures.
>
> (Fordham 1976a, p. 287)

James's difficulties stemmed from failures in his deintegrative activity primarily and the consequent mobilization of total defence systems, which treated new experiences as alien and having to be annihilated. In discussing why this case failed many factors could be brought forward, from the desirability of residential treatment, of daily treatment, of more refined interpretations and less interaction of a physical kind. The positive aspects of the work, the times when James could seem almost normal, to have understood something and to engage in play and real exchange, might hold out hope for a method of treatment more educative and less psychotherapeutic, but Fordham's attempts to follow these up left the essential core of the disorder untouched. What James exhibited was what Fordham was later to call a defence of the self. Originally this concept was introduced by him as part of his study of delusional aspects of the transference. Later he was to suggest tentatively that defences might be grouped in two classes:

> In one, parts of the psyche are rendered unconscious, isolated, etc; in the other, the whole organism seems to be threatened, abandoned, or in danger of being split into pieces, and then defences of the self come into operation. A tentative classification might be a) defences of the ego: isolation, reaction formation, undoing, rationalisation, conversion, repression, some regressions, dramatisation, displacement; b) defences of the self: projective and introjective identification, some forms of acting out and regression, idealisation, somatisation, etc.
>
> (Fordham 1985b, p. 20n)

THE BARRIER HYPOTHESIS

Analytic investigators into secondary autism, that is, autism which is characterized not by brain damage but mainly by psychotic withdrawal, have almost all hypothesized some sort of barrier behind which it was thought the child lived (see Fordham 1976a, pp. 77–8). Some investigators have suggested that the barrier was the sensitive child's response to impingement, its purpose to protect the inner world. Others have suggested that the barrier developed later. In trying to understand the nature of the barrier, workers in this field have extensively studied the autistic child's relation to objects. Features which recur in all studies of these children are that the objects must comply with what the child wants to do with them; and when they do not, then the child becomes enraged or throws them away.

Autistic children's behaviour is often compulsive, repetitive and dissociated. Attempts to interpret the meaning of their activities can often lead to their agreeing but this does not produce the expected integration of the insight; instead it seems that the child's inability to symbolize results in further obsessive repetition of the behaviour. The level of dissociation is such with these children that often it is only by referring to parts of their own body as if they were independent and impersonal entities that is it possible to get through to them. Various explanations are offered as to why this should be so, from Bettelheim's suggestion that the child is defending himself from the mother's unconscious wishes for the child to be dead (Bettelheim 1967), to Tustin's view that autism develops out of an infantile psychotic depression (Tustin 1972), to Bender's that there is some disorder of intra-uterine life (Bender 1953). All the investigators have noticed that the autistic child uses objects as if they were an extension of himself. Similarly, the obsessional controlling aspect of the autistic child's relation to the world has been well documented.

The early onset of autism seems also to be fairly well established, with accounts of the mother's noticing after the first feed that something was amiss with her child. This observation supported Fordham's view of Alan and James and other children he worked with that explanations in terms of a retreat into an inner world were unlikely; rather the problem was to do with the dynamic of the self. This is because Fordham thinks that a first feed antedates the formation of an inner world. Arising from the deintegrative and reintegrative experiences of the first feed's distinctions between good (satisfying) and bad (frustrating), experiences gradually take hold as the ego begins to develop, as a result of the rudimentary awareness which accompanies this. When this begins it then becomes possible, in theory, to talk about an inner world, since with the operation of other ego functions, such as memory, there then arises the likelihood that inner and outer will become part of the discriminatory equipment of the child. But if the reintegrative experiences are qualitatively more painful than pleasurable, if, for instance, the baby is drinking in the mother's depression with her milk, then it is possible that these experiences will give rise to a powerful defensive reaction.

Fordham did, however, want to understand the autistic child's interest in real objects and his need to maintain an environment which did not change. As he observed,

> one must bear in mind that defences are both undesirable features of mental life, but they also contribute to growth of the psyche. Here it may be reflected that the circular outline of a mandala is an impenetrable magic circle and so is a defence as well as a containing symbol.
>
> (Fordham 1985b, p. 20n)

He hypothesized that the conventional barrier hypothesis presumed an inner world for which there was inadequate evidence. By that he meant Alan, James and the others did not behave as if they lived in a world which they perceived as 'inner' to them. He argued instead that the activities of the self could better help us to understand the development of a barrier, arising from a defensive response to external stimuli.

If for instance a baby is submitted to noxious stimuli of a pathogenic nature (either in utero, during or after birth) a persistent over-reaction of the defence system may take place; this may become compounded with parts of the self by projective identification, so that a kind of auto-immune reaction sets in: this in particular would account for the persistence of the defence after the noxious stimulus had been withdrawn. Not-self objects then come to be felt as a danger to or even a total threat to life, and must be attacked, destroyed or their effect neutralised.

(Fordham 1976a, p. 91)

So normal stimulation would have the opposite effect from that desired: rather than opening up access to the autistic core it would shut it off, provoking a fierce defensiveness designed to obliterate what is mistakenly identified as an enemy. If, as sometimes happened, interpretations were understood by the child and were followed by behaviour indicating that the interpretation was correct they were not followed by maturational developments. It seemed that the experience was not sufficiently symbolized to be integrated into the child's self. What occurred was compulsive repetition of the behaviour in the service of a perverse attempt to master it, since it was felt to be impinging on the self.

James could remember where he had put things from one session to the next (evidence of ego activity) but the objects had no symbolic representation. Similarly, he was fascinated by clocks and had noticed the lettering on Fordham's watch, which he drew, but investigation of his acute observation of the outer world for inner-world significance drew a blank. There was no evidence that his accurate time-keeping, his need for regularity and sameness were experienced by him as an inner clock, nor that the hands of the clock had phallic significance. Rather his interest seemed to express his repetitive manipulation of a self-object. Far from there being an inner world the autistic child seemed to live in a state where the

essential core of autism represents in distorted form the primary integrate of infancy, and that idiopathic autism is a disordered state of integration, owing its persistence to failure of the self to deintegrate.

(Fordham 1976a, p. 88)

TECHNIQUE

One aspect of the work with these psychotic children concerned their use of language. Fordham noticed that often the lexical meanings of words were not primary, as part of the process of communication. He developed an understanding derived from his countertransference feelings as to when words were experienced as containing and when persecuting. When approaching the core of an autistic child he found that what was important was for him to tolerate and manage feelings of being isolated and being treated as if he were not there. He began to consider technique as residing not so much in interpretative skill as in paying attention to countertransference and empathic understanding. This led him to suggest that interpretations which approached the core of the autism usually produced no overt response. This was because Fordham hypothesized that 'correct interpretations are experienced by the child as if he and they were one and the same thing' (Fordham 1976a, p. 147). Thus they were not identified as enemies but felt to be unremarkable because already known. This suggests that one of the ways the self behaves when mobilizing total defences is to behave in an immunological manner like a macrophage. (This thought of Fordham's, in my view, is similar in structure to the idea that underlies contemporary post-Kleinian analytical thinking about pathological narcissism. Segal [1983] has pointed out that Klein's views of projective identifications which get into and take over an object's quality are essentially a narcissistic defence against envy.)

It is congruent with his description of the failure of the self to deintegrate in autism that he should have encountered this difficulty, since for a child to make use of interpretations parts of his self would have had to have developed ego structures. When early oral or anal material and their affects predominated, Fordham found that talking to the child out of his empathic feelings had the best results, almost as if he was behaving like a mother to an infant. This contrasted with interpretations derived from his past experience. Many years later he was to reflect on this in a different way when thinking about the importance of 'not knowing beforehand' in each interview so as to remain open to the affective processes of the moment, especially when working with patients who had had a lot of psychotherapy or previous psychotherapy with someone else.

Chapter 8

The discovery of the syntonic transference, and of the importance of analysing childhood

THE HISTORICAL CONTEXT

Historically, one difficulty which held up discussion of transference in the Jungian world was the absence of accounts in the literature of what analysts actually did – an absence due in considerable part to Jung's attitude to technique, which he treated as something which 'did violence to the individual nature of the analytic process' (Fordham 1969d, p. 96). The reason given by some Jungians at this time for not revealing what they did was that this would be a violation of the patient's individuality. The context for this was the idea that the analytic process was like a private chemical reaction going on in the retort of the analytic space, and scrutiny of this by outsiders would interfere with the outcome. Fordham's view was that secretiveness not only made critical evaluation impossible but also bred an undesirable culture of transference and countertransference anxieties, kept secret, as he wrote later, 'because of the infantile anxieties attached to it' (Fordham 1974k, p. 261). He based his approach on Jung's idea that transference was an archetypal process and that the apparent lack of transference, initially, may be due to the analyst's and, later, to the patient's unawareness of it, rather than to its absence.

Fordham's significant writings on transference began in 1957 with the publication of his 'Notes on the Transference'. In this paper he observed how Jung in his 'The Psychology of the Transference' (*CW* 16) assumed that the clinical phenomena of the transference were well enough understood not to need discussion. In the foreword to 'The Psychology of the Transference' Jung wrote that:

> the reader will not find an account of the clinical phenomena of the transference in this book. It is not intended for the beginner who would first have to be instructed in such matters.
>
> (*CW* 16)

But a Jungian beginner would have had difficulty finding an account in the Jungian literature of these clinical phenomena. Fordham wished to promote a climate which would reverse this and bring out into the open what was happening in consulting rooms. For 1957 his statements seem farsighted even if they are now taken for granted.

He clarified that the therapeutic content of the analyst's personality was in his unconscious, and so Jung's

> theory of transpersonal archetypes may be expected to orientate us here. With it we can explain why the patient apparently calls out suitable or adapted therapeutic reactions in the analyst which, together with the unadapted ones of the patient, form the main substance of all intense transferences.
>
> (Fordham 1957a, p. 64)

He examined whether transference was a natural phenomenon as Jung had described. He concluded that the phenomena of analysis are released, not induced, and

> what is 'artificial' in the analysis is more than matched by what is distorted in the patient, particularly at the beginning of any analysis.
>
> (Fordham 1957a, p. 71)

He began by outlining two basic considerations which need to be taken into account when meeting a new patient:

> (1) The patient comes with a presenting symptom for which he seeks a solution. It is the aim of the analyst to elucidate this, and one of the results of this process is the development of a transference in which the energy previously directed into the symptom is now transferred to the person of the analyst. (2) The problem then is how to handle and ultimately resolve the transference.
>
> (Fordham 1957a, p. 72)

He discussed the nature of the dependent transference and contrasted it to the archetypal transference. In the former 'repressed infantile contents are released', which first have to be attended to and projections sufficiently withdrawn from the analyst so that 'emergence of the self and its realisation in consciousness' can occur through analysis of the archetypal transference (see Chapter 9 for a fuller exposition of this). He noted the discomfort Jungians felt about the dependent transference, which was thought to lead to undesirable regression. He suggested that by making use of Jung's concept of 'the actual situation', a term he had used to describe the factors contributing to the contemporary neurotic conflict of his patients, fruitless regressions could be avoided.

> If, however, the actual situation be defined as the totality of present causes and the conflicts associated with them, then the genetic (historical) causes are brought into the picture in as much as they are still active in the present as contributing to the conflicts there manifested.
>
> (Fordham 1957a, p. 82)

That apparently unremarkable statement was significant for Jungians because Jung had distinguished his approach from Freud's, for historical reasons, by emphasizing the prospective nature of the unconscious and the undesirability of a historical quest for the cause of the symptom or problem. His focus had been in the present and not in the past. Fordham had wanted to include the personal genetic (meaning ontogenetic) factors without being 'heretical'. This formulation whereby he reinterpreted Jung's 'actual situation' added significantly to his modernization of analytical psychology while keeping it in touch with its origins. In this as in so many other areas of analytical psychology Fordham was a standard bearer for the critical examination of Jung's legacy, while at the same time remaining close to the essence of Jung's thinking about analytical psychology.

THE PLACE OF TRANSFERENCE

The place of transference is central to the analytic endeavour. Discussions of its significance in analytical psychology have been closely linked to different interpretative methods. On the one hand there was the reductive approach, which meant analysing childhood as part of the transference, and simplifying complex structures. Jung recognized the importance of this method and identified it primarily with psychoanalysis and the doctrine of analysing repression. He was critical of this method mainly for its 'nothing but' approach and the tendency of Freudians to be dogmatic about the sexual theory, as if that was the whole story. He recognized its place in the early periods of all analysis but felt it could be destructive if continued for too long. He was more interested in the inner world as a phenomenon deriving from what he called 'affectivity'. He thought that the complexes he had discovered in his patients through his association experiments were linked by emotion – that feelings were the currency of the mind and fantasy its material form. Because he thought of libido as a neutral energy he did not subscribe to the Freudian theory of sublimation as the displacement of sexual energy into a desexualized form. He compared sublimation to the 'alchemist's trick of turning the base into the noble' (*CW* 15, para. 53); nor did he think that the unconscious consisted of only personal repressed material. For him 'the true reason for a neurosis always lies in the present' (*CW* 10, para. 363) and while detours into the past of the patient could be of interest to him, the search for explanatory causes was not, in his view, primary in psychotherapeutic 'cure'. The prospective nature of the unconscious was the focus of his psychotherapeutic technique, and to access this he deployed another method.

The other method combined amplification of the archetypal images with active imagination and was called synthetic or prospective. Amplification involved the elaboration of the impersonal associations of the image, for instance by reference to literature or myth. Active imagination was described by Jung as 'a sequence of fantasies produced by deliberate concentration' (*CW* 9, i, para. 101); within analysis it 'is a method of introspection for observing the stream of interior images' (ibid., para. 319). This involved the analyst's and patient's contemplation of the impersonal archetypal features of the dreams and images the patient produced. It treated the material as symbolic rather than concrete and its perspective was teleological. It saw the archetype as something which could not be reduced and the analytic task as finding a new route out of an old impasse. It was as if Jung, the hermeneut, steered the patient out of the anchorage of memories into the channel of the next period of his life. This method, he thought, was not suitable for people who were young or who had not integrated their childhood experiences.

Discussions about the prospective method and what distinguished Jungian analysis from Freudian analysis were a feature of the early years of analytical psychology, when trainings and teaching programmes were being worked out. Fordham was in the thick of this as a founder member of the Society of Analytical Psychology in London. He tried using the technique of active imagination with a variety of different adult patients. During the sessions the imagery produced by the patients was related to historical, alchemical and mythological parallels, but not to personal history and experience. The purpose was to integrate the images into the self. In doing this he was proceeding in a similar fashion to Godwin Baynes who had been his first analyst. Fordham writing about this in 1993 said:

> No attention was paid to the transference. I went at first three times a week and wrote down my lengthy dreams in a book. Baynes dis-

coursed on them at considerable length and sometimes analysed them. Then there came a point where I went into a sort of trance and Baynes told me that a good way to catch my fantasies was to try and paint them. I found that easy to do and a long series of pictures emerged, which went on for about seven years and periodically after that. I found that I could orientate myself in emotional crises by painting, to which I added imaginary conversations with some of the figures which emerged.

(Fordham 1993e, p. 71)

Baynes's approach to Fordham's material was mainly educative. He suggested books he should read and even told Fordham that he wanted to use his material for a book he was writing. As Fordham had very little money he offered to accept his material as 'payment'. This complicated Fordham's relationship with Baynes, not least because, as he said, he 'felt obliged to keep on producing pictures to keep up the payments!' (Fordham 1993e, p. 71).

RESEARCHES INTO THE PROSPECTIVE METHOD AND TRANSFERENCE ANALYSIS

Despite his idealization of Baynes and his loyalty to Jung, Fordham was determined to put to the test the prospective method for himself so as to be able to describe from the other side of the analytic duo, in a scientific manner, what its limitations were. Accordingly, he worked with a number of patients using this method. To begin with he described the criteria for active imagination as follows:

1. For active imagination to occur the subject's conscious attitude must be such that archetypal images can be felt to have an autonomous or objective character when they emerge into the field of consciousness. 2. The ego must then react so that the images become a valued experience which can lead to creative work. There are several corollaries to these criteria: (a) the sequence of images can occupy a short or a long period of time; (b) they need not have a numinous or magical quality attaching to them; (c) though understood theoretically as belonging to the inner world they do not necessarily carry with them the feeling of being inner; (d) for active imagination to take place it is not necessary for the subject to consider the psychological significance of the image sequences.

(Fordham 1967b, p. 51)

Fordham's patients were not homogeneous by type, pathology or personality traits. He sat his patients opposite him, working with:

> the emphasis on basic equality of status between myself and patient conceived to be embarking on a joint enterprise of understanding 'the unconscious'. In each case the transference did not feature prominently and this, as I subsequently learned, was due to the emphasis on the here and now relationship in which I and the patient were regarding myself as a person; this masked, but did not eliminate, the transference. . . . The solution was expected to arise from the inner world in terms of a symbolic union of opposites giving increased coherence to a personality which would be better equipped to cope with realistic living.
>
> (Ibid., p. 55)

He thought of active imagination as the ego responding to deintegrations from the self. He found, however, that he had to modify this technique to make room for a reductive analytic method, the results of which he found to be *more* synthetic in some cases. The problems arose from that little caveat of Jung's concerning his method, namely that it was only suitable if infantile affects were not active. Fordham with his increasing familiarity with the affective life of children was becoming adept at recognizing these feelings, which were inevitably, he thought, constellated in the early stages of adult analysis as much by the setting as by anything else. His experience of children had taught him that the opposite of Jung's theory that parents projected their unresolved conflicts into their children was equally true. The child and the child in the adult beamed projections on to and into the 'parental' analyst, which led him to introduce a more transferential approach.

His own analytic experience also supported these findings. Writing of his analysis with Baynes which released his imagination and gave him 'a firm conviction as to the reality of unconscious processes and the relative autonomy of its products' (Fordham 1993e, p. 73), he said that,

> though I was flattered by the astonishing things I was told my unconscious produced: analogies were drawn between my productions, Kundalini Yoga, alchemy and the like. Only the subject of the two women seemed to me especially relevant [Fordham's first marriage was deteriorating and he had a mistress], but here again his method was educative rather than analytic. He gave me an account of Jung's comparable experience in some detail. I do not think that did

much more than increase my sense of inflation in doing what Jung had done, but I succeeded in keeping enough in touch with reality.

(Ibid., p. 72)

What Fordham found in his practice was that the democratic nature of the prospective method could not resolve the delusional transferences which arose. If anything it probably fostered them. (The characteristic of a delusional transference is that the patient develops a fixed idea which is not influenceable by reason or evidence. Further investigation of this in very disturbed patients can often reveal the sense in the delusion, namely how it has arisen.) Sitting opposite the patient often put more stress on them, leading them to avoid saying what was really in their mind. His analysis of the difficulties of using this technique was that it led to the two parties accepting the delusional transference as an objective truth about the analyst (for instance that the analyst was just like the patient). What was happening, he discovered, was that he and the patient were accepting the patient's projection into him (that he was like this or thought that) as a statement which was true of himself rather than something the patient could not see as part of him- or herself but only as an attribute of another. In this way the infantile transference feelings were lost and began to affect the analysis in an undercover and destructive way.

In a recent consultation of mine a middle-aged woman described to me her difficulties in combining being a mother and working, where working meant performing in public. She was an only child. She was extremely competitive, rivalrous and intolerant of anyone close to her having any skills or qualities she could not better. Following a recent confinement she had even managed to persuade her husband to stop his work too, finding his continued engagement in a lively professional milieu intolerable when her world was circumscribed by her infant's needs. We briefly considered the huge division within her personality between the performer, who needed the admiration of her public, and the demands of motherhood, where for her, being a mother meant loss of her position as the most-loved child. This line of investigation became increasingly uncomfortable for her and, as the session progressed, I noticed she began to make personal comments about me, which attributed to me her discomfort at hearing how her neediness and rivalrousness were the emerging problem. So she began to speculate why I did not always return her gaze, or sat back in my chair and withdrew from her intrusiveness. The relevance of this to Fordham's experience of the phoney democracy of the amplification method was that I began to take up her comments about me, thereby giving her the impression that her personal remarks contained an objective truth, like Fordham had with his patients, who sat opposite him. By wondering out loud 'Mm yes, I wonder why you are interested in where I'm looking' I had partially identified with her projection. In this way I lost the focus, which more appropriately could have remained on the way she pushed into me these uncomfortable fears as I got close to what was unbearable. This was that the flakiness she sensed in herself, the deep divisions inside her, the lack of a feeling of being centred were projected on to me, as my way of wondering about this out loud indicated. This was just one consultation. What Fordham was noticing was that once this process had got established between and within him and his patients, it was extremely difficult to shift when they sat face to face, examining their material without considering what was happening between them.

REDUCTIVE ANALYSIS AS THE GATEWAY TO SYNTONIC TRANSFERENCE

Reductive analysis within the transference which is 'the elucidation of complex structures and the resolution of them into their simpler components' (Fordham 1967b, p. 54), by contrast, did resolve those difficulties which arose from the patient's splitting off what they were projecting and denying its source. This method clarified what belonged where, and to whom, within the patient's psychic structures. It is best practised by letting the patient use the couch. It reduces only the complexity of the unconscious structures (it does not reduce the patient from an adult to a child). What his patients needed was to be connected to their individual development through interpretation of their personal unconscious and this was a necessary prerequisite to exploration of the collective features of their psyches. By moving his attitude more towards the reductive he found:

1. In all cases the gains from the synthetic [prospective] approach were recognised by the patient even though it and the therapist came in for critical and often violent attacks during the analysis, for having delayed progress, prolonged the analysis, or failed to analyse the transference etc. These data show that parts of the negative transference had tended to be overlooked. 2. In all cases it became clear that the virtual absence of detailed transference analysis during the first part of the treatment had led the patients, not only to repressing, but also consciously to suppressing (i.e. consciously withholding)

essential areas of their personalities which were felt consciously or unconsciously to be too mean, destructive or shameful to reveal. 3. Prominent amongst these contents were the expression of infantile needs, aggressive and greedy or sexual impulses and fantasies. Many of these had been repressed as well as consciously suppressed by the earlier therapy which, in spite of its 'democratic' aim, had not prevented 'authoritarian' projections.

(Fordham 1967b, p. 57)

It could of course be argued that Fordham's cases, unlike Jung's, were not classical individuation cases – that is, older people whose psychological maturity required something other than investigation of the infantile constituents of their personality. He therefore examined the uses to which his adult patients put the imagery of the active imagination period of their treatment. It revealed that often it was covering 'pathological disintegrations which could only be resolved by penetrating to the source of the splitting' (ibid., p. 60). Translated, this means the patient was feeling broken up inside but keeping knowledge of this from himself by cutting off from it and putting it elsewhere. When he analysed his patients from the perspective of the affective relationship he had with them, such that he became the carrier of the images which were not exclusively personal, then Fordham made progress. He called the use he made of what was projected into him about the patient's state of mind syntonic transference/countertransference. This was similar to Jung's approach to 'individuation cases'.

The patient, by bringing an activated unconscious content to bear upon the doctor, constellates the corresponding unconscious material in him, owing to the inductive effect which always emanates from projections in greater or lesser degree. Doctor and patient thus find themselves in a relationship founded on mutual unconsciousness.

(Jung, *CW* 16, para. 364)

Fordham, combining his experience of child analysis with his investigations of Jung's amplification method, had arrived at a position similar to Jung's later teleological approach to analysis with adults but which included the analysis of childhood.

SYNTONIC TRANSFERENCE/COUNTERTRANSFERENCE

The term syntonic transference/countertransference referred to the analyst's experience of parts of the patient which had been projected into him and which therefore could be treated as information about the patient's state of mind. Fordham now pushed on the work with a more detailed examination of what happened inside the analyst during the analytic hour. Two main constituents underlined his approach. Both derive from Jung and both now are part of analytic practice across all schools. First, Jung was pioneering in his statement of the necessity that interpretations have to be created anew out of the analyst's unconscious for each patient. Second, he was one of the first to describe as the therapeutic factor in analytic cure, the analyst's relation to his unconscious at those points where the patient lacked it. This was the area Jung wrote about in terms of the analyst's reaction to his patient as a person. It is different from transference, Fordham thought, because it was not so compulsive and could be more easily integrated. An example of this would be when the analyst notices he is behaving in a way which is unusual for him with a patient and continues until such time as he recognizes what it is that is happening between them. Fordham early on recognized this as an essential feature of analysis but one that needed clarification. In particular:

> In analysis there are reactions on the part of the analyst which are syntonic and can make the patient more conscious, but these are different from the countertransference illusion, where the increase in consciousness will come about only if the analyst himself examines his own reaction.
>
> (Fordham 1957a, p. 91)

Fordham's work on the dynamic of the self, deintegration, led him to observe his own behaviour with his patients from this perspective. He noticed that if he listened attentively both to what the patient was saying and to what internally he was experiencing he became aware of an appropriate response arising from within him.

> There were two ways of behaving: (1) trying to isolate oneself from the patient by being as 'integrated' as possible; and (2) relinquishing this attitude and simply listening to and watching the patient to hear and see what comes out of the self in relation to the patient's activities, and then reacting. This would appear to involve deintegrating; it is as if what is put at the disposal of patients are parts of the analyst which are spontaneously responding to the patient in the way he needs; yet these parts are manifestations of the self.
>
> (Ibid., p. 97)

Fordham understood from these experiences what Jung meant when he described analysis as a dialectical procedure:

based on processes which neither I nor my patient can control consciously, and that analysis depends on the relatively greater experience
of the analyst in *deintegrating* so as to meet the patient's *disintegration*.
(ibid., my italics)

At the very deepest levels this process can give rise to states of
identity between patient and analyst. Why this is thought of as making
available a part of the self is that much of this process is going on
unconsciously with the analyst respecting the autonomy of this unconscious process and not imposing 'knowledge' on it.

In the following clinical example of syntonic countertransference and
its relation to dialectical procedure Fordham described an analytic session with a female patient who had been deprived of sexual knowledge
by her parents in her childhood and who deeply resented this (Fordham
1974k, p. 279). The patient's behaviour produced in him a response
which was partly syntonic and partly disabling because it induced him
to react in a way which did not allow him to analyse her until he had first
analysed what was happening to him. In this session the patient gave an
account of bathing her son and how his playing a game with the little
fishes and the big fish created an opportunity for her to talk about babies,
but not, Fordham noted to himself, about intercourse and penises. Her
son became most interested in this talk and asked to see his mother's
'little door down below' but she refused his request. Fordham commented about this in a somewhat defensive manner comparing her
parenting (seductive) with his knowledge of her parents' attitude to her
(rigid). This produced the response from his patient 'It is you who wants
to look', referring to her son's request but applying it to Fordham as if
he was the little boy who wanted to look at her genitals. He pushed this
away with a piece of remembered information about her husband only
having to look at her to desire her. What he wasn't able to work on was
the transference implication of the story, namely that here she was being
a good mummy telling her son about the facts of life while he (Dr
Fordham) continued to behave just like her parents, withholding
essential information necessary for her development.

What had happened was that Fordham had lost his analytic attitude
when listening to this interesting story about the boy in the bath and so
stopped paying attention to unconscious processes. Thereby he missed
the reproach in the story. His patient's response to him meant she
unconsciously knew that. His retreat into himself was part of his syntonic countertransference response to this patient whose unpredictable
behaviour often led him to retreat and wait until he understood more. It

was syntonic because he had found, in the past with this patient, that making room for what he initially experienced as intrusive from her led to his being able to describe in terms of the dialectic what the meaning of the interaction had been. The pathological part of the countertransference, however, was in his masochistic submission to her which led to him wondering if she was right and he really did want to 'look' as she had suggested. In other words this masochistic response obscured his being able to differentiate her projection from his own position.

It was experiences like these which led him to understand that in the unconscious patients are experienced by the analyst as parents. Fordham is here including in the concept of the syntonic transference the patient's knowledge of him, that she can silence him by her attacks. By publishing these experiences he was demonstrating his understanding of the process summarized by Jung as the need to create for each patient an individual response. He is also giving descriptive substance to Jung's abstract statement that the patient and analyst are in a state of mutual unconsciousness.

THE VALUE OF MUTUAL UNCONSCIOUSNESS

Over many sessions an analyst can find himself behaving in a particular way with a patient which he does not initially understand, but is allowing to happen, while waiting for his understanding to arise out of the interaction with them. Fordham gives an instance of a patient who endlessly asked him questions, which he found himself unwilling to answer, not just for the usual analytic reasons. Then one day she started talking about her father, who also did not answer her questions. He then realized she had used him to embody her relationship to her father and together they needed the experience of this for its emotional resolution. He had to allow himself to be influenced by her feeling of which she was unconscious. She was defending against this knowledge and Fordham's response was to know but not to know, to allow the foreign body of her projection a place in his mind in a syntonic way. Gradually he then became aware that his behaviour (in not answering) was irrational, so the feeling that the patient was having, namely defending against knowing that she was furious with her father, became projected into Fordham. Then she came up with the information about her father and he was able to bring it all together for her and show her she had been re-enacting her relationship with her father in the transference. To have known this on the first day and told her so would have pre-empted her working it out in the transference. Fordham is proceeding by trusting that the deintegrates will give rise to consciousness and not letting himself be overwhelmed by the feeling that he has to know what his patient is really saying and understand it forthwith. It is almost as if a feature of this approach is to be able to think of getting stuck in an analysis as the beginning of the real analytic experience.

Dr A. Plaut, a colleague of Fordham's, working on the transference at this period, the mid-1950s, when countertransference issues were to the fore, referred to the analyst 'incarnating' the archetypal image for the patient at those times (Plaut 1956, p. 15). He referred to some analysts who accepted the projection from their patient

> in a whole hearted-manner making no direct attempt to help the patient to sort out what belongs to him, what to the analyst, and what to neither as well as both. On the contrary they will allow themselves to become this image bodily, to 'incarnate' it bodily for the patient.
>
> (Plaut 1956, p. 15)

Fordham linked this state to primitive identity and to the deintegrating actions of the self and asserted that provided the 'affective stability of the analyst is maintained', he 'will inevitably find the right form or response so long as countertransference projections do not obstruct its development' (Fordham 1957a, p. 99).

COUNTERTRANSFERENCE ILLUSION

Fordham's response to the woman who told the story about her son at bathtime contains an element of countertransference illusion, in contrast to syntonic transference experiences. This arises when the analyst has not examined his own reaction to the patient but is aware of something lodged in himself emanating from the interaction. If he continues not to pay attention to this, Fordham realized, he can either behave as if he has not heard what the patient is saying, as in the following example, or it can lead to his making plunging intuitive comments which seem 'brilliant' but are really instances of the analyst projecting material he has not yet digested on to the patient in an omnipotent manner. In this example Fordham's aggression towards his patient, an eleven-year-old boy, gets in the way of his understanding, such that he misses the subtlety of what the child is saying. (The session had been recorded on tape.)

John: Why did they block that door up? (Referring to an area in the wall of the room where the doorway had been built up.)

M.F.:   Imagine. (Long silence.) I expect to keep somebody out!

John: I don't! (Then after hesitations and much fidgeting.) Better to have the door there. (Where it is at present, leading into the passage.)

M.F.:   I suppose you thought my idea wasn't sensible. I think that from the way you went so quiet.

John: They could have easily come that way (referring to where the door is now).

M.F.:   I still think I am right in believing you thought your remark was more sensible – you didn't think I would agree – you didn't think I would make *stupid* remarks!

John: Beg pardon. (Followed by a long silence.)

M.F.:   (Repeats the statement.)

John: It isn't really stupid, it could have been. It's unlikely. (After a further silence he went on to talk about electric trains, inferring by asking me questions that I was ignorant on this topic.)

M.F.:   You must think I am an *awfully ignorant boob* if I have not heard of Meccano, because everyone has.

Fordham gradually stops making these remarks and gets more in touch with what John is worried about, leading him to the following reflection:

> My aggression against this boy had interfered with my getting to understand what was going on in his mind. I had misinterpreted the child's feelings, replacing more subtle ones by a cruder statement, owing to the repression of memories relevant to a particular period of my own childhood. Then I used to attack my mother calling her 'stupid', a word I had repeated in my transference interpretations to John. Evidently I had identified with the memory images and John had represented myself as a child while I, ceasing to be the analyst, represented my mother.
>
> (Fordham 1957a, pp. 91–2)

ASSESSING THE VALUE OF SYNTONIC TRANSFERENCE/COUNTERTRANSFERENCE

Fordham's work on the syntonic transference put forward, with clinical examples, the thesis outlined in Jung's work that the whole personality of the analyst is involved in analytic work. He distinguished affects recognized as syntonic to the patient's difficulties from countertransference illusions, which can only be resolved by the analyst examining himself for understanding of his patient. This work on countertransference paved the way for the tentative beginnings of the Jungian study of the Kleinian concept of projective identification (see Chapter 10). If this now seems rather tame and if the reader's background is in psychoanalysis then this work on the transference could seem like Paula Heimann's or Roger Money Kyrle's. But it was arrived at independently and, in the context of Jungian psychology, it filled an important gap left by Jung. Jung himself thought well of it and in his foreword to *New Developments in Analytical Psychology* (in which the paper on transference was published) he praised Fordham's 'feeling for essentials', and recognition that 'the problem of the transference occupies a central position in the dialectical process of analytical psychology', adding that 'It makes the highest demands not only on the doctor's knowledge and skill but also on his moral responsibility' (*CW* 18, para. 1170).

Fordham, like Jung, felt that far from the affects stirred within the analyst being undesirable (the original meaning of countertransference) they were a useful source of information about the patient. In working at the difference between countertransference which is syntonic with the patient's needs and countertransference which is more a manifestation of the analyst's pathology, Fordham was recognizing the truth of Jung's contention that:

> because of the archetypes the analyst inevitably be- comes sooner or later involved with the patient in an unconscious process, which is first experienced as a projection and then further analysed.
>
> (Fordham 1957a, p. 96)

One consequence of this view of analysis is that analytical psychologists treat the fantasy material genetically as *reactivations* of past fixations, and think of the material as a purposeful attempt to resolve the conflict which exists in the present in the consulting room. If this sounds like recognizable contemporary psychoanalytic practice then it is curious that current psychoanalysts do not acknowledge Jung's early pioneering contribution to their present practice. For when Jung was setting this out in 1912 he was being vilified by the Freudians who have subsequently scotomized his writings.

In addition, Jungians do not conceive of analysis as only concerned with the ego and consciousness but also with the self. Realization of the self, referred to as individuation by Jung, as a later stage of the analytic process, was now brought forward by Fordham to include the early reductive periods of analysis. Theoretically the implication of this was that something more to do with the wholeness of the person rather than their consciousness alone was activated in the analytic process, even when it was the analysis of childhood.

Twelve years after first publishing this work Fordham summarized the change in his views on the syntonic transference/countertransference as follows:

I have come to think that the clinical experiences subsumed under this heading seem better considered in terms of an introject that has failed to become reprojected. The two unconscious processes, projection and introjection, are thus considered valuable processes, and together with information gained by listening and observing, form the basis on which technique rests. A syntonic countertransference is thus part of a more complex situation. Because the introject is of little use at the time, it becomes negative, since it deflects the analyst from his aim of working at the level the patient has reached. It is relevant only to what is right under the surface and well defended by the patient. Conceiving analysis as including not only the unconscious content being resisted but also the resistances themselves, it can be asked why does the analyst have the experience? If through introjection an analyst gets indirect experience he often cannot understand, could it not be that he defends himself against the patient's own defences by knowing beforehand? Since he has no evidence of the source of his experiences, the conclusion I would draw is that he has ceased to listen to what his patient has been saying, because of his unconscious hostility to the defences that the patient seeks to communicate to him. In other words he treats the patient as if his defences do not exist. This illusion can lead to brilliant 'intuition', and the like that sometimes produce exciting results. It does not belong to analysis of the patient because the defences are ignored.

(Fordham 1974k, p. 276)

In taking his readers through his own learning experiences Fordham has provided vital stepping-stones for apprentice analysts who, inspired by Jung but puzzled by his clinical legacy, need firm ground to stand on as they pick their way to their own synthesis. In this process they will have learnt too that theories outgrow their usefulness and need renewing from clinical experience.

THE CHILD WITHIN, AS THE SHADOW OF THE ADULT

Having drawn the attention of the Jungian community to the relevance of the syntonic intra-psychic experiences of the analyst during the session, Fordham now addressed the significance of the analysis of childhood for the assimilation of the shadow. Naturally his earlier work with its descriptions of the reductive analysis of transference drew the reader towards the importance of ontogenetic factors. But why this should be important for Jungians had not been spelled out in the context of Jung's model of the psyche.

The Jungian concept of the shadow ('the thing a person has no wish to be' (Jung, *CW* 16, para. 470) is the term used to describe those aspects of one's personality (usually repressed) which one feels to be embarrassing, awkward, shameful, aggressive, ungenerous and unlovable. Fordham described the benefits of analysing the infantile transference in the context of Jung's model. In society it is the antisocial people and the outcasts who make up its shadow. For the patients who have not had any reductive analysis much of the shadow consists of infantile feelings, and the assimilation of these aspects of the shadow of the personality cannot be accomplished without analysing the infantile transference. For if wholeness is the goal of individuation then the shadow of maturity, infantilism, has to be assimilated into the personality. Fordham felt strongly that it was not enough to leave this area to the psychoanalysts. Jungians, he argued, needed their own ontogenetic psychology, for a shadow unattended to increases in potency until it becomes unmanageable. And perhaps more importantly he argued that by understanding the nature and content of the shadow, and its primary affective patterns, regression can be turned into progression. This approach grasped the issue of whether reductive analysis was compatible with the individuation process. Wasn't it really a historical canard to think of individuation and reductive analysis as being in opposition? His view which he summarized later was:

> What therefore is the essence of individuation? It is surely the progressive realisation of our own worth, both positive and negative, in relation to the realities of spiritual and instinctual life, i.e. the contents of the inner world, and the outer world comprising people and the society in which we live.
>
> (Fordham 1979c, p. 108)

Analysis of the infantile aspects of the transference is an essential element in this process of differentiation, because:

> 1. A basically fluid state of mind is induced. 2. The affects which emerge are produced in a situation where another person reacts in a way that is basically safe. Further, he provides understanding

interpretations where necessary – many or few according to what is appropriate. 3. The analyst remains there, he does not die nor is he seriously damaged when very destructive fantasies and impulses are persistently directed at his person. 4. In this situation the primitive affects that develop can be tested for reactions in the analyst and then, when and only when they are well enough integrated, they can be used in the outer world. These are conditions in which every sort of basic, i.e. original, conflict situation can come under review, or otherwise be reflected upon, and no collectively imposed standard can remain untested, uncriticized.

(Fordham 1979c, p. 109)

The integration of the shadow is the route which leads to the self, since it is conceived that the uniting functions of the self enable whole reactions to occur, making it possible for us to react as individuals to experiences. He described his second analyst, Hilda Kirsch, as embodying this quality. He felt she 'had a good capacity for containment and so I felt safe and her statements seemed to come right out of her experience: they represented genuine emotional experience that she had assimilated' (Fordham 1993e, p. 73). As part of this integration of the shadow, he thought, the Freudian fixation points could be usefully understood as 'centres of developing consciousness round which archetypal motifs, as deintegrates of the self, centre in alluring profusion' (Fordham 1957a, p. 83). This was important as it allowed the Jungians to use a more embodied language to describe their patients' conflicts. For he was aware of the limited effectiveness of interpretations which had become detached from the actual physical reality of the content of the experience. Thus Jung's interest in the dual aspect of the mother could be linked, where appropriate, to early feelings for the breast as either loving, receiving and nurturing, or witch-like in its starving, persecuting and attacking attributes.

Fordham linked his experience of the special nature of the transference relationship – namely the way it constellated in whatever form aspects of the parent–child relationship – to Jung by drawing on Jung's description of the analyst's personality as the patient's bridge to the real world (Jung, *CW* 16, para. 290). By doing this he focused a discussion occurring in the Jungian world on to the dynamics of the defences activated by the analytic process. This discussion had been in danger of veering towards interpreting the importance of the analyst's personality as a licence to behave idiosyncratically. By doing this Fordham deepened the analytic understanding of a practice deriving from Jung's statement that there was therapeutic value in the analyst's personality. Fordham took Jung's recognition of the patient's need's for a real relationship and squeezed it for the juice of therapeutic insight. He emphasized Jung's recognition that the total involvement of the analyst in the process was relevant to a successful therapeutic outcome – a point of view now widely acknowledged by psychoanalysts but not attributed by them to Jung.

One feature of this discussion about the analyst's own personality was the frequency with which some analysts found themselves giving information to their patients when this was undesirable because not sufficiently examined in context. Fordham's recognition of the continuing presence of transference phenomena at these times, when others thought a more 'human' response was necessary, could seem 'inhuman'. His reply to this was as follows:

> Analysts are inhuman because of the transference, and we need to know how to be inhuman; this is surely one of the main reasons for undergoing an analysis, so that we may understand the patient's need and, at the same time, maintain our humanity.
>
> (Fordham 1957a, p. 94)

For instance:

> Suppose a patient evokes warmth and compassion in the analyst; that needs scrutinising, because it may be a grave mistake to provide it. That is so because the supposed feeling in the analyst can be a response to his patient's projective identification, and then it is the analyst's job to feed it back to the patient so that he or she becomes capable of such feelings as well.
>
> (Fordham 1985a, p. 216)

At the same time he was mindful of the archetypal nature of the transference relationship, which he mainly described in terms of interaction, a concept he was later to refine and distinguish from countertransference.

CONCLUSION

Fordham's work on transference analysis showed that reductive interpretation and analysis of the infantile transference promoted individuation. The significance of this was that it could have been understood theoretically that the synthetic methods of the analysis of the archetypal transference as described by Jung in 'The Psychology of the Transference' stood in opposition to reductive methods associated historically with psychoanalysis. In examining Jung's method, whether revealed anecdotally as in the statement 'I am unsystematic by intention' or in the detailed study of his writings, or in the microscopic examination of patient–analyst interactions, he evaluated Jung's legacy and compared it to contemporary practice, which often meant psychoanalysis. But while at a descriptive level different practitioners can agree about the phenomena under examination, Fordham never forgot he was a Jungian, with the result that he clarified, when necessary, the theoretical differences between psychoanalysis and analytical psychology. These differences may now in practice have disappeared, although often without acknowledgement of the modifications introduced by Jung (see Fordham 1985a, p. 95 and 1995, p. 26).

Descriptively Fordham demonstrated both the need to integrate archetypal non-personal contents, and the need for greater adaptation as expressed in analysis through the projective/introjective processes. This led to the distinction between identifications which were syntonic and those which were delusional, a distinction he was later to change as his understanding of projective identification took hold in his clinical work. When first introduced, this earlier distinction had greatly expanded and clarified Jung's statements about transference, such that analytic flesh and clothing were put on Jung's often pithy but incomplete skeletal outline.

Chapter 9

Countertransference, interaction and not knowing beforehand

FORDHAM'S FURTHER DEVELOPMENTS OF JUNG'S WORK ON THE TRANSFERENCE IN THE ANALYSIS OF ADULTS

Two particular contributions to transference and countertransference were made by Jung. The first was his early recognition of the importance of the way the analyst was affected by the unconscious of the patient. And secondly, in relation to individuation processes, how important it was to acknowledge the transpersonal elements in the archetypal transference. He wrote as if his patients fell into two categories: those who wished to achieve a greater normality in their lives and those for whom individuation was their objective. The procedures Jung thought appropriate for those wishing to be more adapted included psychoanalysis, as distinct from analytical psychology. And although he recognized the central part the transference played in analysis his attitude to transference was complex:

> The transference is the patient's attempt to get into psychological rapport with the doctor. He needs this relationship if he is to overcome the dissociation. The feebler the rapport, i.e., the less the doctor and patient understand one another, the more intensely will the transference be fostered and the more sexual will be its form.
>
> (*CW* 16, para. 276)

He conceived of a time in analysis when the analyst would be able to move from focusing on the infantile transference to the 'problem of the individual relationship', which is one of the ways he distinguished his psychology from Freud's psychoanalysis.

> The touchstone of every analysis that has not stopped short at partial success, or come to a standstill with no success at all, is always the

person-to-person relationship, a psychological situation where the patient confronts the doctor upon equal terms.

(Ibid., para. 289)

What Jung was drawing attention to was the need to recognize that patients also have a relationship with their therapists, which for each of them includes their knowledge of his personality. He emphasized the personal relationship within the impersonal framework. He often used a chemical metaphor:

> For two personalities to meet is like mixing two chemical substances; if there is any combination at all both are transformed. In any effective psychological treatment the doctor is bound to influence the patient; but this influence can only take place if the patient has a reciprocal influence on the doctor. You can exert no influence if you are not susceptible to influence.
>
> (Ibid., para. 163)

In addition, he recognized that the doctor had to engage with the patient as a real person. 'The patient's claim to . . . human relationship still remains and should be conceded, for without a relationship of some kind he falls into a void' (ibid., para. 285).

Jung frequently described his patients as being special; by this he meant that they were socially adapted (even successful in the eyes of the world) but their reasons for seeking help were that their lives lacked meaning. He thought that it was wrong to analyse such patients from the point of view of the history of their experience; rather, what they needed to have emphasized was their individuality. For these patients, 'the therapist must abandon all his preconceptions and techniques and confine himself to a purely dialectical procedure, adopting the attitude that shuns all methods' (ibid., para. 6).

The dialectical procedure here refers principally to that which happens between the ego and the archetypes. It is exemplified by the practice of active imagination. His understanding of the archetypal aspect of transference was that there came a time in the analysis when the imagos needed a response from the analyst which was symbolic. He gave examples of this; perhaps the best known one is of the female patient who dreamt he was a giant of a man and she was a little girl in his arms. He was standing in a field of wheat and the wind was blowing and he was swaying with the waves of the wind in the field.

> And she felt as if she were in the arms of a god, of the Godhead, and I thought, 'Now the harvest is ripe, and I must tell her.' And I told her,

'You see, what you want and what you are projecting into me,
because you are not conscious of it, is the idea of a deity you do not
possess. Therefore you see it in me.'. . . . But the idea of a deity is not
an intellectual idea it is an archetypal idea. . . . . She did not have the
idea of a Christian God, or of an old testament Yahweh. It was a
pagan god, a god of nature, of vegetation. He was the wheat himself,
He was the spirit of the wheat, the spirit of the wind, and she was in
the arms of that numen. Now that is the living experience of the
archetype. It made a tremendous impression on that girl, and instantly
clicked. She saw what she really was missing, that missing value
which she projected into me, making me indispensable to her. And
then she saw that I was not indispensable, because, as the dream says
she is in the arms of that archetypal idea. That is a numinous experience, and that is the thing people are looking for, an archetypal
experience that gives them an incorruptible value.

(Jung 1978, pp. 346–7)

Fordham thought that this understanding of the archetypal nature of
transference comes later in an analysis when infantile transferences have
been sufficiently worked over. His concern originally was to ascertain
that analysts in training in the UK did not rush prematurely into thinking
that this stage had arrived. He questioned the usefulness of maintaining
the distinction between those patients wanting to be more 'normal' and
those seeking individuation. This was because the transference relationship contained archetypal as well as personal constituents. It could also
lead, he thought, to overlooking the fact that patients who came seeking
individuation often felt they needed to be more adapted. Fordham
pointed out that dialectical procedure can also mean the more general-
ized process the analyst engages in with his patient when drawing on his
own experience of individuation and interacting out of it.

Jung, because of his respect for the individual and his need to
differentiate his method from Freud's, frequently wrote as if having a
technique was undesirable. But in Fordham's view Jung's objection to
technique was mainly historical in that it was part of his disagreement
with Freud, whose technique he felt was identified with his method,
such that he felt that psychoanalysis became the analysis of infantile
sexuality. And Fordham also observed that an 'attitude which shuns all
methods' is of course a method.

Fordham mistrusted the excessive reliance on the personality of the
analyst as this could lead to idealization of the analyst, and to 'intrusive
displays of his personality or acting out his countertransference'. He

wanted analysts training in the Society to be well enough grounded in analysis of the infantile transference. Further, by relating it to his dynamic of the self he demonstrated that this sort of analysis extended Jung's concept of individuation. To that end his pioneering work on the micro-analysis of countertransference opened up the discussion of what analysts did with their patients and made possible the teaching of technique for future generations of trainees. Technique became not so much what was imposed on patients, as Jung had originally feared it might become, but rather 'the distillate of habitual behaviours by an analyst with differing kinds of patients' (Fordham 1974k, p. 270). The purpose of technique was shown 'to increase the capacity of the patient for reflection about himself, first in relation to his analyst, and, as a consequence, to his wider environment and his inner world' (ibid., p. 271). The further refinement of Jung's statement about the significance of the personality of the analyst – since he was as much in the analysis as the patient – came from this work. This showed him that it was not so much the qualities of the analyst *per se* which were therapeutic as his abilities to manage them. Communication between him and his patient was both conscious and unconscious but not, as Jung had sometimes implied, symmetrical. The analyst, by virtue of his training and experience, was clearer as to what was happening. Fordham's contribution to the understanding of technique therefore was that:

> if *all* valid techniques are personal interactions between analyst and patient, then the individual element becomes an essential part of all interpretative and other analytic procedures. But this does not mean that all cases are the same; indeed, Jung's distinction still stands, as it were, macroscopically. It is only when the detailed microscopic analysis of the analytic situation is gone into that his distinction comes to be seen as quantitative rather than qualitative.
>
> (Fordham 1974k, p. 271)

He clarified that Jung's emphasis on the therapeutic value of the analyst's personality principally meant his unconscious. This was one reason why Jung was emphatic that all analysts must have a thorough personal analysis before working with patients. The meaning Fordham saw in Jung's statement that all patients had a claim on their analyst for a human relationship was that the doctor had to refrain from hiding behind his authority. He had to recognize that his patient was having an effect on him, knew quite a lot about him psychologically and influenced him. As I have discussed in Chapter 8, Fordham is clear that the human aspect of the relationship did not mean giving information to patients:

When I have objected to this practice or attempted to draw analysts' attention to their motives, I have been asked: 'Why do you find it necessary to withhold information about yourself from the patient?'
(Fordham 1957a, p. 93)

He wanted to know why those analysts thought it was in the patient's interest for them to 'be more human' or make mistakes, as it seemed likely that this behaviour masked a countertransference illusion. In setting out his objections to this practice Fordham argued that the patient did not see the analyst as the analyst saw himself, and therefore to give information avoided analysis of the patient's projection. Because Jungians were still trying to distinguish themselves from Freudians they were muddling spontaneous reactions from the self with inappropriate revelations. Fordham found himself having to explain that at times like these 'Analysts are inhuman because of the transference, and we need to know how to be inhuman' (Fordham 1957a, p. 94). His objective was not to make his patients more normal or adapted, but to increase their capacity to think about themselves, first in relation to the analyst then to the wider environment.

NOT KNOWING

Fordham's clinical experience with children and adults confirmed for him Jung's statement that the whole of the analyst's personality was engaged in the process of analysis. This included the irrational processes. It was this, for instance, which led him to meet his patients first and read their notes afterwards. He did not want his head filled with preconceptions and explanations. He wanted to meet the person and then later add in the history as an aid to understanding. In his child guidance work he used to come into the waiting room and announce himself to the family. Then, calling the child by name, he would suggest he came along with him. This inevitably provoked a reaction and what happened next depended on what this was. Sometimes the child came with him, sometimes the mother came too. The manner in which this occurred provided valuable information about their relationship and their way of dealing with stressful situations.

Fordham's way of approaching his child patients recognized that he was part of their fantasy. Going to visit the doctor is an event full of preformed transference implications. If the mother has not told the child the purpose of the visit the unconscious content will be even higher. Doctors, physical or psychological, try to find out what is inside the patient and can employ invasive techniques – from surgery to asking questions. They can also be expected to make right what is wrong, whether it is bad insides or bad thoughts. The first interview also provided a concentrated example of the problem the patient had come with. Fordham, by proceeding in this way, was allowing the archetypal nature of the transference to be experienced by himself and his patient.

This way of initiating contact with a patient is what Jung referred to when writing of the doctor risking his authority, since he is not making the patient conform to his expectations but letting a situation develop from which both will learn something. The long case study of Alan in *The Self and Autism* (Fordham 1976a) (see Chapter 7) is set out in this manner: first we meet the child, only at the end do we learn of his history and background. Similarly in the consulting room with children Fordham wanted them to have an experience of the self, to discover and integrate those aspects of their personality which were giving rise to their difficulties. Underlying this attitude is his valuing of Jung's view of the purposiveness of archetypal activity, and that 'illness' contains an attempt to heal the psyche.

Within the interactions of the consulting room this attitude leads to an approach that acknowledges within the transference 'a creative element, the purpose of which is to shape a way out of the neurosis' (Jung, *CW* 16, para. 277). Locating this creative element is where the skill of the practitioner lies. Some practitioners encourage their patients to paint or draw or find expression for their conflicts in plastic arts. Fordham, while not opposed to this, has understood it as potentially concealing the transference with some adult patients rather than illuminating it. It can be used defensively, as well as tending to encourage the patient's feeling of being identified with the collective aspects of the material to the detriment of discrimination. The analyst can compound this problem if he brings forward fascinating parallels from his prior knowledge of myth or legend. Fordham preferred a dialectical procedure based on interaction with the patient, rather than that more supervisory approach to the patient's unconscious processes. This is to say that, for instance, in the analysis of psychoses in childhood, and probably in all analyses which penetrate the deeper layers of the psyche, there is a measure of presiding over a process as well as enabling a process. This is because the actual analytic situation is such a powerful instrument for the investigation of the psyche that once the conditions are in place the process has its own momentum, guided by the archetypes.

One of the constituents of this investigation is the analyst's own countertransference. In the previous chapter I described how Fordham made use of this to separate out what was his own pathology and what was a part of the patient lodged in him, which he had to work on to make sense of for his patient. Subsequently he came to realize that the process of mutual projective identification meant that the patient also 'knew' about the analyst's unconscious. This experimental attitude to himself had earlier led him to recognize that while there were many interpretations he could be making to his patients he was often holding back from doing so until he became clearer as to why he felt this reluctance. With Alan, for instance, when he was in the manic phase of his analysis, Fordham understood that in his activity in the consulting room he was working out his inner conflict but was not experiencing it as inner to himself. It had the quality for Alan of a heroic deed. Therefore to have interpreted in usual analytic fashion that the outside activity was a manifestation of his inner world would have

> confirmed the idea that I understood nothing, so what I said would not have carried any weight. It is only an adult who could think of his experiences as part of his internal world; for Alan it was a world of imagination and play that he entered when he came into the therapy room and it was always related to objects in the room.
>
> (Fordham 1976a, p. 207)

EPISTEMOLOGICAL REFLECTIONS

What Fordham was here recognizing, and later was going to develop, was that analysts often spoke out of their own need not the patient's, and that what they said was frequently based on assumptions arising out of their training or theories. Jung recognized that patients infect their analysts, and that it was useless for the analyst to deny this. He described how it happened from a partial identification with the patient's material. But he noted that since this was accompanied by 'inner disharmony' the route to understanding was in place as the analyst had additional information deriving from the study of his own feelings and thoughts. In the above example of Alan, the assumption would have been that he had an inner world because Fordham felt Alan's conflict inside himself. But to intrude assumptions of this kind into the analysis, he thought, did not foster the analytic aim of Jung as described above. Caution, however, had to be taken to distinguish that from occasions when not interpreting would have been a way of avoiding facing the patient with some unpleasant truth.

These reflections set Fordham thinking about the interactional nature of the analytic process. Was the dialectical process, in its more general sense, an example of an open system and was this what Jung had in mind in his theory of archetypes? This would mean that the common substrate in all people could lead to a situation where the differences between people were minimized and it was this process in action which would enable the analyst to take on those parts of the patient wherein the conflict lay. Arising out of this, it would follow that if the analyst was paying attention to the patient's particular difficulty this in turn would emphasize the difference between the patient and the analyst, i.e. their individual features, and consequently facilitate the assimilation of the archetypal features common to all. (This line of thought naturally presupposes that the neurosis in the patient has not disabled the analyst.)

Fordham's study of these consulting-room dynamics had so far produced his work on syntonic countertransference and countertransference illusion, which he subsequently revised. Two colleagues of his had further demonstrated that what Fordham had called countertransference illusion could be understood as the patient making the analyst behave in a way which was right for the patient but unusual for the analyst and therefore still part of the syntonic countertransference.

NOT KNOWING AS A TECHNIQUE WITHIN THE DIALECTIC

Subsequently Fordham reconsidered the value of countertransference illusion. He pointed out that it placed the analyst on the same level as the patient and this kept the analyst on his toes as he must ensure that it did not go on too long. If the analyst denied this, it might lead to him using technique in a split-off way, intended to ward off the affective content of what he had introjected from the patient. His work on countertransference illusion made clearer the occasions when it was necessary for the analyst to withdraw his projections from his patient. Fordham gives an example of this process in his paper on countertransference and interaction.

A patient over sixty years old gets up from her chair when I come into the waiting room. She looks bright, with eyes sparkling like a little girl's. I feel annoyed about something hungry about her and think that she wants to be met with a hug and a kiss – it seems inappropriate and I don't want to do it. She lies down on the couch and says nothing. I feel a growing frustration and become aware that it is I that am hungry. She is not going to feed me with associations and I reach for my pipe. Then she starts talking and I put my pipe down. I am able to listen comfortably as the interview proceeds.

These incidents and reflections would not have become conscious had I not emptied my mind. This patient had been in analysis for some time and I actually knew well enough what this was about. I could have documented each of her actions. She was a somewhat narcissistic personality and easily felt angry if her virtues were not appreciated. I knew enough about her childhood to know why she had regressed when she came to her sessions and could have interpreted it without difficulty. But if I had done that, none of the affective content of the meeting would have been felt and my underlying irritation would have been missed. Also my projective identification and the way it was withdrawn to discover my own hunger would have been lost sight of. Finally I might very well have not noted that she started to talk out of competition with my pipe. . . . In short instead of resolving my own state of mind I would have developed a concealed countertransference.

(Fordham 1979c, pp. 201–2)

As Fordham understood, here was an instance of him projectively identifying with his patient and how he worked at locating the identification accurately, so as to be able to continue to analyse his patient effectively. It provided both knowledge about himself and also knowledge about his patient since she was leading him towards a different understanding of her. By continuing to work on this within himself he arrived at a reformulation of countertransference. He argued that:

apart from an analyst's appropriate reactions, his transitory projections and displacements cease to be called countertransference since they represent the analyst acting on and reacting to his patient. . . . It is when the interacting systems become obstructed that a special label is needed and, to my mind, it is then that the term *countertransference* is appropriate.

(Ibid., p. 208)

Where this work begins in the consulting room is in the analyst's effort to empty his mind, and not know anything about his patient before each interview.

As I mentioned in Chapter 2, Jung in his description of psychic processes described something he called compensation. He defined it as

an inherent self-regulation of the psychic apparatus. In this sense, I regard the activity of the *unconscious* as a balancing of the one-sidedness of the general *attitude* produced by the function of *consciousness*. . . . The activity of consciousness is *selective*.

Selection means *direction*. But direction requires the *exclusion of every-thing irrelevant*. This is bound to make the conscious *orientation* one-sided. The contents that are excluded and inhibited by the chosen direction sink into the unconscious, where they form a counterweight to the conscious orientation. The strengthening of this counter-position keeps pace with the increase of conscious one-sidedness until finally a noticeable tension is produced . . . in the end the tension becomes so acute that the repressed unconscious contents break through. . . . As a rule, the unconscious compensation does not run counter to consciousness, but is rather a balancing or supplementing of the conscious orientation.

(Jung, *CW* 6, para. 694)

Fordham applied this concept to describe the analyst's compensating for his conscious knowledge when with his patient. Jung urged analysts to find a new theory for each patient, Fordham for each interview. His ideal analyst forgot his previous knowledge of the patient each time he met him and began afresh each day. For while it is true that an analyst has a repertoire of conscious techniques which include his knowledge of his patient, the unconscious interactions also give rise to information about the patient and the analyst. He investigated whether there was a method of using the information this unconscious source provided. While this is not exactly a technique, since it consists mainly in digesting unconscious material, he studied what happened in single interviews. As with all advances in method, it is only when it becomes difficult to do what you are trying to do that understanding its complexity increases. In his paper entitled 'On Not Knowing Beforehand', he gave examples of his successes and failures in applying this non-method.

A tall distinguished-looking young woman came to my consulting room door that is made of glass, she tapped on the door, entered and lay down comfortably on the couch looking at me with pleasant eyes. In order to be seen I do not sit right behind her. Her look was friendly and affectionate. That event was pleasing and I was surprised since it had not taken place before (intrusion of a memory) which I knew to be true (a piece of knowledge). I wanted to enjoy the experience of her being like that (intrusion of desire). . . . I succeeded in blocking off all that material but I had to be very alert to do so, for I could soon have had enough material to make quite a number of interpretations and so relieved myself of the effort involved in not knowing. My point is that if I had started intervening I would have shaped the interview myself instead of leaving the patient to do so. It turned out that none of my memories, knowledge or desires were relevant to the shape of the interview as she developed it.

(Fordham 1993b, p. 130)

Fordham made three points about this example. First, that if proceeding in this way is what an analyst habitually does anyway, then it is because it has been learnt. Second, that the learning process necessitates putting to one side the previously gathered data about the patient, which is retained in some imagined mental filing cabinet. And third, that while there is nothing wrong with using filing-cabinet material in sessions it is preferable that its use is determined by the relation to the patient on the day.

In the above example it became clear as the session continued that the filing-cabinet material was not relevant. It had not disappeared; Fordham described it as existing in 'a space in my mind', not repressed but accessible to be worked on. Included amongst it was a tentative inter- pretation along the lines that she was glad to come today; that this derived from her previous session and the feeling she was having reflected her increased capacity to love and trust the analyst; or an interpretation based on a mixture, as he wrote, 'of knowledge, theory and conjecture which would have been intrusive'.

It is equally possible, as Fordham pointed out, to begin the session making the effort not to know beforehand but ending up speaking out of previous knowledge of the patient. For instance, a patient whom he knew well stayed silent for forty-five minutes of his fifty-minute session. During this time Fordham became aware that the silence had a particular quality, a numinosity. So he told the patient before he left that his silence was the best possible way he had for conveying what he was feeling. Fordham had spoken to this patient in many other sessions about the preverbal nature of his silences, his fragmentary thoughts or ones which were too dull, shameful or personal. What he said on this occasion came out of knowledge pushed by the desire to say something. It was not memory. The line Fordham is tracing is a thin one between listening to what is being communicated unconsciously, and, in the process of paying attention to it, trying to avoid imposing on the patient material arising from the history of their analysis. To do this he had to eliminate what was not key to each day's session.

Central to his examination of this process is the experience that while he may begin every session having made an effort to empty his mind, what comes into it will develop as the hour progresses and the risk of it being an imposition will be kept to a minimum. It can happen of course that what the patient is communicating is almost unbearable, and even if the analyst knows what it is about, the patient's intention may be solely to affect the other person; then it can become necessary for the analyst to unburden himself of whatever it is he is being filled up with. When this happens the analyst is speaking out of *his* desire. Another example of this is when the analyst's anxiety about the patient's life outside the sessions intrudes into the sessions and he starts to inquire how he or she is coping. All of this Fordham is aware of but does not feel it invalidates his ideal of trying not to know beforehand.

This work of Fordham's is, in my view, a summary and brief clinical description of a development in him of what Jung calls a transformation of libido. This term refers to relinquishing some ego position or achievement to let in more consciousness, a psychological *reculer pour mieux sauter*. Jung described transformations at different times in the life of the person and how they had different purposes. Fordham later described how he arrived at this 'not-knowing position' out of his efforts to integrate his two analyses, his experience of patients' delusional transferences, his study of Jung and his understanding of projective identificatory processes (Fordham 1993d). All combined to help him 'build up a formula about arriving at an interpretation which was not based on theory but which came out of the self. That involves trusting one's unconscious, in which projective and introjective identifications are active' (ibid., p. 637).

To work in this way requires a conscious effort and in its application it has features which are similar to Bion's ideas (see Bion 1970). 'On Not Knowing Beforehand' represents Fordham's mature analytic stance and while it is always difficult to identify the precise influences of a particular approach (see Fordham 1993d, pp. 636–7) Fordham's immersion in clinical work, Jungian literature and thoughts about the self suggests that the predominant influence in this formulation was not Bion's work, although he was undoubtedly aware of it. In my view the source derives from his historical awareness of the progression, from Freud's 'evenly suspended attention', to Jung's 'not knowing', to Bion's 'absence of memory and desire', and that his contribution fills out Jung's statement with a more detailed description of the process. This later work is very different from the earlier quest for scientific rigour expressed in his papers on transference and countertransference. In those papers he was trying to describe his empiricism as an analyst. In this later paper on the analytic process he puts to one side what he 'knows' and describes his trust in the unconscious. In his earlier papers he had been comparing his position with that of his psychoanalytic colleagues with whom he was in regular discussion in the forum of the British Psychological Society's Medical Section. In this paper he is saying what he thinks analysis is in contrast to psychotherapy. Jung refers to the transformations of libido in later life as a sort of sacrifice (*CW* 6) and this paper of Fordham's describes the way he gave up the superior ego functions of knowledge and memory to allow unconsciousness into consciousness.

There are also, however, occasions when the analyst finds himself simply reacting to his patient. Examples of Jung behaving in this way have been collected and presented anecdotally in a way that stresses the individuality of his method. For instance Henderson described Jung striding up and down the room during sessions, only to swoop down and sit very close to him to make some uncomfortable observation. Jung also gave him a conducted tour of his house in response to a dream of his about trying to reconcile his family's colonial and his own contemporary architectural styles (Henderson 1975). Fordham has sought in his published work on this aspect of Jungian psychology to stress the relation between the action and the process. There is, for instance, the well-known example of Jung's patient who was in the habit of slapping her employees – including her doctors:

> She was a very stately and imposing person, six feet tall – and there was power behind her slaps, I can tell you! She came, then, and we had a very good talk. Then came the moment when I had to say something unpleasant to her. Furious, she sprang to her feet and threatened to slap me. I, too, jumped up and said to her, 'Very well, you are the lady. You hit first – ladies first! But then I hit back!' And I meant it. She fell back into her chair and deflated before my eyes. 'No one has ever said that to me before!' she protested. From that moment on, the therapy began to succeed.
>
> (Jung 1963, p. 140)

Now, while Henderson's examples were presented in the context of Jung's flexible approach to analysis, Fordham understood this example of Jung's emotional reaction as a statement of his limits and the necessary limits within which therapy can be conducted. This he argued was containing, and, as Jung wrote, 'From that moment on, the therapy began to succeed.' He compared it to Little's description of the analyst's total response, which she called 'R' (Little 1957). Little's patient went on telling stories about children who came to visit her and whom she could not stop coming. The patient could not say no to these children. Little told her she would not listen to any more of these stories. This was a great relief to the patient, who subsequently was able to say no to the children. Not all responses, however, are necessarily so easily related to the progress of therapy. Fordham has observed that sometimes out of frustration he can find himself unconsciously saying something which has the quality of a verbal countertransference enactment. He wrote:

> During an analytic hour what was to me an especially frustrating patient was talking about wanting to be calmer, and complained of her Karma. As the end of the interview drew near she became increasingly desperate and started picking to pieces anything I said. We had often worked on her difficulties over the end of the interview, and I had interpreted the meaning of it frequently, to no avail. This time she claimed that I was muddled and in particular, she could not tell whether I meant 'calmer' or 'Karma': 'Which do you mean?', she demanded. To which I emphatically replied, in a half conscious state, 'Karmer' and spelt it out. As I did so I realized, to my satisfaction, that I was making a malicious joke.
>
> (Fordham 1978b, p. 129)

The extent to which this impinged on the patient is difficult to estimate. Fordham said of this incident that the patient took it as an example of his madness. Over time what it may have contributed to was the patient's awareness of Fordham's non-judgemental attitude to his own malice, something which could have helped her integrate her own.

His reflection on this and other instances of idiosyncratic behaviour is to refer them to the internal oscillations that occur within sessions between an open system (the patient and the analyst interacting in a context of not knowing) and the closed system, exemplified by the culmination of this process when the analyst makes an interpretation, thereby signalling where the boundaries are between them. The malicious joke of the above example arose from the effect within the open system when the feeling within the analyst was not modifiable by his own self-analysis and in desperation he relieved himself of his frustration.

Underlying Fordham's attitude to these experiences were his continuing interest and thoughts about the analyst's responsibilities to his patient and the process of analysis. To this end he gives an example from Jung's practice where Jung was finding himself increasingly perplexed by a patient of his (*CW* 16, paras 549–64). Then he had a dream about her which revealed an unconscious attitude of his towards her. Subsequent to this dream the patient began to develop a sequence of psychosomatic symptoms. Jung made it clear to his patient that he did not know what was going on and that perhaps she would be more helped by a therapist who did. The patient's response to his suggestion was astonishment, telling him that while her dreams and symptoms were crazy, as far as she was concerned the treatment was going splendidly. Quite by chance Jung then discovered a book about kundalini yoga in which the progression of his patient's symptoms corresponded closely to the centres of consciousness described in this book. From his study of this he was then able to elucidate the patient's symptomatology and help her in the integration of these experiences. Fordham's point is that this is an example of how the patient was able to tolerate the analyst not understanding her symptoms until he could catch up with her and learn from them. He is refuting the clichéd thinking which states that patients can only develop as far as their analysts.

These contributions which his approach makes to analytical psychology further refine, fill in and bring up to date Jung's statements about the analyst being in the analysis, that a new theory has to be created for each patient, and that the psyche has an almost physiological system of self-regulation. Fordham's work gives those statements a practical application. They also pave the way for recognizing the centrality of the unconscious process of projective identification, an important psychoanalytic discovery, which has been in the centre of Fordham's most recent developments and is closely linked to Jung's use of empathy and *participation mystique*.

Chapter 10

Defences of the self, projective identification and identity

DEFENCES OF THE SELF

In 1974, Fordham wrote what was to become one of the most quoted papers in analytical psychology, *Defences of the Self*. In it he described in a manner similar to Jung's a phenomenon he called 'a total defence exhibited by patients in a transference psychosis' (Fordham 1985a, p. 152). It aroused so much interest because he described a situation where whatever he said to his patient was reinterpreted 'in the light of the projective identification that held sway at any particular time' (ibid., p. 153).

> First, I proceeded on the ordinary basis that it would be enough to name the projection and suggest, even if I could not prove, how it had arisen in the expectation that the analysis would then proceed. However, since the interpretation itself was submitted to reinterpretation, this did not work . . . in the patient's view, the analyst was using his technique as a shield behind which to hide himself.
>
> (Ibid.)

The paper described how the patient persistently attacked the analyst, trying to divide him into a 'bad technical machine' and a 'good hidden part'. The sense of time, what is past and what is present, got lost. Memories of childhood remained isolated emotionally from their context. Fundamentally the patient ruthlessly treated the analyst as if he was the 'patient'. A consequence of this was that, if this was not detected, 'an amalgam of analyst–patient is set up, and it is very difficult to dissolve: it is a malignant form of countertransference' (ibid., p. 155). The analyst could become masochistic, confused, frustrated and feel like abandoning the work.

> All these states of the analyst avoid helplessness, despair and depression on his part, so he can begin to consider whether it is not these feelings

that are the state of the patient contained in himself. It cannot be underlined sufficiently that the patient remorselessly plays on any weak points he may discover in his analyst, the effect being to destroy the mature, nurturing, feeling and creative capacities of the analyst.

(Ibid., p. 156)

Fordham counselled the importance of sticking to the method, maintaining an analytic attitude at all costs, not giving in to guilt and keeping in mind that the pain of all this was the sign that 'the patient is struggling and of his will to live'. The patient is trying to relate to the analyst but the relatedness is in a malignant form.

The significance of this paper for analytical psychologists was that it brought together the extremes of delusional transference behaviour and Fordham's studies of infancy in a creative synthesis, which others have been able to draw on when in a similar predicament. Fordham was demonstrating what happened when a deintegrate of the self becomes split off and distorted. He was showing how these deintegrates could with great energy be forced into the analyst, but that what the analyst needed to keep in mind was that his own self could not be destroyed, even if he felt his ego was being overwhelmed at times. Consequently, with experience, he would be able to transform the projective identifications and by developing his interpretative skills help his patient find his way out of the impasse. Within the patient's delusions are 'archetypal forms aiming to re-establish relatedness'. This descriptive paper provided the springboard for analytical psychologists to study projective identification, while remaining true to Jung's individual psychology. Fordham explained:

Analytic practice involves introjecting parts of various people and it may not be possible to find the means of digesting and projecting these parts back into the patients. That is particularly difficult when there is much projective identification. When that predominates my identity may become threatened, boundaries become insecure, and I may be put in the position of 'fighting for my life'. That discovery, which I recorded in 'Defences of the Self', opened the doors for me to the treatment of patients as a whole, and seeing it as a precarious operation for any analyst who opens himself to patients so as to individualize his analytic endeavours.

(Fordham 1988d, p. 12)

The study of projective identification begins with Freud, then moves via Abraham to Rosenfeld, Klein and Bion to the present proliferation of work on the subject. What follows paraphrases the way Fordham compared Freud and Jung and the differing significance to these two pioneers of the place of identification processes in development, defences, and subsequent communication in one of his most recent papers (Fordham 1994b). He confined his Freudian sources to *Group Psychology and the Analysis of the Ego* (Freud 1921), the Leonardo paper (Freud 1910) and *Mourning and Melancholia* (Freud 1917).

IDENTITY AND IDENTIFICATION

The importance of identification in Freudian psychology is well attested. Freud wrote of identification as a valuable developmental process. He described it as 'the earliest expression of an emotional tie with another person' (Freud 1921, p. 105). Psychoanalysts who follow Freud think that the personality is formed through identification processes.

Jung on the other hand thought of identification as a process with a limited serviceability. He thought for the individual truly to be himself or herself he or she would eventually want to free himself or herself of the identifications of childhood and upbringing. He wrote:

> Identification can be beneficial so long as the individual cannot go his own way. But when a better possibility presents itself, identification shows its morbid character by becoming just as great a hindrance as it was an unconscious help and support before.
>
> (*CW* 6, para. 738)

The significant difference between these two points of view contributed to Freud and Jung going their separate ways in 1912. Fundamentally, underlying the Freudian point of view of the psyche is the absence of an internal source other than the super-ego, while Jung's view was that there was an inner source, some sort of internal organizing principle containing impersonal unconscious nodal points which behaved in characteristic ways. In the classical psychoanalytic models the preoccupation is, however, with the relation of the external to the person. So, for instance, the son's identification with the mother becomes important in the development of homosexuality. Subsequent workers, especially Klein, have developed and refined the work on identification, not least by describing projective identification, which has been worked on further by Bion (1959, 1962a, b), Rosenfeld (1987), Joseph (1989) and Meltzer (1992).

But Jung's interest was more in the relation of the archetypes to objects formed in the ego (to which Fordham added a developmental feature by describing how objects were formed on an archetypal basis through deintegration and reintegration). Jung was interested in the inner world, which he called the objective psyche, and in his accounts of active imagination he described dialogues with figures emanating from the unconscious. Sometimes if the ego identified with one of these figures the person could become psychotic. What more often happened was an inflation. This meant that the person became identified with images emanating from the collective unconscious, attributed by Jung to 'a regression of consciousness into unconsciousness' (*CW* 12, para. 563). This could result in either a depression or an extreme mania. Freud saw identification as the primitive process by which the psyche was built up, while Jung stressed identity between subject and object. The differences between the two are fundamental. Laplanche and Pontalis define identification as follows:

> Psychological process whereby the subject assimilates an aspect, property or attribute of the other and is transformed, wholly or partially, after the model the other provides.
>
> (Laplanche and Pontalis 1973)

Jung defines identity as an unconscious phenomenon. He regarded identity as a relic of our 'original non-differentiation of subject and object and hence of the primordial unconscious state' (*CW* 6, para. 741). He thought of it as a precursor to the identificatory process and a characteristic of infancy:

> Identity with the parents provides the basis for subsequent identification with them; on it also depends the possibility of projection and introjection.
>
> (Ibid.)

Developmentally therefore Jung sees identity preceding identifications. But what of projective identification? The term had not been invented when Jung was pursuing his research interests but he knew well enough what the experience entailed. He described it in a number of different ways. For instance he defined *participation mystique* as follows:

> It denotes a particular kind of psychological connection with objects, and consists in the fact that the subject cannot clearly distinguish himself from the object but is bound to it by a direct relationship which amounts to partial identity. This identity results from an a priori oneness of subject and object.
>
> (*CW* 6, para. 781)

He elaborated this oneness in his essay 'The Type Problem in Aesthetics' (*CW* 6) when writing of empathy. He described empathy as

> a kind of perceptive process, characterised by the fact that, through feeling, some essential psychic content is projected into the object so that the object is assimilated to the subject and coalesces with him to such an extent that he feels himself, as it were, in the object . . .
>
> (*CW* 6, para. 486)

Later in the same essay he describes the empathetic type as having a life which is

> empathised into the object, he himself gets into the object because the empathised content is an essential part of himself. He becomes the object. He identifies himself with it and in this way gets outside himself. By turning himself into an object he desubjectivises himself.
>
> (Ibid., para. 500)

These examples show that Jung was familiar with the unconscious processes which are now called introjective and projective identification but was not thinking of them as part of the analytical procedure so much as a characteristic of certain personality types. In his descriptions of the alchemists' efforts to turn the base metals into gold he was essentially describing the way in which these early scientists and psychologists were thinking about their projections into matter. His understanding of these projections is close to contemporary descriptions of the effects of projective identification in its evacuative and controlling aspects although it is misleading to ascribe to Jung an understanding of the psychoanalytical concept of projective identification.

PROJECTIVE IDENTIFICATION

This concept, central now to Kleinian psychoanalysis, was first defined by Klein in 1946 as an unconscious forcing of part of the ego into another person or part of a person for the purpose of controlling them. In the 1950s and early 1960s Bion was to modify this concept to distinguish projective identification which was in the service of normal communication, such as might occur between a mother and baby when their relationship was not suffused with unconscious violent affect, from projective identification which is characterized by the forceful evacuation of affect into another person (Bion 1959, 1962a, b). The more the subject has been studied, the harder it has become to define exactly what it is. Most Kleinian psychoanalysts describe what has happened between themselves and their patient to convey what it is, thereby enabling the projective and the identificatory aspects to be teased out. Mainly, however, the experience is described in terms of the affective quality of the experience as it exists between patient and analyst. This has led to projective identification being described in terms of the phantasies motivating it (see Rosenfeld 1983). In itself, as Jung recognized, projective identification is not a pathological mechanism, rather it is the basis for all empathic communications. It is essential, however, to normal mental functioning that projective identification is reversible, that projections can be withdrawn and that interactions with others are based on one's own identity.

The Jungian development of this concept has needed Fordham's dynamic of the self. His early descriptions of self-objects in autistic development (see Chapter 7) had shown how split-off parts of the self were being projected into another person or object which was then related to as if it were someone else. As the analyst recipient of these projections he wrote out of his countertransference. The Jungian interest in projective identification has mainly been from this point of view. One of the first analytical psychologists to publish on this was Rosemary Gordon (Gordon 1965). Her thesis was that projective identification was a 'drive towards fusion', which she described as 'a striving towards the realisation of wholeness and union'. This idea, that it represents a desire for fusion, is found also in the psychoanalytic investigation of it, but what distinguishes the Jungian use of this is to attribute a benevolent motive to the phenomenon. Where Gordon sees striving towards wholeness, Rosenfeld sees narcissistic, confused and split object relationships. In Gordon's description, the contents of projective identification are deintegrates from the original self and,

> because projective identification involves the getting rid of something which is yet not truly abandoned, the ego finds itself confronted with the rejected or denied complexes; and this may promote the development of a more efficient re-synthesis and integration. It is to this secondary function of projective identification that, I believe, Jung referred when he stressed the importance of projection for the ongoing process of becoming conscious.
>
> (Gordon 1965, p. 131)

All investigators agree that projective identification intensifies when the patient feels least understood. The greater the gap the patient feels between himself and the analyst the greater the projective identificatory content. Consequent upon this is the idea that projective identification as normal communication forms part of the transference–countertransference and can be distinguished from the more aggressive and expulsive aspects first described by Klein.

Fordham's work on this came together in his description of the expulsive and destructive features of some projective identifications in his paper 'Defences of the Self'. In this paper he described a pathological organization which could be reversed with difficulty through analysis. His later work, gathered together by Hobdell, continues his investigation of this phenomenon, which he conceptualizes in terms of Jung's formulations concerning identity and identification (Fordham 1994b). In this book Fordham provided clinical descriptions which indicate that states of identity precede projective identifications, as Jung suggested. The clinical evidence for this came in part from infant observation and in part from the discovery in analysis that when working through states of projective identification some patients arrive at a state of identity. This can be described and distinguished from projective identification. In the following clinical description taken from Fordham's chapter entitled 'Identification' he presented a male patient's struggle to free himself of his pain, which both he and Fordham could describe, but of which neither could understand why it was not modified by the analysis (Fordham 1994b). Then Fordham recognized where it originated from, with consequent implications for his technique. The patient had a series of dreams in which he was in a faraway country where a dictator was in control. The dreams progressed until soon after the liberation of the USSR the patient dreamt of embracing Gorbachev. Underlying much of this material was the patient's deep envy of Fordham's capacity to survive repeated annihilating attacks on the value of analysis.

Fordham now described to this patient how he had made him aware of an assumption which he was applying to the patient, namely that analysis was therapeutic and that analysts were only interested in their patient's 'inner worlds', especially the kind described by analysts. Because of the patient's characteristic pathology (obsessional undoing) he tended to assert that although he valued the efforts Fordham made to help him they were in fact not much use to him. Shortly after the Gorbachev dream there was a session spent in silence. After this session the patient had woken up in the night and had written out a criticism of Fordham's paper 'Defences of the Self' (Fordham 1985a). The silent session, followed by the patient's attempt to use the 'unproductive daytime' (a phrase of the patient's which denoted his wasted days) to organize his critical attack on Fordham, was significant and Fordham concluded that during this silent session 'he was near to bringing his state into relation with me' (Fordham 1994b, p. 67). His criticism was that Fordham did not acknowledge his omnipotence, 'and assumption that I [Fordham] was right' (ibid.). This Fordham linked to the assumptions about analysis being for the benefit of patients. In Fordham's words:

> though I had a very good idea of what it was all about and was able to provide some understanding of material brought to any particular session, I did not understand basically why I could not make inroads on his basic pain. It only became clear when I grasped that the problem centred at the level in which identity was active and so we were in an area in which understanding or insight in the ordinary sense of the word did not operate effectively. We were in fact in a state where consciousness (and unconsciousness) were not relevant. I think Jung may have been referring to this when he writes 'Doctor and patient thus find themselves in a relationship founded on mutual unconsciousness' [*CW* 16].
>
> (Fordham 1994b, p. 68)

Jung's explanation for this is that it is a consequence of the patient's unconscious contents constellating corresponding material in the doctor. Jung suggests that this level of unconscious communication is structured by the archetypes. Fordham, however, does not think this mutual unconsciousness is as structured as Jung suggests but rather that a state of identity exists between patient and analyst which is at a more primitive level of functioning, more akin to a state of very early infancy. The modification in technique which accompanied this discovery was in conveying to the patient, less out of his understanding only and more out of his emotional conviction, what he (Fordham) had seen. This represented a shift in emphasis from interpretation based on trying to meet the patient's need for understanding to one where he is telling the patient what he has understood.

What Fordham seems to have impressed on his patient was that his discovery that he, Fordham, was neither omnipotent nor omniscient had helped free the patient from his claustrophobic dependence on an analysis within which he felt imprisoned. Interpretation was not what was significant here but recognition. What the patient was responding to was Fordham's new-found conviction, not his daily interest and concern. This description expands Jung's statement on the necessity for the analyst to respond as a whole person out of his emotional being, to include how unconscious defences can be met in a way which allows the patient to hear what is being said to him. Fordham understood that what had blocked the analysis was the state of identity, meaning mutual unconsciousness, which he and his patient had got into. It was a relief to his patient, he thought, that by demonstrating his (Fordham's) 'inability to address his [the patient's] pain' he was checking his patient's 'unconscious belief that I believed myself to be omnipotent'. Fordham is here working out the consequences of his ideas about the self in infancy and linking them to the episodic states of non-differentiation, which this patient went into. He is referring these experiences to a state of mind which precedes the structuring necessary for projective identification.

In the Freudian model, early omnipotent delusionary states of identification are thought to contribute to the development of the personality, whereas Jung's early view of non-differentiation as a characteristic of the infant mind is close to Bick's (1968) description of the infant personality, when it is felt not to have the passive containment of a skin to hold it together (Jung's state of identity, Bick's state of unintegration). Bick's descriptions of infants who do not form a psychological skin, however, are in terms of the disintegration of the personality, whereas in Jung's model the personality does not disintegrate as a result of these experiences, since he considers them reversible. Jung is basing this on his experience of psychotic adults who recover from their psychosis. For Jung these states of identity are part of the developmental process in infancy. Fordham sees them differently, as episodic and not the principal characteristic of infancy, which is the dynamic of the self.

In Fordham's model the primary self as such cannot disintegrate and for him these early states of mind would be organized by the self, be episodic and only significant if they were not given up with maturation.

There has been considerable controversy especially amongst psychoanalysts over the question of how early an infant can distinguish the difference between two objects so that the introjections, projections and identifications could take place. It was Bick who, as a result of her studies of infants, concluded that there was at first primary identity of subject and object but that soon the infant discovered the skin and that made an interface and a space both inside and outside himself and his mother, in which mechanisms under consideration could operate. Should the experience of the skin be inadequate, the pathological condition of adhesive identification arises. That was an important proposition for it suggests there was a place for Jung's condition of identity before the more sophisticated processes developed. I should add that theoretically if the idea of the primary self be correct that the self contributes to infant experience by organizing the emotional and perceptive data to which Bick refers.

(Fordham 1994b, p. 66)

Fordham's model of the primary self goes some way to bringing these different observations together, especially if one thinks of it as a two-tier model. First there is the abstract self without characteristics, a concept similar to DNA, which is then followed by the development of a body and a person with characteristics which through interaction with the environmental mother gives rise to self-objects and then self-representations, which brings in the first awareness of self and other and the beginnings of rudimentary ego development.

This detailed working out of early object relations gives a grounding in infancy and childhood to Jung's ideas arising from his work with adult patients. For instance in his description of the psychological complexity of the marriage relationship, what he called in a resonant phrase the problem of the 'contained' and the 'container' is followed by an examination of the to and fro of projection and identification which makes the survival of a marriage so complicated and difficult (Jung, *CW* 17). Among the many subtle points which Jung makes in this paper is his description of the progression from 'the purely instinctive choice of a mate' – what he calls 'a kind of impersonal liaison' which is 'wholly regulated by traditional customs and prejudices, the prototype of every conventional marriage', where 'unconsciousness results in non differentiation, or unconscious identity' – to the struggle ('there is no birth of consciousness without pain') to unravel the complexities of the containing and contained partner's projections and identifications (*CW* 17).

Sonu Shamdasani writing in his introduction to the collection of Fordham's papers on technique has observed that Fordham's clarification of Jung's ideas is of 'more interest than simply that of an intra-disciplinary affair within analytical psychology'.

Through complex political and institutional processes that have yet to be adequately recognized, let alone mapped, the reading of Jung by psychoanalysts, which is still largely regarded as being off limits, has often been conducted in secrecy. . . . Fordham's clarification of Jung's ideas on therapy thus has a great significance for a general psychotherapeutic audience today, as many of Jung's seminal insights concerning the analytic encounter, have subsequently been developed by psychoanalysts, without any reference to Jung.

(Shamdasani 1995)

An example of this is Jung's use of the concept of container–contained which is similar to the model proposed much later by Bion in his work *Attention and Interpretation* (Bion 1970). In this book he elaborates Jung's thesis of the container and the contained to include not only marriage but the way meaning is contained in language and patients are contained within their analyst's mind. He works out in a less abstract and more detailed way than Jung how the container can restrict growth. Meltzer's work on the claustrum has taken this a step further in that he has described a clinical method for working with patients living in that state of mind and in so doing distinguishes intrusive identification from projective identification (Meltzer 1992). Steiner has delineated the characteristics of the place retreated to and its pathological organization, as it exists inside the patient and between the analyst and patient, and has shown the importance of working through a mourning process as part of the recovery (Steiner 1993). The work these Kleinian psychoanalysts have done has separated out the container, where thinking and the potential for transformation can occur, from states of identification, where the object identified with is possessed for a motive, often hostile, sometimes evacuative, nearly always perverse and non-developmental, where the rigidity of the projective process is characterized by its resistance to reversibility.

CLINICAL EXAMPLES

In Fordham's paper 'The Supposed Limits of Interpretation' he gives a clinical example of how he recognized a projective identification and the manner in which he responded analytically (Fordham 1991a). He described how a woman patient began by giving an account of her life abroad which was satisfactory and then contrasted it with her life here in England which was unsatisfactory. She had no work, no companion and no family here. She felt lonely and depressed. Fordham described the thoughts which came into his mind as he was listening to this, but none of them met the urgency of feeling she was evacuating into him. Aware that some response was required from him, he spoke entirely within the transference, out of this feeling, telling her that he understood she wanted him to feel what she felt so that he would be able to help her with it and take away her pain. But whatever he had done he had not achieved this as she had hoped. This was a partial interpretation and it was in response to the patient's inaccessibility to a more complete understanding reflecting the atmosphere of the moment in the session. The interpretation was located in the maternal transference and included

Fordham's recognition that 'Mummy' in the transference was felt not to be able to bear her pain and that the patient's accumulating discomfort, her urgent, ugly feelings, would stay to persecute her if she could not evacuate them into a receptacle which could transform them for her. In giving a full description in the paper Fordham was pointing up the essentially anal nature of this particular projective identification.

In a second example in the same paper he illustrates from his practice the interpretation of a projective identification. By contrast, the example is of a benevolent communication, albeit presented in the context of the patient's persistent negative transference. The patient was silent as he often was at the beginning of the session. Fordham found coming into his mind an observation of an infant whose grizzling stopped once he was spoken to. It did not matter what was said so much as the fact that he was being spoken to. He thought about this as a communication relevant to the patient's state of mind in the session. He recalled that this patient often said he did not understand what Fordham said to him. This encour- aged Fordham to speak. In his description of his interaction with this patient Fordham showed how he moved from talking to the child in him (who liked the sound of but did not understand the words) to talking to the adult about this child and why this was so. He proceeded in this way because the affective content from the child in this adult today ('I need to be talked to') was not primarily evacuative and controlling, but rather communicative.

This paper elaborated a contribution Fordham made to *Jungian Analysts: Their Visions and Vulnerabilities* (Spiegelman 1988). The paper and the short communication in the Spiegelman book are directed towards Jungian readers since Fordham's reading of papers produced by contemporary Jungians, especially those trained in Zurich, had led him to attempt to refocus what they were calling projective identification. What Fordham was drawing attention to was the way some analysts (a) treated projections of a physical, sexual and ultimately childlike affect as if there were some subtle adult quasi-mystical union of body and spirit occurring in a space which existed between them and their patient; and (b) how others limited their understanding of projective identifi- cation to the projected content and treated the identificatory content as fact not delusion.

In his paper 'The Supposed Limits of Interpretation', Fordham ex- amined the former example (a) through the published material of a Zurich-trained therapist who treated a female patient's erotic transference to him in an elaborate and directive way, which essentially abandoned analysis in favour of injunctions and behaviour (Fordham 1991a). The feature of this which concerned Fordham was that not only was analysis abandoned just at the moment when it was most called for, but that the analyst was acting on his identification, and consequently not hearing what his patient was actually describing. Instead he was telling her what to do and when he came to write about it, imposing on the events his abstract formulation. The fact of not analysing but rather acting on the identification was especially significant since the patient was describing an erotic experience of sexual arousal in the session.

In the second example (b) taken from the book edited by Spiegelman Fordham again drew attention to the analyst's response but this time it was to the feeling he has had projected into him that he was a useless parental figure who could not look after his child/patient (Spiegelman 1988). The theme of Fordham's description is that the patient regularly denigrates him, and analysis, but keeps on coming to the sessions. Spiegelman indicates that if he had been the analyst he would have responded to the projective identification that he has nothing of value to give this patient by describing to him what he felt has been put into him from the patient. Spiegelman says he would have said to the patient the following:

> As you say that I give you nothing, I feel as if I am a mother with empty breasts, and feel hurt and guilty. No matter how I try I can not satisfy you. How does my reaction affect you?
>
> (Spiegelman 1988, p. 18)

Fordham responds to this description of Spiegelman's by saying:

> I do not give raw emotional responses, when I have one, which is not often, but transform them into an interpretation.
>
> (Ibid.)

Fordham's point is that this is an example of the analyst failing to analyse the projective identificatory content in favour of reprojecting the projection – i.e. 'How does my reaction affect you?' – and treating the identificatory part as fact rather than delusion. To respond in Fordham's way takes more account of the context of the material in the session and how it has arisen in the patient. My understanding of Fordham's attitude is that the earliest and least verbal aspects of the transference are expressed behaviourally and that it is the analyst's task to find words to contain and transform them, rather than words which enact the patient's projection.

THE SENSE OF SELF

Underlying Fordham's work on projective and identificatory states is his understanding that the self is a continuous and active presence through-out life. Jung worked with adults and had no particular theory as to the significance of the self in infancy. Although he wrote about the self in many different ways, overall his writings convey the desirability of being able to achieve a state where the self takes precedence over the ego in the second half of life. Rosemary Gordon has distinguished Jung's 'big self', which refers 'to the wholeness of the psyche and includes the conscious as well as the unconscious areas of psyche', Fordham's primary self, 'the matrix of all those potential faculties of the organism which await the process of "deintegration" and of reintegration in order to become operative and so actualize themselves', from the 'little self', which refers 'to the awareness of one's own personal identity' (Gordon,1985). Gordon's 'little self' thus is a deintegrate of the self in the context of Fordham's modification of Jung and is in effect a part-self.

Fordham's work brings together the primary self of infancy with Jung's 'big self'. It is not so much concerned with the sense of self, 'the little self'. The main distinction between the sense of self (the little self) and the self as an abstract and imaginary concept (the primary self) is that the sense of self is something we can experience, since it is an aspect of the ego. Critics of Fordham's work point to the way he links the self to the individual, when Jung's descriptions of the self emphasize the way it transcends the individual. That is to lose sight of the repeated emphasis Fordham also puts on the way the self transcends the individual. For instance when he is describing categories of experience which have the feeling of 'being myself' he calls these part-selves, because the overall self transcends these feelings (Fordham, 1979a). Louis Zinkin, a prominent member of the SAP, disagreed with Fordham and described the sense of self as the more important feature.

> The sense of self has always seemed to me to be of more interest than discussion as to whether there is an objective self which exists or not at any particular age.
>
> (Zinkin 1991, p. 43)

In my view this statement of Zinkin's separates him from his Jungian origins. In excluding the self from being a 'given' which can lead to archetypal activity, which can integrate experience and give rise to experiences which transcend the ego, one of the unique features of Jung's psychology is lost. It is almost as if Zinkin is suggesting that the abstract self is the concern of philosophy whereas only the sense of self as we know it is the proper concern of psychologists.

Most writers on the subject of infant development, whether they are psychoanalysts or analytical psychologists, describe an early state of undifferentiation out of which arises something more differentiated. Winnicott, for instance, described this in terms of the self arising out of the ego (Winnicott 1965). This is the opposite of Fordham's description of the infant as a differentiated unit, as Fordham writes:

> It is this unity of the self that leads to early object relations being all parts of the self (deintegrates). At first there is no external object, nor for that matter any internal ones. . . . It is only through maturation and good mothering that the infant gradually recognises the difference between self and not self and it is in this way that the primary self is converted into symbolic representations.
>
> (Fordham 1976a, p. 223)

The particular value of Fordham's work on the self as it relates to clinical practice is that it provides a framework for the conceptualization of the interactions between patient and analyst which are not initially distinct nor clear in their attribution to one person or the other but which come within the ambit of containment, holding, modifying and transforming. What does Fordham's self add to these qualities which have been described by psychoanalysts as aspects of the mature ego? Fordham's model has one quality which is missing from the more ego-based models and that is that a self-based model recognizes gradations within the continuity of experiences which are, in Jungian language, transcendent. The intense conflicts which integration of the opposites give rise to involves the recognition that in the infantile parts of the mind the good internal object feels as if it cannot be protected from the destructive forces within the self. Fordham's analytic technique described above in relation to defences of the self implicitly recognizes the necessity of working through both dependency and loss in the context of the indestructibility (except by death) of the self. The patients who taught him this spent long periods of their analysis denying their fear of losing the good object, rigidly fending off integration of this in wilful and determined ways, and in so doing exemplifying an aspect of the self in its malignant form, which was obstinate, contrary and perverse in its essential behaviour.

Chapter 11

Christian experience, mysticism and the self

Jung's interest in Christianity is well known. He spent the last twenty years of his life working on his interpretation of the history of Christianity, its rites, spiritual exercises and doctrines. He never disguised his personal involvement in this work and he wrote about *Answer to Job* (*CW* 11): 'If there is anything like the spirit seizing one by the scruff of the neck, it was the way this book came into being' (Jung 1973–6, vol. 2, p. 20).

He wrote out of a need to help Christianity change, motivated by a desire to transform Christianity, whose central symbolism, he felt, was in need of revitalization. He perceived Christianity as having lost its way, lost its meaning for modern man, because it did not have a unifying symbol which could reconcile its contradictions. This loss of meaning was close to his home life, for there was also his family experience of his Swiss pastor father losing his faith and dying disillusioned. So Jung's desire to understand Christianity was in part driven by his wish to understand what had happened to his father. But it would be too simple to reduce his major works on Christianity to this level, even if there were some aspects of the oedipal myth contained in it as well as his wish to heal the image of his father inside him. For although Jung recognized his need to understand his relationship to his father and to Freud, he also recognized (in *Answer to Job*) that the God of Christianity was as much in need of transformation as was man. He thought of Christianity in psychological terms as a patient who had become too one-sided, dogmatic and out of touch. His diagnosis took the form of his major investigations, *A Psychological Approach to the Dogma of the Trinity* (*CW* 11), *Transformation Symbolism in the Mass* (*CW* 11), *Introduction to the Religious and Psychological Problems of Alchemy* (*CW* 12), *Aion* (*CW* 9, ii), *Answer to Job* (*CW* 11) and *Mysterium Coniunctionis* (*CW* 14). Underlying his approach was the evidence he gathered to show that the essential features of Christianity were to be found in other cultures, both of non-Christian and pre-Christian kinds. He took this to mean that the patterns he was observing were archetypal and reflected human psychology and its development, or lack of it.

Christianity, he argued, could not be understood as the product of rational thought, a system for the organization of society which would maintain and promote civilizing influences. It was, he said, the conscious elaboration of an unconscious process:

> the history of the Trinity presents itself as the gradual crystallisation of an archetype that moulds the anthropomorphic conceptions of father and son, of life, and of different persons, into an archetypal and numinous figure, the 'Most Holy Three-in-One'.
>
> (*CW* 11, para. 224)

Precisely because of the archetypal nature of the crystallization, it was felt by early Christians to be a revelation. It resonated with their own experience. To Jung its 'Holiness' was evidence of its numinosity and a sign therefore of its archetypal nature. The problem was the Son. He was too good. The dark side of human nature had no place in this structure 'Most Holy Three-in-One'. Christ was an ideal, never a reality. Jung's analysis of this consisted in a detailed argument for a quaternitarian Christianity to replace the trinitarian. The fourth element which was required, he suggested, was God's unruly Son, the Devil. The purpose of Jung's argument was not to put psychology in place of religion but to use the insights of psychology to see religious truths more clearly.

Jung valued religious experience, which offers people an irrational experience of their inner selves which psychology could deepen. In essence Jung suggested that archetypal images and Christian dogma were one and the same and could be investigated in the same way. Almost as if to demonstrate this, his *Answer to Job* was written out of the 'psychic infection' of his identifications with the participants, Job and God. The problem as he saw it was that God, the Father, needed to change. God, Jung argued, was envious of man, who had gone beyond him in consciousness, and so he sent his Son to become a man. For Christianity to develop it must, he suggested, include the fallen angel, the 'natural man', who puts science, knowledge and artistic achievement above faith and belief. Job's greatest attribute, he perceived, was his capacity to see God as combining opposites, especially justice and injustice, faithfulness and faithlessness. He was almost describing in this work a personal resolution of his own struggles towards psychological maturity, as if this was the solution for the destructiveness he perceived in man, which, if not controlled, would destroy the world, now that he had the means to do so with nuclear fission.

Fordham's initial interest in Christianity was also from a psychological angle, but without the conflicts engendered by a pastor father. The Fordhams were country gentry, and Michael Fordham had been brought up in a family where going to church was mainly part of the social fabric and not so much to do with personal belief. God was in his heaven and the squire was in his pew. He had read Jung's researches into Christianity and admired them, but he felt they were being misused to create a personality cult and a religion out of analytical psychology. His point of departure was to focus on Jung the scientist. Fordham described three phenomena of religious experience: one, the belief through faith in the metaphysical reality of God; two, ritual exercises, such as prayer and confession; three, spiritual experiences such as visions and dreams. He considered that the second and third were accessible to psychological examination but that the first depended on faith, and faith, in Fordham's view, was a delusion. A delusion is a belief which exists despite the facts which challenge the belief. Organized religion, for instance, in Fordham's view, is a socially sanctioned delusion designed to contain the less manageable unconscious processes within the personality. Fordham is not an atheist, nor does he think that the delusion of faith has not been without immense cultural value. It is after all quite a cultural achievement to move from sacrifice and cannibalism to the ritual of the Mass. But he regards religious understanding as a speculation which cannot be proved:

> Religion depends upon faith in the transcendental reality of God, and rests upon a kind of reality which transcends every experience. Religion, in particular theology, looks at the phenomena from their metaphysical position and comes to conclusions about the nature of God; psychology looks at them from the theory of the collective unconscious and comes to conclusions about human nature.
>
> (Fordham 1958a, p. 115)

He grounded the psychological point of view in human biology, meaning by this that, in his view, without a body the human animal cannot be examined psychologically. The significance of this is that the survival of the soul after death is outside of the realm of psychological investigation. His approach to this is to examine the ritual of the Mass from the standpoint of its being an act of integration; specifically, that the dedication of the members of the congregation to God involves them giving up something (their egotism) and paradoxically feeling strengthened by this experience (of the self).

Similarly, his examination of the steps towards the mystical union with God which the Spanish mystic St John of the Cross described in *The Dark Night of the Soul* is understood as the gradual relinquishment of egotistical needs leading to a mysterious and enriched state. The mediating factor in the experiences of St John of the Cross begins with images of the mother. To the analytical psychologist this is understood as the anima mediating between the ego and the unconscious. In this description, therefore, God becomes equated with the unconscious, and the appearance of the anima with the withdrawal of projections. The word of God is the milk of knowledge, a head-breast. Fordham was especially interested in mysticism (but only in one mystic) and nowhere does he really define what it is. The nearest he comes to a definition is when he summarizes the steps the mystic St John takes, but it is more of a description:

> *The Dark Night of the Soul* is a description of the soul's journey in search of God. This journey is an introverted process which involves as a fundamental tenet renunciation of the world, the flesh, and the devil, from which the soul is protected by the three virtues of faith, hope, and charity. Starting on a human plane, it gradually becomes more and more remote from earthly life till the climax is reached with the ascent of the *scala mystica* and the final union with God – the *unio mystica* – after the death of the body. Though the final union takes place only after death yet the soul is able, in this world, to come into an intimate relation with God, through which relation many sublime results are said to accrue.
>
> (Fordham 1958a, p. 131)

Before I continue with this exposition I would like to consider the term 'mystical experiences' as it is one which, applied to psychology, frequently denotes mystification, rather than a distinct experience with recognizable qualities. The first thing to be said about mystical experiences is that they are a form of consciousness which have a quality of reconciliation about them. All descriptions of mystical experiences combine references to the impact of the experience, its clarity and importance, yet at the same time retain something inexpressible about them.

William James (1902) has identified four characteristics of these mystical experiences: ineffability; a noetic quality; transience; and passivity. Ineffability, in itself a negative characteristic, is the first and is more a state of feeling than a state of the intellect; its quality has to be experienced. As to the noetic quality, these experiences are accompanied by the feeling of having understood something, a revelation, an insight, a new truth. The third, transience, acknowledges that the state rarely lasts for long, although its recurrence is not without development. Finally, passivity is the feature which accompanies the feeling of having been in the grip of a superior power.

Mystical states are often recorded by poets, scientists and imaginative people and are experienced by them as an irrational form of consciousness, usually with a revelatory content. The truths communicated in these states are not exclusively religious: instances are recorded of sudden understanding of obscure texts, predictions of future events and even truths about the created world such as the medicinal properties of certain herbs and plants. Christian mysticism is a special version of mysticism which has within it an idea that the devout person by vocation, training and application of a rigorous regime of denial can overcome the physical limitations of the body and step by step approach nearer to God. As a historical phenomenon it flourished in Europe during medieval times. The church had considerable difficulty assimilating mystics and the penalties for unorthodoxy were severe. Most were not canonized.

How to evaluate these experiences? Might we not, after all, say that those who have them suffer from over-vivid imaginations and delusions? In my view our attitude to them is best compared to our attitude to the creative and artistic. If we ourselves have never had an experience of the beauty of the world then it is difficult to know what the person who has is referring to, but we can note some consequences of it. For the person who experiences it, it is a true experience, it leaves them feeling optimistic about the world. Peculiar to this mystical tradition is that it is defined by negation, for by saying what it is not the mystic asserts the limitations of language to describe what it is. Its truth is that it bears witness to a kind of consciousness which is not rational and based on understanding and the senses alone. Like the poet's experience of beauty it enlarges and challenges the known facts, adding another truth, the individual's own experience.

Fordham makes parallels between mysticism and analysis, using the comparative method. His object of study is St John's commentary on the 'Stanzas of the Soul'. Fordham's first account was published in 1958 (Fordham 1958a); later, in 1985, he was to revise this work (Fordham 1985a). I shall set out his thesis as explicated in the first version and then comment on the differences in the second version. In the mystical experience God is active, the soul passive. The soul has to be purged. The first phase is preparatory and those in this phase are called beginners;

the next phase is the first Dark Night when the senses are purged; the third phase is the second Dark Night when the soul is purged of all its spiritual activity. Between each phase there is a quiet period.

First, St John describes the effect of the stirrings of the soul of the beginners in terms of the sensual pleasures of the infant at the breast:

> It must be known, then, that the soul, after it has been definitely converted to the service of God, is, as a rule, spiritually nurtured and caressed by God, even as is the tender child by its loving mother, who warms it with the heat of her bosom and nurtures it with sweet milk and soft and pleasant food, and carries it and caresses it in her arms.
>
> (St John of the Cross, quoted in Fordham 1958a)

To St John the pleasure experienced by the beginners before the first Dark Night constitutes the problem. To enjoy the workings of God on the soul is a dangerous state to be in, much like intoxication. The comparison Fordham makes with analytical psychology is with inflation. The consequence of this state for the apprentice mystics, the beginners, is that they become recalcitrant and in St John's words 'peevish as children'. This is a description, Fordham suggests, of the infantile aspects of the transference. St John goes into the problems of the beginners in some detail, and Fordham considers this to be similar to analysis, in that St John is trying to understand his students' difficulties from the point of view of the inner conflict they engender. What he mainly seems to be stressing are the dangers inherent in the pleasure of the spiritual exercises. Fordham links this to the psychoanalytic pleasure principle and says of this phase of the beginners' apprenticeship into the ways to scale the heights of mystical experience that it is not unlike psychoanalysis. That the experiences are manifestly not identical need not colour our attitude to this exposition of Fordham's, since we can orientate ourselves round Jung's statement that the differences between theologians and psychologists are that

> both appear to speak the same language, but that this language calls up in their minds two totally different fields of associations. Both can apparently use the same concept and are then bound to acknowledge, to their amazement, that they are speaking of two different things.
>
> (Jung, *CW* 11, para. 454)

The next stage has God withdrawing the breast; this heralds the beginning of the first Dark Night of the senses. St John writes,

> as the child grows bigger, the mother gradually ceases caressing it,

and, hiding her tender love, puts bitter aloes upon her sweet breast, sets down the child from her arms and makes it walk upon its feet, so that it may lose the habits of a child and betake itself to more important and substantial occupations.

(St John of the Cross 1953, vol. 1, p. 330)

Fordham's interpretation of this in his 1958 analysis is characterized by distinguishing Freudian concepts from Jungian ones, and here he emphasizes the 'separation anxiety' of this weaning experience.

St John's description of the beginners' difficulties returns often to those that arise from the pleasure felt when practising the spiritual exercises. Fordham considers this pleasure from the point of view of the psychoanalytic concept of sublimation, that the incursion of sexual thoughts, feelings and desires can be repressed and sublimated in religious exercises:

In St John's experience, the soul is divided into two parts, a spiritual part and a sensual or sensitive part. It is the sensitive part from which apparently psychosexual manifestations arise. These are most insistent and obstinate in their activity, and there can be little doubt that sexual feelings get into the most sacred rites.

(Fordham 1958a, p. 135)

Fordham goes on to quote from St John that 'impure acts and motions' intrude 'even when the spirit is deep in prayer'. Again this is attributed by St John to the pleasure of the spiritual exercises and the mystic's response to this is to try to repress these feelings (the opposite of the analytic technique). Fordham points out that while psychoanalysis (as distinct from analytical psychology) is opposed to mysticism, in his view, expressed in 1958, there are common areas which overlap and which he recognizes as having the same archetypal basis. Thus he links the Freudian death instinct, Thanatos, which arises out of the body and whose aim is to die, with the mystical concept of the need for the death of the body for the final union with God. He then connects the sexual instinct, Eros, to the mystical notion of eternal life since the sexual instinct perpetuates itself and could therefore be said to be eternal.

Both these speculations of Freud's (Thanatos and Eros) contain mystical elements, although it is known that Freud's criticism of religion was in terms of its function in the development of civilization. At this point Fordham is stressing the differences between Freud and Jung, and is drawing attention to Jung's archetypal psychology, which he characterizes as emphasizing the internal integrating experiences of the spiritual struggle and as being less dependent on explanation related to phenomena of the external world. Writing later, in 1966, for the journal *Theology*, Fordham was, in his discussion of the similarities and dissimilarities between Jung and Freud, not only to include more instances of their similarities, but also to stress that their differences over mysticism stemmed from their personal and cultural experiences (Fordham 1966f).

Jung has written in his autobiography of his mystical and religious experiences as the son of a Swiss pastor who had lost his faith. Freud had a different cultural tradition: Jewish, and without any direct experience of God. This naturally led to their putting a different emphasis on religious experience. Putting Freud's and Jung's understanding together, however, Fordham writes of the mystical experience as follows:

> The whole development is similar [to analysis]; there is the separation from infantile dominants which St John understands in terms of separation from God's breast, the resolution of the transference in its infantile aspects, but most striking of all is the experience of the soul which, if stripped of its theological interpretation, is simply identical with Jung's description of the anima. The soul in both cases is purely objective, a female 'person'. We are not concerned in the Dark Night with what happens to a living man, but to the soul which is conceived of as a separate entity.
>
> (Fordham 1958a, p. 138)

Once we have got this far, the final two stages of the Dark Night begin. In the first stage the soul is purged 'according to sense', meaning of all its relations to the outside world, especially love relationships but also objects of the imagination. In the second stage the purgation is spiritual and the soul is 'subdued and made ready for the union of love with God' (St John of the Cross 1953, vol. 1, p. 349). Fordham delights in St John's detailed descriptions of how the soul now becomes fixed on God, relinquishes mental activity, desire, thought and argument. In its place arises contemplation. This Fordham compares to active imagination, noting that whereas the objective of this process for the psychologist is greater consciousness, for the mystic the desired outcome is complete unconsciousness in the blissful union with God. In his later examination of these texts he distinguishes these experiences from active imagination, pointing out that the requirement for the soul for these experiences is absolute passivity, so that there is no active interference with the soul's entry 'into the Dark Night of unknowing' (Fordham 1985a). This is quite different from active imagination, where active interchanges are encouraged. Added to this is the fact that St John makes considerable use of biblical stories, not as analogies, but as illustrations, thereby recognizing the truth of the myths and stories – true, that is, of the unconscious processes he is trying to describe. At this juncture Fordham writes:

> It appears to me that this is a striking anticipation of Jung's concept of the objective psyche and the collective unconscious, whilst St John's method is to be compared with that used by Jung in his researches and which he called amplification.
>
> (Fordham 1958a, p. 141)

In Fordham's view the second stage of the Dark Night, the spiritual purgation, is where analytical psychology and mysticism begin to part company. St John calls this experience the Secret Wisdom, and it certainly meets William James's criteria for a mystical experience in its ineffableness. For the Secret Wisdom which

> is so simple, so general and so spiritual that it has not entered into the understanding enwrapped or cloaked in any form or image subject to sense, it follows that sense and imagination (as it has not entered through them nor has taken their form and colour) cannot account for it or imagine it, so as to say anything concerning it, although the soul be clearly aware that it is experiencing and partaking of that rare and delectable wisdom.
>
> (St John of the Cross 1953, vol. 1, p. 429)

Undaunted by the incomprehensibility of this and challenged by its mysteriousness, Fordham returns to first base and examines why man would want to create a dogma such as we have in Christianity. He suggests that the need for Jesus to be a historical figure derives from the unconscious value which his supposed historical existence gives to the objectivity of Christ and the way this (a) prevents identification of the ego with the unconscious and (b) locates the power of religious experiences in the hands of the church. The development of this thesis leads Fordham to restate Jung's assertion that the unconscious is deeply mysterious, only partly known, terrifying to most people and Godlike in its awesomeness.

Whatever the route taken, whether psychological or theological, the quest is assumed to be the same: namely, what is the significance of the irrational, whether instinct or spirit, in the shaping of the destiny of the individual? But as Fordham argues, for St John's brand of mysticism to work, the renunciation of instinctual gratifications requires a belief in the dogma of heavenly bliss since there is no satisfaction to be had in corporeal life. Finally, what are we to make of the *unio mystica*? Fordham likens this to the *conjunctio*, the union of the conscious and unconscious, with the qualification that the *unio mystica* – because a transcendental reality – can never be equated with the *conjunctio*, which is psychologically and biologically based. We are still left with the unaddressed problem of the Devil. He seems to have disappeared in this pursuit, and yet we know he's still there and this is where, for Fordham, Jung's recognition that while experiences may change (medieval Christian mysticism has had its day) the archetypes of the unconscious remain unchanged. God may no longer be enthroned and He has certainly descended into the ordinary man.

The theological rebuttal of this psychological approach is contained in the argument that the religious person's experience begins at that point when psychologists feel they have arrived at an internal resolution of the opposites in the unconscious. The religious then go on to claim, using detailed theological argument, that matters of the spiritual relationship of God to man are their province, not the psychologists'. Buber, for instance, described Jung's claim to be only an empiricist as a disguise for his greater claim to be the interpreter of a new world religion of pure psychic immanence (Buber 1957). At this juncture the discussion becomes, in Bion's language, one of vertices. In other words, while there might be agreement about the phenomena, there is disagreement about the interpretation of it, which depends on the vertex of the inquirer. This takes the argument straight back to Jung's statement quoted earlier, about the difference between theologians and psychologists: they 'are then bound to acknowledge, to their amazement, that they are speaking of two different things' because of the associations the phenomena stir up. The question is, however, do Jung and Fordham, who is closely following Jung here, accept the nature of the phenomena? Neither, to my mind, accepts the transcendence of God, which is fundamental to Christian faith. Fordham is clear, however, that Jung's psychological approach is 'individualized religion', thereby making it part of man's evolution and, as such, part of the continuing study of the unconscious.

In his later revisions of his writings on mysticism and the Dark Night Fordham is much clearer in his analysis of the symbolism of the Dark Night. His orientation is to its infantile roots, though he states that he does not identify mysticism with infancy. He translates God as the self and understands much of the mystic's experience as being a manifestation of deintegrations of the self. There is more emphasis on the suffering of the mystic and what Fordham understands as the psychic pain of maturation in the context of the gradual realization of the self through deintegrative and reintegrative experiences. The deintegrative manifestations are equivalent to the action of God on the soul in the purgative nights, the reintegrative occur both in between these nights of terror and during the periods of quiet contemplation which follow the successful purgation.

Fordham's reflections on these experiences in his 1985 text are in tone less assertively 'Jungian' and more quietly descriptive of his experiences of the self, which he digested over the intervening twenty-seven years (Fordham 1985a). Thus he writes of St John's experiences as the working of the archetypes within him rather than as the mystic trying to embody and struggle with the Christian dogma. He now brings out more clearly his understanding of God as the self and the various manifestations of this Godhead in the Trinity.

The problem of the Devil and evil remains controversial with the psychological and theological points of view diverging fundamentally. Fordham sees the Devil as necessary to God. When St John describes the soul being tempted, and the Angel of God not intervening, as God wanting to test the strength of the soul, it seems to Fordham that God and the Devil are a pair working together. St John sees this differently, putting greater emphasis on the cunning and subtlety of the Devil. How then to understand the eighth step up the *scala mystica* when the soul becomes immune to the Devil? Fordham offers alternative interpretations: one has the Devil split off, going about his business elsewhere, tempting other souls (the religious vertex); the other proposes what he calls 'an individual solution', in which the soul becomes whole in God. This means the symbolic bringing together of the opposites through what Jung has described as the transcendent function. This seems to Fordham to be the most satisfactory resolution of the mystic's journey, looked at from the vertex of individuation. From the point of view of Christian dogma it would not be acceptable, since it goes out of the domain of Christian morality.

The major revisions in Fordham's later work on the Dark Night centre round his own analytic developments in the intervening years. The main concept he now introduces is transformation. Transformation is the term he uses to describe the fact that experiences are not finished and done with but, like phases in development, they mature and take on new forms. This is especially true of the infant's experience of the breast. Within the mystical vertex St John describes the transformations of the soul within God. To the mystic, the soul's desire to unite with God can become divine through transformation. As has already been noted, St John describes the beginning of the mystic development in terms of the impact of God's breast.

Employing the concept of projective identification Fordham compares the mystic's transformations of the soul with those which occur within the infant in relation to the mother's breast. He begins with the pleasurable satisfaction of instinctual needs, accompanied by the increasing awareness of the breast as transformer and container of experience, including, with its nipple, the unconscious fantasy of the father's penetrating penis. As development proceeds, the characteristics of the mother and the father become differentiated, the father becoming more identified with Logos, the mother Eros. In the beginning the breast combines the opposites in such a way that they are undifferentiated. Gradually Logos and Eros separate out only to be later joined together in the symbolic union of opposites represented as the internalized parents in good intercourse, an intercourse which nurtures the child.

There is a further cogent link to be made to the stimulation to development which the withdrawal of the breast produces, both in mystical development, where it initiates the first Dark Night, and in the infant, where it initiates the beginning of weaning and the emergence (it is hoped) of depressive concern. Fordham makes use here of the formulation of the psychoanalyst, Wilfred Bion, who described the absence of a good object as the presence of a bad one. Bion described how this bad object can be dealt with, either by primitive forms of evacuation or by having thoughts. This is similar to the mystic's experience of the first Dark Night, where his pain is transformed into mental life. The further comparison to the mystical experience is to be found in the role of the spiritual adviser who continues over time, much like the mother, to help the child/mystic contain and manage his experiences.

In conclusion, Fordham's exposition of the links between medieval mysticism and analytical psychology derives principally from his empirical scientific approach to analytical psychology. This means that Victor White's criticisms of Jung also apply in part to Fordham (White 1960). White found that Jung repeatedly interpreted in psychological terms the theologians' metaphysical statements, but from a position which failed to understand the religious need to maintain the transcendence of God. Jung was stuck on immanence, as is Fordham, combining it with a form of reductionism. Because Fordham feels himself to be outside of the Christian tradition he does not identify with the meanings Christians assign to their symbolic world. This leaves him free to use his own categories, especially those relating to the infant and its development. While this, in Fordham's language, may individualize Christian experience, to a religious person it limits the understanding of Christian experience to personal and impersonal insights.

Chapter 12

Synchronicity
An interpretation

INTRODUCTION

Jung was interested in the connection between events for which there was no cause but which had a significant meaning for the person or persons experiencing the event. This realm of parapsychology he called synchronicity, which he defined as:

> The coincidence of a psychic state in the observer with a simultaneous objective, external event that corresponds to the psychic state or content where there is no evidence of a causal connection between the psychic state and the external event and where such a connection is not even conceivable.
>
> (*CW* 8, para. 984)

He gave a number of different examples of this. For instance the story of Monsieur de Fortgibu and the plum pudding:

> A certain M Deschamps, when a boy in Orleans, was once given a piece of plum pudding by a M de Fortgibu. Ten years later he discovered another plum pudding in a Paris restaurant, and asked if he could have a piece. It turned out, however, that the plum pudding was already ordered – by M de Fortgibu. Many years afterwards M Deschamps was invited to partake of a plum pudding as a special rarity. While he was eating it he remarked that the only thing lacking was M de Fortgibu. At that moment the door opened and an old, old man in the last stages of disorientation walked in: M de Fortgibu, who had got hold of the wrong address and burst in on the party by mistake.
>
> (*CW* 8, para. 830n)

He also described the interaction between a patient's dream and an event in a session (which I will discuss later), prophetic dreams and 'out of body' experiences. He gave an example of a patient who, while unconscious, was able to give a precise description of a doctor's agitation, where he was standing and what precisely happened during her unconsciousness. In addition he included as examples of synchronicity mantic experiences, especially those associated with the use of the *I Ching*. He collected anecdotal accounts and made notes of his own experiences, but it was twenty years before he dared formulate his thoughts in print. He was thinking of synchronicity as a complement to causality. From his understanding of contemporary physics he knew that the validity of natural law was no longer absolute, but was now relative.

> The philosophical principle that underlies our conception of natural law is causality. But if the connection between cause and effect turns out to be only statistically valid and only relatively true, then the causal principle is only of relative use for explaining natural processes and therefore presupposes the existence of one or more other factors which would be necessary for an explanation.
>
> (*CW* 8, para. 819)

He wondered also whether synchronicity was specific to the psyche or an instance of a general 'acausal ordering in nature'. His interest in and knowledge of Taoist philosophy led him to discuss with his colleague and friend Professor Pauli, the eminent physicist, a revision of the classical triad in physics of space, time and causality such that it might be better presented as a quaternio in which causality and synchronicity were one pair of opposites, and indestructible energy and the space–time continuum the other (this was Pauli's suggestion) (*CW* 8, para. 963). The importance of this was that Jung was tentatively suggesting a radical theory for a new way of conceptualizing a scientific picture of the world, which took into account modern physics.

SYNCHRONICITY

The special phenomenon of synchronicity as opposed to synchronous events is that there is a lowering of ego consciousness allowing unconsciousness to flow into the space created by this *abaissement du niveau mental*, with a concomitant experience of a meaningful kind. Having fish for lunch on Friday 1 April, thinking of making an April Fish of someone (April Fool), noticing an inscription with the word fish on it, being shown a piece of embroidery with a fish on it, and being told a dream by a patient in which a large fish swam towards her and landed at her feet – all these happened to Jung on the same day but this was emphatically not an experience of synchronicity, but rather of synchronous events. He said of it: 'There is no possible justification for seeing in this anything but a chance grouping. Runs or series which are composed of quite ordinary occurrences must for the present be regarded as fortuitous' (*CW* 8, para. 826).

The only example he gives from his clinical practice of synchronicity is of a female patient who was rationalistic and argumentative. She had been to other analysts without resolving her difficulties and one day she told a dream in which she was given a golden scarab. While she was telling the dream Jung heard a tapping on the window and let in, catching in his hand, a rose chafer, a type of scarabeid beetle not usually found at this latitude. He described what happened.

> I handed the beetle to my patient with the words, 'Here is your scarab'. This experience punctured the desired hole in her rationalism and broke the ice of her intellectual resistance.
>
> (*CW* 8, para. 982)

There followed, he said, a gradual diminution of her Cartesian rationality in a beneficial way. Jung, with his interest in Egyptology and classical symbolism, recognized the scarab as a symbol of rebirth, which he pointed out was what one would expect to accompany the beginning of a process of psychic transformation such as that event initiated in his patient. The implication of this, for Jung, was that synchronicity was derived from an archetypal foundation. The telling of the archetypal image of the scarab in the dream came together with the rose chafer tapping at the window to let in what was a numinous experience for the patient. Jung wrote:

> Synchronicity therefore consists of two factors. (a) An unconscious image comes into consciousness either directly (i.e. literally) or indirectly (symbolised or suggested) in the form of a dream, idea or premonition. (b) An objective situation coincides with this content.
>
> (*CW* 8, para. 858)

The beetle appeared in her dream and the rose chafer at the consulting-room window. Today what is immediately striking about this account is the charismatic behaviour of Jung in the session and its impact on the patient. For here he was behaving like a shaman beguiling his patient with his personality and erudition.

There are two other features of Jung's discussion of synchronicity which are relevant to our understanding of Fordham's examination of this phenomenon. The first is the use he makes of J.B. Rhine's experiments in the 1930s and 1940s. The second is his own astrological experiment (*CW* 8).

In Rhine's experiments there was an experimenter in one room turning over cards (twenty-five in all, five different patterns), and a subject in another room or across the ocean in another country who had to guess which card had been turned up. Rhine's results were significant; they disproved the null hypothesis. Jung considered these results were evidence of synchronicity(!), which reveals that he did not appreciate the nature of statistics and the significance of disproving the null hypothesis. The most significant variable was the subject's enthusiasm: the more enthusiastic the better the result.

In the second experimental study Jung reported, he used horoscopes of married couples to ascertain whether astrological correspondence conformed to any law. The astrological correspondence to marriage has since Ptolemy been the three degrees of harmony:

> The first is when the sun in the man's [horoscope], and the sun or moon in the woman's, or the moon in both, are in their respective places in a trine or sextile aspect. The second degree is when the moon in a man's [horoscope] and the sun in a woman's are constellated in the same way. The third degree is when the one is receptive to the other.

> (*CW* 8, para. 869n)

He investigated the conjunctions and oppositions of the sun and the moon, the moon and the moon, and the moon and the ascendant. He looked at the conjunction or opposition of Mars and Venus in their descendence and ascendence in these couples' horoscopes since this, he wrote, 'would point to a love relationship'. Over a large sample the astrological constellations and the married state were not statistically significant. Jung then classed the three most frequent conjunctions, which are mentioned in the old astrological literature as marriage characteristics, as one group, re-examined them, and found that the likelihood of their occurring in this pattern was statistically highly improbable. He therefore restated his findings as evidence not of chance but of meaningful coincidence, and since the source of data arose from meaningful connections, the married couples, he considered the conjunctions were synchronistic, stating the while:

> Because the statistical method shows only the average aspects, it creates an artificial and predominantly conceptual picture of reality.

That is why we need a complementary principle for a complete description and explanation of nature.

(*CW* 8, para. 904)

From this it can be seen also that Jung's objection to statistics is their nature – they average out exceptions which to the individual psychologist in him meant statistics did not give a 'true picture'. There are innumerable problems here, particularly with Jung's cavalier treatment of statistical analysis, and Fordham was one of the first to point them out to Jung.

FORDHAM'S INTERPRETATION

In his first approaches to Jung's interest in parapsychology Fordham was tentative in his criticisms of Jung. Contained in the 1957 revision of his 1955 article were the seeds of his real puzzlement with Jung's approach to statistics (Fordham 1957a, 1955f). By 1962 he was more explicit in his reservations and had become clearer about his own interpretation (Fordham 1962e, republished in Fordham 1985a). In a personal communication to me (6 September 1993) he wrote:

> I thought CG did not understand statistics. . . . I think that what I was trying to say was that if Jung had wanted to show that his conjunctions were not caused then his [astrological] experiment makes sense i.e. statistics can tell us whether a cause is improbable. Then he could have taken this as evidence that the meaningful conjunctions were an example of synchronicity. But he did not think like that because in a muddled way he was trying to make the subject respectable.

The core of the problem was that parapsychology without a firm base in scientific method could be taken as just so much fashionable malarkey. Jung's method was his individual psychotherapeutic one, but in his approach to synchronicity he seemed to feel it was necessary to apply 'objective' scientific methods such as statistical verification. He thought that without these methods there was a danger of seeming to be a crank, a believer in ESP and flying saucers, who found significance in coincidences and applied these ideas in the consulting room. His interest could seem to be an instance of archetypal phenomena being the source of the supernatural rather than of his investigations contributing to an understanding of the relationship between archetype theory and parapsychology. But despite his wish to connect it to current scientific theory there was no substantial theory in Jung's writings on this subject.

He gave examples, recorded facts and treated statistical evidence in what Fordham, being diplomatic, called 'an unusual way'.

Fordham considered one of the problems with synchronicity was this credulity factor. Jung himself referred to the archetypal readiness in all of us to believe in miracles, which evokes oscillating responses between belief and incredulity. The *I Ching*, which Jung was interested in and experimented with, can often give quite startling answers. This book of divination, which works, according to Jung, on a principle of synchronicity, can therefore evoke resistances to its significance in the person asking the question. Fordham described asking the *I Ching* a second time the same question and getting a judgement which effectively said 'I've answered this once, I shan't answer this again' (Fordham 1957a). He did this as an experiment but suggested from it that the *I Ching*'s replies could lead to the questioner arguing away its significance, if the answer was not to his liking. The second difficulty is that if a synchronicitous event cannot be repeated it can lead to the sceptic in us pushing it away. But Fordham pointed out that the problem is not one of exactness so much as the definition of the class of phenomena under consideration. The same atom cannot be split twice but no one doubts you can split the atom.

Fordham called Jung's approach to statistics 'highly original, and peculiarly his own'. Later, in a comment in the margin of the first draft of this chapter, Fordham wrote 'it was just mistaken and I saved his face'. This is because Jung saw meaning in uncaused events, which 'cuts right across the duality chance–cause axiom on which statistics is based' (Fordham 1957a, p. 36). Fordham discussed chance and probability, pointing out Jung's ingenuity in treating events which are improbable, on a null hypothesis, as meaningful, as the 'region in which synchronistic phenomena are most likely' (ibid., p. 37). What Jung was in effect doing was to turn a negative result, for instance that the astrological experiment was not significant statistically, into a reason for looking again into those events, which were no better than a chance occurrence, for 'significance' in their meaning. Of course if they had been statistically significant then a causal explanation would be likely. And if so then the meaningfulness would no longer have archetypal significance.

In 1957 Fordham considered that Jung was right to proceed in this way but Jung did not know it because, as Fordham pointed out, the principle of convergence made statistical procedures more reliable when large numbers were involved, 'for as the figures became larger he converged towards the true probability'. So by reducing the numbers in his astrological experiment, by grouping the data in the way he did, it was more likely to show what the empirical probability was as opposed to the true probability. True probability ($p = n/N$) is the value to which p will converge as N becomes infinitely large, where N is the number of times the event is tried and n is the number of successes (ibid., p. 38). He pointed out how Jung, by grouping the astrological data in the way he did, had increased the likelihood of synchronistic events since 'if we want to observe synchronicity, large numbers are undesirable'. He explained this as Jung's psychological standpoint which 'makes it much easier for him to remain unmoved by the logic of statistics which is based on the abstraction of opposites which synchronicity transcends because of its symbolic (archetypal) associations' (Fordham 1957a, p. 41).

Fordham was avoiding being openly critical of Jung in 1957 but there is no doubt in my mind that he had reservations about Jung's method in attempting to justify his evidence. Jung himself wrote the preface to the book in which this article appeared and described Fordham's approach to the problem as having a 'feeling for the essentials', which was true in the sense that he recognized the experience Jung was referring to while doubting Jung's attempt at proving it by statistical verification, which was impossible (Fordham 1957, p. xii). Fordham wrote to me in September 1993 as follows:

> There was a statistician who asserted that the whole experiment was nonsense and wanted the article suppressed since, supported by Jung's authority, it would be taken by many to support false ideas. As editor I did a lot of work on the article filling in details of Jung's exposition. They demonstrated more clearly that the data were not significant. Consequently I had to become something of a diplomat and that obscured my thinking. Many of Jung's data convince me but not his understanding of the experiment.

Returning to Jung's use of Rhine's experiments, which, as I mentioned above, were statistically significant, the most important variable was the subject's enthusiasm and credibility, a factor which nowadays might be classed as an experimenter effect. Jung was not troubled by this result as he seized on the fact that as these experiments transcended space and time they therefore could not be a phenomenon of energy and so causally related. Consequently he deemed them acausal and coming into the category of synchronicity. Fordham had reservations about Rhine's experiments but it was not until his 1962 article that he stated categorically that Jung was wrong to make use of Rhine's work. This is because the statistical analysis of Rhine's data makes causality more rather than less probable.

What Fordham did begin to develop in his earlier paper was the significance of examining the data of synchronicity in the context of the individual patient, his analysis and personality type. His own experience confirmed that there was a relationship between all those elements and the relative unconsciousness of the patient. He even suggested that Jung's patient who had the scarab experience was responding out of her transference to Jung and his behaviour during the session. This led Fordham to pay particular attention to the patient's conscious attitude. Jung's patient was rationalistic; an irrational event was needed to break through this. So, not impressed by Jung's use of statistics, Fordham concentrated on individual analytic experiences to evaluate the acausal meaningful principle, paying particular attention to where the meaningfulness lay.

FORDHAM'S CLINICAL EXAMPLES

Case one

Fordham described a man of thirty-one who was the part-owner of two boats, one a racing yacht, the other a converted lifeboat. This patient, unlike Jung's, was insufficiently conscious and reasoning in his attitude to what happened to him. His share of the racer came from his father, of the lifeboat from his mother. He preferred the lifeboat. His father had ambitions for him as an ocean racer. The most important race of the season approached and the patient's father came to see his son race. Soon after the start, however, the mast fell overboard and so his participation in the race ended. The patient was not getting on with his father at this time and was in conflict with him. It was hardly credible that his hostility to his father had made the mast collapse although there was a coincidence. He decided to join the other boat which his partner, H, and two girls were sailing down the coast. He arrived at the harbour he knew they would have got to and found the converted lifeboat had been run aground and its mast was projecting over a cottage near to the jetty. This made a great impression on him, not least because the cottage over which the mast projected was where his old housekeeper lived when he had been at college with his friend H, with whom he shared the boat – another coincidence. She (the housekeeper) had thought, on seeing the boat, that it must be H on board. The combination of all these coincidences, Fordham stated, contributed 'a severe blow to his racing career and he soon decided to sell his share in the boat', as he understood it to be meaningfully associated to his difficult relationship with his father.

Further examination of the material revealed that a possible reason why the boat ran aground was that it was being steered by one of the women who had been H's lover and who now knew that H wanted to end the affair to marry the other woman (so she had plenty of reasons to sink his ship). The reasons for the mechanical failure of the mast were not uncovered. All these events running together had meaning for the patient which he acted on by selling his racing boat. Fordham understood from this that it was possible to consider synchronistic events from the point of view of the patient's conscious attitude as well from the unconscious archetypes. His patient was inclined to emphasize the unconscious and not pay sufficient attention to the conscious. He began to note synchronous events which he reported in the sessions and which he defensively called further instances of synchronicity when they were not. Fordham concluded from this that:

> Under these circumstances it does not necessarily matter whether the material events are proved to be chance or caused, since the synchronicity occurs in an individual; but *it is important that the individual's belief in a cause be undermined* where this is used in the service of repression.
>
> (Fordham 1957a, p. 50)

This is the beginning of an interpretation which Fordham worked out later, which put the significance of synchronicity in the context of object relations. He thought of synchronicity as a particular form of 'uncaused subject–object relationships' (Fordham 1985a, p. 131). When it is clear to the subject that there is no cause for the connections, then with the diminution of consciousness referred to by Jung as the *abaissement du niveau mental* the affective significance of unconscious processes can emerge. Synchronicity is one of those manifestations. Jung stated that a feature of synchronicity was that the space–time continuum became relativized. How does this occur? Fordham put forward the following argument:

> There is a correspondence between the external event and the archetype itself, which becomes manifest in meaningful relations with the material object in the external world. It appears certain that it is the archetypal imagery which makes the correspondence meaningful, but the synchronicity is essentially the correspondence and is not (necessarily) produced by the projected archetypal image.
>
> (Fordham 1985a, p. 132)

To Fordham the significance of Jung's thesis is that it brings parapsychology into the analysable realm of relations between ego and archetypal objects and images.

Case two

The cases most likely to exhibit synchronicities would then be those whose level of ego consciousness was low, who were psychotic, borderline or fragmented people with whom there were often countertransference features in analysis. A male patient of Fordham's became preoccupied with the ornaments on his mantelpiece. He became convinced that there was significance in the way they were in different positions from one session to the next. The patient thought Fordham was doing something 'to test him and play on and stimulate his passive homosexual trends'. The objects were in fact changing places but it was due to the activities of a cleaner who was not obeying Fordham's instructions not to move them. Fordham began to feel quite persecuted by this and realized that it would not have been difficult to believe that some spirit had got into the cleaner and was deliberately playing tricks:

> The spirit can be conceived of as the unitary being, evidently intended to create a confusion in the patient and myself by using the cleaner for his purpose – that conclusion could still be in the field of causal explanation. If I had started looking at the overall pattern and had been able to see through the magical projection, then I might have arrived at synchronicity, of which the spirit could have been the symbolic perception. But I should have needed to deintegrate far enough for the synchronicities to become conscious. In retrospect I could not do this for fear of being disintegrated by my patient's projective identifications.
>
> (Fordham 1985a, p. 134)

What these fantasies about the spirit add to the total situation is the recognition that reducing it to a causal explanation, that the cleaner moved the objects, ignored the complexity of the countertransference feelings, which were taken more into account by the fantasy content. This was because the fantasy content constellated the archetypal nature of the homosexual transference. This example is not striking – intentionally. Fordham wanted to contrast two ways of thinking, causally (magically) and synchronistically, because the question which he was interested in was whether synchronicity was unusual, rare, odd or special, or whether it was an ordinary form of object relating which most of the time we overlook. Jung thought the latter. Bringing it down to earth and into the consulting room removed it from the pseudo-scientific areas of psychical research where fashionable belief and credulousness predominate.

In the discussions of the self at the beginning of this book a substantial account was given of the self as combining and transcending opposite features, functions and attributes within the personality. Among these were the rational and the irrational. The self combines both, integrates them, and is comfortable with contradiction, because not taking sides. The self has also been described as an integrating centre within the personality different from, but complementary to, the ego. One attribute of synchronicity is that its manifestations are associated with a lowering of ego consciousness. Fordham described how this would have occurred in him in the example of the patient who gave rise to the persecutory feelings in him about the ornaments. If he had allowed himself to treat the material as evidence of synchronicity then the archetypes which were active would have unsettled the space–time continuum, giving rise to a new perception based on these irrational elements. In analytic practice Fordham contends that is the part the self plays, when there is evidence of meaningful coincidences.

Case three

Fordham had been thinking about states of being alone, and while he was doing this his colleague D. Winnicott had sent him a draft version of a paper he was writing on the capacity to be alone. (An internal state in Fordham and an objective fact, the arrival of the paper on the same theme, come together.) Fordham's thoughts had focused on how in certain states of mind, connected to feeling alone, symbols of the self arose. At this time he was preparing a talk and needed some clinical material for it, when a patient whom he had been analysing for some time came for her session and was quite silent. When she did talk it was quite empty in feeling. He pointed this out to her and she told a dream:

> I am floating on the water, on the surface of the sea; I am undressed and have nothing on at all, my genital was like a flower, only not so beautiful.

Fordham without waiting for associations said,

> The dream seems to have a sense of being alone that you have experienced in the past after a satisfying orgasm in intercourse with a man you loved.

(Fordham 1985a, p. 121)

(An objective fact, the patient telling the dream, and Fordham making this penetrative interpretation come together.) The patient was quite startled by this because she felt it was true although, as Fordham later remarked, it passed over the transference content. He had derived the interpretation from the image of a flower being associated in his mind with the self which emerges following a conjunction, the intercourse. It was also connected to his previous thoughts about being alone, Winnicott's paper and his need for some clinical material for his talk. His interpretation too, as he noted, was quite penetrating and she was receptive to it. He called it a 'conjunction generating wholeness in the unity of the sexual opposites' (ibid., p. 122). There are synchronicities in this material (his thinking about states of aloneness, and symbols of the self, and her then bringing this dream) which, while they may have contributed to the numinosity of the experience, were not the salient feature. This was the linking function provided by the self.

> Something linked all these events into a sequence as if there were a unity in them outside my control. This something is what is meant by the self. It is as if bits of my internal world were not separate from the outer and other people but both were part of a whole which was not myself only.
>
> (Fordham 1985a, p. 122)

This was an action of the self which took precedence over all other aspects of the interaction. Consequently the synchronicities became part of Fordham's self which was functioning in a transcendent manner in bringing together rational and irrational elements. The implication of this is that the synchronicities are part of object relationships operating at a level of unconsciousness not usually attended to in the analytic process until they give rise to archetypal images (e.g. the genital as flower, which is symbolically a mandala image). But the significance of these images is better understood in the context of the whole pattern rather than as parapsychological phenomena. Fordham is stressing that in analysis what is important is the total situation.

As an intriguing additional idea about this puzzling phenomenon Fordham wrote:

> It is the meaning of an often very diffuse collection of data which leads to the emergence of a conscious expression either found by the patient or made known to him in an interpretation. It is also a matter of interest that most of the formulations of analysts are not of the kind which renders their conclusions suitable for statistical investigation.

These reflections give a special cogency to the idea of synchronicity – it may be that we work much more on the basis of meaningful coincidence than we like to admit.

(Ibid., p. 136)

Intuitive interpretations would come into this category, as would the products of reverie and what are reported in the literature as projective identificatory states occurring in sessions and recognized as such, which lead to a deepening of the analyst's understanding of the patient. I understand also from this that Fordham is suggesting that to approach this problem from the experimental vertex, as Jung did to give credibility to his thoughts, is irrelevant. The inquirer who looks into his own subjective experience is likely to approach more nearly the problem. Why Jungians are especially attached to synchronicity is that its acausality puts it in the territory of the individual solution rather than the causal explanation. Fordham's contribution is a development of this in the context of individuation, analysis and the self.

Afterword

Fordham led the way in setting up the foundations for Jungian analysis in the UK. He set up both an adult and a child training, and he established rules and principles which have ensured that these trainings will continue to develop along the scientific lines he has set out. Foremost amongst his bequest is his attention to the detail of the interactions between patient and therapist. In this he is close to Jung.

When Fordham began to think about establishing a training based on Jung's ideas, the analysis of transference was not a primary feature of Jungian therapy. Today it is. In large measure this is due to the scientific atmosphere he in part created and in part fostered in the Society of Analytical Psychology, which made possible the scrutiny of what took place in analytic sessions both between patient and analyst and within the patient and the analyst (see Appendix). Scientific is the word Fordham prefers for his approach. What this means in essence for him is thinking about and working on emotional experience. The learning will come from the change in the mind resulting from this process, a kind of internal reorganization akin to growth – a change in the mind which he called deintegration and reintegration.

He will also be remembered for his studies of infancy. What he has achieved is to give Jungians their childhood and a way of thinking about it and analysing it – not as one aspect of the archetypal relationship, but as the basis for the analysis of the transference within archetypal forms. It is not that he has put childhood in the place of the impersonal archetypal features of analysis, so much as he has shown how the psyche oscillates between states of mind – sometimes mature, sometimes immature – which continue with greater or lesser strength throughout the life of the individual.

In his work on autism he showed how the failure of adequate deintegration gave rise to a mad world of self-objects, where all non-self-objects had to be annihilated, a view agreed with by Frances Tustin, one of the major workers in this field. In his work with adults he described the defences of the self in their perverse and negativistic forms. He showed how by using the body language of childhood and infancy he was able to relieve the anxieties arising from the childlike and infantile structures in the minds of his adult patients. By doing this he showed the continuity of archetypal structures in the mind and the need to speak to them directly.

If I have dwelt on Fordham's work with children at the expense of his work with adults it is because it is through his work with children that he discovered that Jung's concept of the self applied throughout life and was based in the psyche-soma, as Jung eventually thought. Fordham's task was to elucidate this, and in doing so he changed for ever the Jungian model of ego development. His work with adults shows him applying to them not only his understanding of ego development but also what he had learnt from children of the pathology of the self.

Like Jung, he has understood that the instability of the mind gives rise to fierce struggles internally, principally against negative forces of mind-lessness, cynicism and all their derivatives and perverse clothings. Throughout these struggles the beauty of the continuity of the self, of what Jung called the 'prospective' nature of the psyche, with its capacity to heal itself, can carry forward the interested inquirer who does not give up the struggle. Fordham's legacy is to have shown us, through his example and published work, that the self in its unifying characteristics can transcend what seem to be opposite forces and that, while it is engaged in this struggle, it is 'exceedingly disruptive' both destructively and creatively.

He has occupied himself with detail, working out in the micro-analysis of sessions what the movement of the dynamic between him and his patient has been and what this means. He has been true to Jung's spirit in his manner of changing Jung's model of the mind, in that he has let the empirical experience of the clinical work lead the changes. When he has published a major discovery it has always been with sufficient accompanying evidence for the reader to understand how he has arrived at the change he is proposing. His discovery of the syntonic counter-transference and his subsequent discarding of it, his redefinition of countertransference and his clinical descriptions of what Jung meant when he referred to the 'danger of knowing beforehand' have been inspired by Jung but not constricted by his eminence. Rather Fordham has thought out his own solutions, guided by Jung's originality.

In part he seized the moment, using the unique opportunity of the forums in which psychoanalysts and analytical psychologists met, to make Jung's ideas more widely known to psychoanalysts and to learn more of Freud's and Klein's ideas and their relevance to analytical psychologists. His character and personality are those of a natural leader and his experience within his family and of Jung had alerted him to the dangers of becoming isolated. He valued his father's qualities and Jung's and was puzzled why his loved mother should have died so young. His investigations into childhood brought together his wanting to know why his mother's death had such resonance in his life, with wanting to reattach Jung to the significance of the childhood he (Jung) had turned away from because of its remembrance of psychotic anxieties. Following on from this original work which showed the importance of the self from infancy to the grave, he imported the knowledge psychoanalysts had acquired into analytical psychology, in a creative and open minded way, in the context of the further development of Jung's ideas. Loyalty to Jung meant that he sometimes played down the significance of Jung's weaknesses. Nowhere is this more noticeable than in the tightrope he walked in his work on transference. Jung's attitude to transference was ambivalent. He knew it was the 'alpha and omega' of analysis but disliked the experience of it in practice. This ambivalence continues to be a feature of some Jungian trainings.

Many Jungian analysts do not see patients several times a week and prefer less intense transferences (see Spiegelman 1988). Might there be another historical and characterlogical feature here, that reductive analysis within the transference is historically associated with a Freudian causal reductive model and consequently resisted? Maybe the early struggles which Fordham was engaged in to clarify what the relationship was between synthetic and reductive analysis are formalized at an institutional level but unresolved in individual practice.

When the Society of Analytical Psychology was established few of Jung's works were available in English. As a consequence of this, and of the fact that many of the original members were medically trained and interacted in the psychiatric field with Freudians, the early members of the SAP turned to psychoanalysis for the knowledge needed for their work. Now that nearly all of Jung's work is available in English and the majority of SAP members are no longer medically trained, few begin their training by studying psychoanalysis. I do not mean that psychoanalytic method is not part of Jungian trainings, but rather that the exchanges enjoyed by the founders of our society through the common forum of the British Psychological Society and the Royal College of Psychiatrists is no longer part of the professional development of Jungian analysts. As a result many contemporary Jungians do not keep up to date with developments in psychoanalysis. For instance the Kleinian development of the Oedipus complex, with its discovery of the importance of the pregenital characteristics of early object relations within the personality, does not form part of the core curriculum of Jungian analytic trainings, although Jungians and Kleinians can agree about the significance of fantasies and imagoes in the development of character.

Fordham enjoys thinking about feelings and has lots of thoughts. This is not a characteristic which is common among those attracted to Jung. This difficulty with thinking among Jungians is often presented in the form of denigrating thinking as a defence against feeling. Jung's psychology is an individual psychology, and his reluctance to foster the institutionalization of his ideas arose from his knowing that an individual method could only be taught with difficulty, and often attracts people who are working out an individual solution to their own lives. Much of Fordham's work has countered this religious aspect of Jungianism. In understanding the complementary nature of Jung's contribution to Freud's, Fordham has drawn attention to the need to be well grounded in the analysis of transference as a prerequisite to a deeper analysis of the self, and his example has demonstrated the enriching qualities of psychoanalytic concepts in this task.

Fordham recognized that there were gaps in Jung's work and his deep engagement with both Jung and psychoanalysis allowed him to fill many of them, in a way that more recent trainings cannot sustain. He knew also that Jung's work was short on detailed accounts of his practice and long on abstraction from his experience. He knew from his study of Freud and Klein that they gave sufficient detail of their method to demonstrate what they did. He determined to publish clinically based material. Towards the end of his clinical working life he became preoccupied with one aspect of the tradition of analysis. Freud called it listening with 'evenly suspended attention'. Jung called it 'not knowing beforehand'; Bion called it listening 'without memory or desire'. Fordham described his experiences of this process, and of when it had to be modified. His essay on this problem (Fordham 1993b) does not quite bring out, because of his way of writing, that there comes a time in most sessions when it is appropriate to know, rather than go on not knowing, to have what Fordham calls filing-cabinet material (see Chapter 9) to draw on and amplify and interpret the patient's conflict. His struggle with this demonstrates that there is much you need to know before not knowing is of value.

I wrote in the Prologue that Fordham had reversed the traditional Jungian method of using myth as metapsychology to using clinical

material to illuminate contemporary personal myths. This, as Fordham
has pointed out to me, was what Ferenczi said Jung should have done,
when he was deputized by Freud to review *The Psychology of the
Unconscious* (revised as *Symbols of Transformation*, *CW* 5). Perhaps
this also reveals the fundamental difference between Fordham and those
who have studied Jung without studying Freud and his followers.
Fordham knows that clinically some Jungian methods, without modification, are deficient in addressing personal psychopathology (infrequent
interviews, use of the chair, mythological amplification and active imagination – see Chapter 7) while nevertheless finding Jung's prospective,
rather than Freud's causal reductive, approach invaluable as an analytic
attitude for promoting individuation.

In his memoir he described taking a dream to Jung, which contained
much of his fury and perplexity at Jung's attitude concerning the
transference in analysis: did Jung say one thing and practise another?
wondered Fordham angrily (Fordham 1993, p. 118). Jung proceeded
analytically and Fordham understood that Jung recognized the transference content, but when he came to the figure of Hercules in the dream
then Jung jumped out of his chair and insisted Fordham came back the
next day to go into that archetypal figure. Fordham records that this
second interview was disappointing; the work had been done in the first
when he had accomplished his heroic task by confronting Jung. Jung's
analysis missed the personal significance of Fordham's Herculean task
as expressed in the dream in relation to him. In discussing this with
Fordham, Jung described how when he got on to an archetype he thought
that the analyst should become more involved. If primitive layers of the
psyche are reached, Jung thought that what is normally understood as
transference was no longer a relevant concept. This was because there
was not enough structure in the psyche. This is the area where Jung's
concept of identity operates and which Fordham has tried to describe in
clinical practice (see Chapter 10). What I draw from this is that Jung had
forgotten that in analysis it is more important what the patient knows
than what the analyst knows. Fordham's work has shown us how to
bring this understanding of the personal and the archetypal together in
the consulting room by attending to the very details Jung was less
interested in.

Fordham's breadth of interests, love of Jung and scientific inquiry led
him to write on the occasion of Jung's death:

> His name is still almost automatically linked with that of Freud as
> most nearly Freud's equal, and if his main life's work was in the end

to be founded on a personal and scientific incompatibility with Freud, there are those who believe, like myself, that this was a disaster, and in part an illusion, from which we suffer and will continue to do so until we have repaired the damage.

(Fordham 1961d, p. 168)

Fordham's life has been open to this task of repair. He has given papers to psychoanalytic groups, demonstrating to them the value of Jung's archetypal psychology. He has promoted discussions and conferences with speakers drawn from Jungians, Freudians and psychiatrists. Through the careful study of the clinical work of Freud and those who have come after him, he has equipped himself to disseminate psychoanalytic ideas in his analysing, his teaching and his supervising, and to show where the connections and differences lie between the two great pioneers (see Fordham 1994b).

Sam Naifeh, a Jungian analyst and psychiatrist, has emphasized that it is not only Fordham's assimilation of psychoanalysis and his recognition of the individuality of the infant years before Stern which has made his work so important but,

By understanding the self through working on its role in child development as well as in the here-and-now symbolic elaboration and amplification, Fordham has contributed what amounts to a unified field theory in place of one that splits life into a first and second half, and infancy from adulthood. The unified field is in fact the self.

(Naifeh 1993, p. 6)

Fordham is the last of the founders of a movement in analysis, and like the other founders, for instance Klein, Winnicott or Bion, he has tapped into something essential in analysis. Certainly the historical circumstances which gave him the opportunity will never be repeated, any more than the Freud–Jung collaboration will ever be repeated. Fordham seized an opportunity and positioned analytical psychology between psychoanalysis and Jung's original formulations. He has grounded Jungian analysis of transference in infancy while highlighting the distinctive features of Jung's contribution to analytic practice. His work has been a turning point in Jungian studies. What I have shown in this book is that Fordham has been true to his own thoughts about Jung that 'the best monument that can be raised to Jung's memory is to make use of and develop his work rather than let it be passively accepted and sterilized' (Fordham 1961d, p. 168). In this he has succeeded.

Appendix

Notes on some early discussions of transference 1953–4

This appendix consists of the notes recorded by one or other of the group members of a transference group, initiated by Fred Plaut, which Fordham in his chairman's address for July 1954 described as follows:

> A new sign of activity within the society has been the continued interest in the transference, round which is tending to centre some of the conflicts within the society. If my reading of these conflicts is correct, they turn on the question, not of the existence of transference phenomena, but upon the desirability, or otherwise, of interpreting some of them in personal terms, and on the ways of handling and reacting to transpersonal contents. These I believe to be fruitful conflicts because they are ones capable of conceptual and methodological solution. The transference groups are, however, not just composed of persons interested in a topic; they are the equivalent of the growing vitality of committee members.

He went on to describe the way in which the society was organized and the time which the members were giving to evening meetings. The context of these discussions is interesting. Fordham joined the Analytical Psychology Club in 1935 when there were four other active analysts in England, Drs Godwin Baynes, Culver Barker and Hellen Shaw and a lay analyst, Elsie Beckinsale. Then there was no training and no society. He said 'we were, with the exception of Dr Baynes, without position in medical circles, a supposedly defunct remnant of the Jungian deviation'. In 1954 the society had forty members – twenty-two medical, eighteen lay analysts – and had representatives in ten hospitals, three psychiatric clinics, four child guidance clinics, one infant welfare clinic and one appointment at Wormwood Scrubs Prison. Quite an achievement for a 'defunct remnant' and one of which Fordham was justly pleased.

The members of the transference group, which met in 1953/4, were Mrs Hella Adler, Dr Fordham, Dr A. (Fred) Plaut, Dr Gordon Prince, Mrs Ruth Strauss and Mrs Mary Stein, also referred to as Mary Williams. These discussions give something of the professional atmosphere in Jungian circles that Fordham was working in, where he was 'the master', a position he half enjoyed and half did not. The group seems to defer to him, while also gently teasing him. Sometimes their compliance leads him to make provocative statements – such as that the analyst is God.

In the first session Dr Plaut describes his technique with a woman patient. His contemporary perspective on this session is that he 'no longer subscribes to the view he held then'. He has pointed out to me that the transference was maternal, not oedipal, and that he was then influenced by J. Rosen's *Direct Analysis* (1953) and Sechehaye's *Symbolic Realisation* (1951). The point he raised about the manner in which countertransference feelings are best made use of continued to be discussed in the next meeting. In this meeting, the second, Fordham observed that the objective psyche is manifested in analysis 'by the way in which large parts of the transference had to be worked through as if it were true'. Whether the analyst is presiding over a process, reducing a complex to its components or providing in the transference a different quality of emotional experience are all issues contained in these discussions but in an embryonic form.

Another theme which appears in this second group meeting is the vexatious issue of trying to discover how colleagues work with patients. There were two main threads here: one was to do with the confidentiality of the analysis and the need to protect the patient's privacy; the other with the analyst's feeling of being exposed in discussion and revealed to be not conducting the analysis 'properly'. The material which would reveal this is called the 'unconscious transference' in the discussions. Later, in the eighth meeting, the 'unconscious transference' was represented diagrammatically in relation to the analytic hour. The reference in the notes to the second session is light-hearted, but this issue concerning how to conduct an analysis became an important one contributing to the divide between the Zurich analysts and those who trained in London. Hella Adler's allegiance was to the Zurich school. She was never, in the language of Dr Plaut's thirteenth session report, a 'daughter', in the sense that Ruth Strauss and Mary Williams were 'daughters' of Michael Fordham.

Examination of transference processes brought up Jung's cases and his meaning of transference analysis in the context of his individuation cases and the dialectic between 'I' and 'thou'. This topic of the difference between individuation cases and those people needing more analysis of the personal unconscious was taken up in the ninth session, where there was a vigorous discussion of the importance of the relationship to the analyst in the individuation process. Fordham asserted that because individuation is a psychological process it needs a person to receive the projections. This was felt to be helpful as it bridged the gap between reductive analysis and individuation processes as described by Jung. In the sixth meeting arising from Fordham's remark that analysts were 'not necessarily male or female psychically' reference was made to the 'peculiar ideas emanating from Zurich'. This refers to the custom in Zurich of candidates in training having part of their analysis with a male analyst and part with a female analyst.

These discussions, especially in the diagrams, also touch on the tentative thoughts Fordham is working out on ego development. In the early diagram (session five) he places the ego in the centre of the self and elaborates this in his statement in the tenth session when he describes consciousness as the centre of the self. Neither of these statements can be supported by evidence and they are inconsistent with Fordham's later views. They are, in the categorical language of these discussions, just plain wrong. They show also how when Fordham is playing about with ideas he can follow a wrong tack for quite some way. What is also noticeable is that his authority silences opposition. Thus when he makes the statement that consciousness is the centre of the self he adds the assertion that this is evidenced in children's dreams, without producing that evidence. Examination of the children's dreams he has published does not support this assertion. Today Fordham's view is that the ego is the most significant deintegrate of the self.

The self of the analyst in the analytic process is returned to in several of the discussions. This seems at times to push Fordham into making provocative statements, especially about the magical projections of the patient on to the analyst. The transcription of the notes capitalizes the 'G' of God, incorrectly in my view if one is taking the discussion seriously, but correctly if the tone is tongue in cheek. What is meant in the discussion is that when a patient has a strong transference to the analyst powerful projections, sometimes even of aspects of the patient's self, are an important feature of the work, until the patient develops a stronger ego.

The thirteenth meeting has been written up as a play by Fred Plaut to illustrate the group dynamics. The cast consists of two sons and two daughters, the master and a middle daughter who is absent. Elder Son is Fred Plaut (E.S.), Younger Son is Gordon Prince (Y.S.), Elder Daughter is Ruth Strauss (E.D.) and Younger Daughter is Mary Williams (Y.D.); Hella Adler is absent, Fordham is the Master and the photograph on the mantelpiece of the presiding patriarch is, of course, a photograph of Jung. According to Dr Plaut on the first page (p. 213) the E.S. who speaks first is him and second E.S. is Ruth Strauss (E.D.) but on the second page (p. 214) E.S. refers to Dr Plaut; from then on the abbreviations remain constant. Dr Prince's review of the play begins the notes for session fourteen, a session which particularly interested me as it ends with the observation that the account of a part of an analysis the group had just been listening to revealed that the analysis had been reductive 'and the group ended the session in agreement that its members often did this but seldom discussed it'. This is to be taken hand in hand with Fordham's observation that the transference has to be lived and worked through with the patient, in what is essentially an archetypal process, presided over by the analyst.

The predominant feeling these notes convey is that the playful atmosphere in which these discussions were conducted masks a host of hidden agendas. I am grateful to the surviving participants for their permission to publish these informal notes.

TRANSFERENCE GROUP MEETING, 13 OCTOBER 1953

The first meeting of the group was held on the 13th of October, 1953. It was decided to have weekly meetings at the homes of the various members.

Dr Fordham suggested to read up existing literature about Transference. Dr Plaut suggested that each member of the group should take their turn and discuss case material.

We agreed that what we understand by transference is 'an unconscious content which is projected into the analyst' and therefore the analyst is a phenomenon within the patient's psyche.

Dr Plaut expressed the view that transference needs a countertransference. He brought the case of a woman patient of 35, a spinster, who had no sexual desires and experiences towards the other sex (it simply did not occur to her). He described how the patient developed a sexual transference. He also described his feelings and reactions towards the patient. At one point of the analysis Dr Plaut decided to let the patient express her emotions and allowed her to hold his hand. After that experience he found to his relief that the patient developed sexual phantasies towards other men.

Other members of the group do not agree with that technique and rather feel that the analyst 'misses' the transference if the analyst allows the patient to express his emotions actively and responds to them as well. The analyst leaves his 'position within' and therefore may upset and endanger the analytical position and security of the patient.

Dr Fordham described the sexual phantasies of a woman patient. The patient feels that her analyst is deeply in love with her. Dr Fordham describes his negative countertransference towards this patient. The atmosphere the patient created during that phase of the analysis seems to be that of an unreality and unrelatedness towards the analyst.

We seem to be moving towards the problem of 'handling' the transference and countertransference.

TRANSFERENCE GROUP MEETING, 20 OCTOBER 1953

The meeting started by attempting to define the criteria of countertransference and the following indicia were considered:–

(a) Reactions continuing after the analytic interview;
(b) Dreams and fantasies about the patient.

The members were apparently satisfied by this for they now plunged with some vigour into the study of transference, covering such subjects as the patients' fear of the sexual transference becoming actual and defences against the fear by leakage and acting out.

This leads on to further elaboration by Fred Plaut of his liking for expressing countertransference love in a physical manner, weak ego development and comparison with the case of children were brought in on his side, also the inadequacy of words and the need for toys. On the other hand, Michael Fordham considered the comparison with children fallacious, for whereas children needed responsibilities taken for them, the analyst relied either implicitly or explicitly on the adult patient's maturity. Ruth Strauss then instanced a case in which she deliberately expressed her controlled hostility to her patient's behaviour by asserting her belief in the importance of patients taking responsibility for their infantilism. The countertransference soon returned.

Ruth Strauss then went on to describe how, in spite of this, she sometimes allowed patients to express physical affection. Hella Adler gave the case of a woman whose impulse to touch was not allowed and who then dreamed her conflicts in such a way that the impulse ceased to have a hold over her. She regarded this as an example of the action of the objective psyche. In both of the cases, the one cited by Ruth Strauss and the other by Hella Adler, the mother archetype had been constellated but in Ruth Strauss's case the transference was positive. In Hella Adler's, it was evidenced only in the impulse to touch. This showed the difficulty of generalising without careful consideration of the case. Michael Fordham then elaborated his view that the objective psyche could be very well demonstrated by the way in which large parts of the transference had to be worked through as if it were true. He gave a case to illustrate his point.

Fred Plaut talked about the importance of life experience in relation to transference content. This was not taken up. The discussion again gradually veered away from transference towards countertransference.

A high point was reached when the humanity and inhumanity of analysts was broached and this prompted Mary Stein to describe graphically her inhuman behaviour with cups of tea. The result, a test of the patient's progress, was gratifying. On the contrary, however, Fred Plaut described a disastrous consequence to his positively diabolical manoeuvre of bringing a paranoid delusion to bear on a teacup.

What do analysts do, led back to: what are they like in analysis? This perennial inquisitiveness came into the limelight. Why not discuss cases which other analysts have tried to analyse and thus show how different personalities produce different fantasy transference reactions? Why not indeed! Because if you talk about patients they get blocked! Thus Hella Adler triumphantly leaping into the fray, brandishing Freddy Meier in one hand and parapsychology in the other.

Electrified by the spectacle, a combined assault by all was made. Cries of countertransference rent the air. Could the behaviour of our Society in encouraging students to discuss their cases be so disastrous? Thanks be to God the Society was in some measure exonerated by Mary Stein springing forward with examples of cases who had been benefitted by seminar discussions.

The meeting ended soon after 10 pm in high spirits.

ADDENDUM: Diagram overleaf of Transference–Countertransference phenomena drawn at the meeting by Michael Fordham (improved and amended).

TRANSFERENCE GROUP MEETING, 27 OCTOBER 1953

While M. Fordham was reading his most comprehensive summary of the previous meeting, S. Prince joined the group; ill-health having prevented his attending the first two meetings.

M.F. then stated that he was afraid of giving personal details about

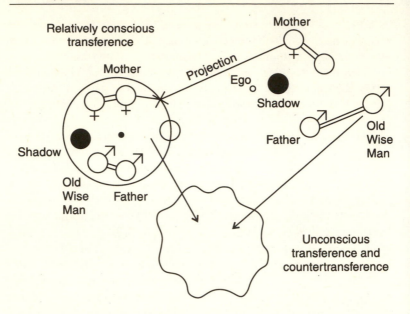

transference cases, his reason being that patients might easily be identified by the rest of the group, this leading possibly to discussion outside the group and jeopardising the analysis in this way. F. Plaut said that he felt safer if more than one member of the group were 'incriminated', e.g. by two analysts having had a share in the analysis of one patient at different times. While this defence was soon shown up to be obvious nonsense, the theme of personal exposure through discussion of transference cases, which had been in the air since the first meeting, seemed to persist. It had been there at the end of the last session in the shape of the 'retort', or, as some preferred to call it, 'Counter Transference "Telepathy"' or even 'Parapsychology'. Nor had the theme quite vanished at the end of to-night's meeting when M. Stein divulged that she had proposed R. Strauss should present a case 'because she always looked so cool and collected'. R.S. rejoined that appearances were likely to be deceptive. M. Fordham said that he felt no longer afraid now that he had voiced his fear.

It was found that behind the question of personal exposure lay the fact of the 'Unconscious Transference', i.e. that part of the transference of which both analyst and patient were mutually in the dark and which therefore could not be discussed. The existence of this Unconscious Transference was nevertheless sensed by members of the group (other than the analyst talking about his case) and this made them inquisitive, uncomfortably so, as their curiosity concerned an area likely to be charged with affect. F. Plaut wondered whether an ethical question arose when the analyst of a case was pushed by the inquisitiveness of his colleagues to become more aware of his Unconscious Transference which he shared with his patient. The latter, after all, was not here to take his share in the growing awareness. H. Adler nodded assent but no further comment was made about the ethical aspect. (Could the old problem of personal exposure have been hidden behind the latest guise of an 'ethical aspect'?)

S. Prince then remarked that it was a moot point whether the patient would not benefit when, through having discussed it with his colleagues, the analyst had become aware of the transference, as presumably he was bothered about the case; otherwise he would not have brought it up for discussion. F. Plaut doubted whether this presumption held necessarily for this group. It now looked as if S.P. and Mary Stein were in favour of open discussion, F. Plaut and H. Adler were against and M. Fordham presumably was also against because he said that we hoped to arrive at generalisations, to crystallise common factors. Inquisitiveness about personal details was to be deplored!

The main theme of the subsequent discussion centred around active imagination and its relation to transference analysis. Whereas passive imagination could be said to be at work in patients' fantasies, paintings, sculptings, dancing and such like, M. Fordham pointed out that a dialogue between patient and analyst required the patient's active participation as a separate being *vis-à-vis* the analyst and this could not be achieved until the transference of material belonging to the personal unconscious had been analysed. This necessitated the patient being seen frequently. F. Plaut remarked that he felt much more comfortable about an analysis if he saw the patient frequently, as only then could he feel sufficiently aware of what was going on. S. Prince, on the other hand, quoted the case of a schizophrenic patient whom he only saw every three weeks, yet immediately after the beginning of each session he felt in rapport with this patient. F. Plaut replied that rapport was not equivalent to transference analysis. He had not made himself sufficiently clear when speaking about his comfort in analytical situations. On the other hand, he agreed with S. Prince that patients frequently carry on imaginary conversations with the analyst outside sessions. In such dialogues they even stood up against an analyst whom they saw infrequently. Perhaps the difference was that such conversations were taking place outside the analytical sessions. Moreover, such patients were frequently immature.

This brought up the question of Ego development. A certain maturity was required (and presumably acquired during the initial stages of analysis) before the dialectic between 'I' and 'You' and 'Non-You' could be carried out. This is the kind of transference analysis Jung is mainly concerned with but other analysts presumably do not see so many individuation cases. M. Fordham pointed out that it was important to distinguish between these two varieties of transference, as otherwise personal and individuation analysis would get mixed up. In the individuation case, impersonal material was transferred on to the analyst and the distinction between archetypal and personal content required a certain ego development on the side of the patient and maturity of the analyst.

R. Strauss would have preferred the discussions to proceed in the way in which they had so far gone but F. Plaut thought that concepts had been sufficiently clarified to apply these to actual case material. This would also help to keep one foot on the ground. R. Strauss agreed to present a case from the aspect of transference at the next meeting.

Adjourned at 10.20 pm.

TRANSFERENCE GROUP MEETING, 3 NOVEMBER 1953

Present: Mrs Strauss, Mrs Williams, Drs Fordham, Plaut and Prince. An apology was received from Mrs Adler.

Dr Plaut, in spite of a tale of lost notes, read his summary of the proceedings of the previous meeting, which was acclaimed as an accurate record.

Mrs Strauss, confessing to anxiety that she had not anticipated, then presented some case material as a focus for the evening's discussion. This concerned the first phase of four months in the analysis of a young woman of Eurasian extraction. In spite of a traumatic early history – in which loss of the mother at birth, an unpleasant stepmother, infrequent contact with her father, and the experience of boarding schools from the age of four feature – the analysand had made a good superficial adjustment to life, attained a successful professional level and was unaware of symptoms except for a lack of adequate relationship with men. Her conscious motive for coming into analysis was the idea of doing therapy with children.

Mrs Strauss, achieving the difficult task of giving in brief a clear and living picture of several months of analysis, described the analysand in this phase as being very tense and anxious, unable to produce associations, afraid that the analyst would have nothing to work with because she was 'empty' and feeling that Mrs Strauss was 'aloof'. She mentioned a recurrent dream which occurred both before and during analysis. In this the analysand saw herself as mutilated in some way and experienced a fear of touching a small bird or animal in case it would crumble.

The second dream she mentioned was that of the analysand having a session with Mrs Strauss in Hyde Park. Mrs Strauss asked the dreamer if she remembered a telephone number that she had given her at the first session and asked the dreamer to phone a maladjusted school, asking for some girls to come along to form a group, since the dreamer needed group treatment. The group of adolescent girls arrived but the dreamer tried to avoid them; she was kicked and pinched by one girl and ran away but could not get through a succession of park gates because they were blocked by boys playing around bonfires.

At about four months of analysis came a dream which Mrs Strauss felt contained all the dreamer's problems. In it she brought a picture to Mrs Strauss of a snowcapped mountain, at the foot of which were gathered people of every creed who were concerned with the business of living. Half way up the side of the mountain there projected a silvery lotus plant with a golden centre. Mrs Strauss returned the picture, having signed it across the base of the lotus, the signature consisting of a maroon box with a window in the centre and a leaf being severed by a sword. She returned it with a story: that the moon shone for many decades on the mountain and it was eternal night. The lotus flower was born of the union of moon and mountain; the golden day dawned and the flower awoke. Men wanted the flower. Enterprise arrived amongst them in the shape of a young girl but she was unable to attain the flower because she became entangled in the passions of the people.

At this stage of Mrs Strauss's presentation, Dr Fordham suggested that enough material had been heard for a discussion of the transference to begin and this was agreed. In spite of the agreement, several members of the group had difficulty in resisting the fascination of the symbols in the dreams and in the pictures which illustrated the last dream.

Dr Fordham pointed out that both the dreams above mentioned were transference dreams and asked for details of the patient's behaviour in the transference situation. Except for the fact that the patient had brought over 300 dreams and many pictures during her year in analysis, I did not feel that Mrs Strauss supplied these details but may have failed to register this in my somewhat despairing efforts to keep notes.

Dr Fordham stated that the patient had a concept of development divorced from the realities of her nature (equating this with the phrase: 'passions of the people'). Dr Plaut, referring to the pictures, felt that she had a positive or animus evaluation of detachment and felt that only a woman could have painted the pictures, especially the smaller one which showed the details of the 'signature'. Mrs Strauss was inclined to disagree with this, because of the patient's conscious exploitation of her femininity, but seemed to concede to Dr Fordham that there was an element of Masquerade Femininity.

Dr Fordham dragged us back to the transference by saying that the patient transferred the Self on to Mrs Strauss and again asked for details of the interview behaviour. Being denied these, he stated that it seemed that the material simply emerged and that the content of the transference was found in the material. He continued that the patient had come with an attitude of foreknowledge about analysis.

Mrs Strauss brought us back to the Hyde Park dream. She referred to the conflict illustrated as being the patient's internal conflict and was taken up on this by Dr Fordham, who pointed out that taking images as internal can lead to the patient using this concept as a defence against having a content analysed, for example in relation to a mother image. There ensued an argument between Dr Fordham and Mrs Strauss about 'outside and inside' but unfortunately the scribe was well outside this. This Hyde Park dream was agreed by Dr Fordham and Mrs Strauss to illustrate that the dreamer's ego was absent or evanescent but Dr Plaut voiced doubts about this (with which Dr Prince agreed). It was admitted that in many ways the patient showed a considerable development of ego and agreed that the ego was evanescent in the transference only.

Dr Prince offered some woolly ideas, mainly from his phantasies about Hyde Park and about the French tongue in which the patient had once dreamt she could with difficulty communicate with an analyst-figure, on the lines that the patient needed an appreciation of the infantile and erotic elements in the Transference. Mrs Strauss agreed but pointed out that she did not feel that these could be used effectively in the stage of analysis under description. Dr Plaut said that the transference was that the analyst would know about the sort of material the patient produced and that the analyst would not destroy the archetypal material by reductive interpretation.

Dr Prince suggested that the same material form the nucleus of our next discussion but Dr Fordham thought we should have further material from the same analysis and this was agreed.

TRANSFERENCE GROUP MEETING, 10 NOVEMBER 1953

Present: Mrs Strauss, Mrs Adler, Drs Fordham, Plaut and Prince. An apology was received from Mrs Williams.

At the beginning of the meeting Dr Fordham gave a diagram, follow-ing the question of Mrs Adler about the outside and inside images mentioned in the last report. The idea of the diagram grew out of his work with children and shows the Ego in relation to the Self and the Ego-bits split off. The second diagram shows the Ego and Father and Mother Archetypes. The Archetype has become an internal figure.

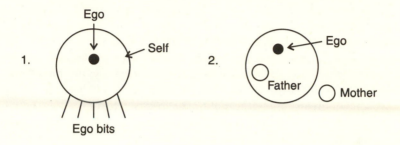

Dr Prince points out that the Ego is missing in the Transference, whereupon Dr Plaut remarks that the patient has Ego-fragments only and one could not therefore give her any transference interpretations.

Dr Prince quotes the case of a woman patient of forty, where the 'father was missing'. Transference interpretations to make the absence of feeling towards the analyst conscious were accepted by the patient with a good result.

Mrs Strauss disagrees with this suggestion. She continues to give further details about the case. The patient in question referred to her stepmother in an infantile way as 'Mummy'. She was talking of the stepmother as of a very good mother. During the course of the analysis, this positive feeling about the stepmother changed into a less positive figure and after 13 months of analysis the patient seemed to experience the stepmother as a very bad mother. (The father had remarried when patient was 4 years old.) Mrs Adler points out that the patient can obviously afford to do so at this point of the analysis, after a relationship with the analyst has been established.

At this stage Mrs Strauss shows two pictures in which she and the patient appear. The first picture shows the analyst on the top left side; in the middle of the page a question mark and right at the bottom a child (the patient) sulking, turning her back to the analyst and the question mark. Picture 2 shows a white, embryo-like figure, which is surrounded by black spirals. At the bottom is some black and on top some black hands across the opening seem to have a dual aspect to the patient. They are protecting and holding the embryo enclosed at the same time. Picture 3 (not reproduced here) is a cube made of glass. The patient is like a cocoon enclosed in this. That was how the patient felt.

Dr Plaut enquires with what part of herself the patient painted this picture. Dr Prince suggests that the picture shows how the patient felt towards the analyst. Mrs Strauss thinks that the patient had transferred the Self on to the analyst and that the picture was "How the Self sees the Ego". She explains that these pictures formed the turning point of the analysis. Before, the patient seemed to be tense when coming without dreams and pictures. She could not imagine that the analyst would turn up for the interview. Dr Prince asked: "Would the patient be likely to feel this tension had she not had this traumatic experience with her mother?" Dr Fordham expressed the view that the patient dealt with her experiences in a kind of 'living through her split-off-ego-bits'. He further stresses the importance to be clear on which level the interpretation is given.

Mrs Strauss continues with a dream:

> I had just begun to attend a new school. The headmistress had put me into a C stream which contained the least intelligent pupils. We had all had to sit for an examination and most of the girls were discussing it. I was alone reading. A phone-bell rang and someone said the headmistress's secretary wanted to see me and that she sounded very cross. I went to the headmistress's room and she was extremely angry. She held my paper and said that it had been selected by the examiners as the best paper written by a pupil in her school. She asked me how I dared write such a paper and she was furious with me for getting the top marks. I apologised profusely and explained that I had not meant to write a good paper but that I had just put down what came into my head and that I really couldn't be blamed if the examiners liked it. I felt very contrite.

Mrs Strauss pointed out that the patient belittles her position. The headmistress in the dream is not pleased. Her bad opinion is projected on to the mother (headmistress-analyst).

Dr Prince wondered whether her devaluation has to do with her guilt feelings of having 'killed' the mother during the birth process.

Mrs Strauss cannot agree with this suggestion.

TRANSFERENCE GROUP MEETING, 17 NOVEMBER 1953

Present: Dr Fordham, Dr Plaut, Dr Prince, Mrs Adler, Mrs Strauss, Mrs Williams.

After Mrs Adler read the notes of the last meeting, the discussion centred on the effect on the patient of losing her mother at birth. Dr Prince thought that she must feel responsible and that was why she was punished by figures such as the Head Mistress. He favoured a reductive interpretation. Dr Fordham said it would depend on the level at which the patient was experiencing things. For instance, if she were on the omnipotent, magical level, you might hit it off but not otherwise. Dr Prince then argued for a transference interpretation. Mrs Strauss reminded him that she had asked the patient how she felt about her and the spiral painting resulted. Here the white embryo is in a spiral with hands below pushing it up and hands above keeping it down. Mrs Strauss believed in keeping in the here and now rather than referring to the past, as many patients were only too pleased to get away from the present by explanations in terms of the past. Dr Prince then changed his ground again and wanted both so that the present and past were linked. Mrs Strauss agreed that where it was possible to analyse content and behaviour together it was ideal but in her experience the opportunities were rare.

Mrs Adler was interested in the difference of the effect of the early death of the father and of the father's attitude to the child if the mother dies in childbirth. Here Dr Plaut brought up the problem of the sex of the analyst in relation to the early loss of a parent and its effect on the transference. After this dead parents lost their charm and the body of the analyst loomed for the rest of the evening.

Mrs Strauss quoted a case in which a woman was alarmed by the strong sexual feelings towards Mrs S, which the patient herself interpreted as homosexual. Directly afterwards the patient flew into the arms of a male colleague, a Jew, who was quite prepared to have an affair with her but who wouldn't marry her because he could not have children by a non-Jew. She then dreamt that she was having intercourse with her father. Mrs Strauss felt events proved that the so-called homosexual feelings hid a father transference which was even more taboo. Dr Fordham mused about what would have happened if the analyst were a male and supposed that the father transference would have been well hidden by the patient's insistence that the analyst was a lover. Dr Plaut felt there might have been a risk of the patient running away if the analyst were a man but Dr Prince thought that the taboo on homosexuality was much stronger than the incest taboo. He instanced a male homosexual who had rushed into marriage in the early stages of analysis.

Dr Fordham reminded us that we were not necessarily male or female psychically, just because we happened to have male or female forms.

We were blinded by our bodies. Dr Plaut hung on to his and felt sure that his male body made it more difficult for a male patient to project his anima, which tended to get projected outside the analysis. Dr Fordham did not agree. In his experience, male patients with an anima problem adopt a passive, feminine role towards the analyst.

The discussion then turned to the peculiar ideas emanating from Zurich. Mrs Strauss said they thought that certain problems could only be worked out by a change of sex. Dr Plaut reminded her that she had sent him a patient for this reason but she declared that this was only the good reason given to the patient, not the real one. Mrs Williams murmured something about countertransference problems and Dr Fordham said it was a question of personality, not sex. Zurich, however, is said to declare that the whole constellation is different. Dr Plaut insisted that the body was very important in the early stages at least and Mrs Adler agreed. The analysis might break up because of it.

After more discussion about patients, Mrs Adler appealed for personal experiences as she believed that most of us had worked with a man and a woman. Dr Fordham was the only one to come clean and in his case the body hadn't come into it for a very long time with either. Dr Prince wondered whether this had to do with function types but Mrs Adler was more inclined to think it had to do with the constellation of a particular archetype, an idea which appealed to Mrs Strauss as archetypes are apparently not interested in the sex of the analyst. Dr Plaut did not agree and doggedly asserted that sex mattered. He instanced a woman schizophrenic who had been to three male analysts and left because she could not cope with her incestuous feelings. Dr Fordham relented a little and said it makes the analysis easier or more difficult but as far as schizophrenics were concerned, they often left because the analyst was too sane.

Dr Prince recalled seeing Rosen at work with a schizophrenic girl who ran away from him and his interpretations because he was right. Dr Plaut was pleased, for here was a case which showed that the reality and the myth together were too much. The body may be too much of a reality.

The meeting closed in confusion, at least as far as the scribe is concerned!

TRANSFERENCE GROUP MEETING, 26 NOVEMBER 1953

Present: All members of the group.

After some dilatory discussion, the group returned to Ruth Strauss's case, which occupied its attention for some time. Ruth Strauss started by saying that giving the case does not do her much good. She felt confused with her patient because she was constantly thinking would the material the patient produced fit in with what she had said, or would it not. Thus, the difficulty raised by Hella Adler had come up in a different form, and gave an opportunity for Hella Adler to say that her previous statements had been concerned with a single experience. Mary Williams pointed out that Ruth Strauss's difficulty arose from a transference to the group. Ruth Strauss could then proceed to her case.

She pointed out that the threatening mother had been black and that the embryo had been white according to the patient's picture. She then retailed a transference dream which she felt was pathetic because Ruth Strauss was away and the patient wanted to come and see her. She put on her best clothes and brought along a picture of a mountain with snow on it, which she wanted to show Ruth Strauss, but there was doubt concerning the appointment. Was it tomorrow? Tomorrow was Sunday; she went on Saturday instead of Monday. It therefore appeared that the patient wanted to come on Saturday or Sunday. Members of the group interpreted this in two ways. Firstly, that she wanted to come on a day when she would not be seen; secondly, that she wanted to fill in a gap between Friday and Monday. Other interpretations were given as well. Ruth Strauss reported that the patient felt for her for the first time at this point. Before this, her attitude had been one of interest in analysis and of fears of boring Ruth Strauss.

The next dream was a long one in which the patient was applying for the post of 'chief therapist' and was walking up a road. Another figure appeared who was going for the interview. The second figure was nervous and wanted the patient to be there in the background during the impending interview. The figure gave the patient a story written like a cheap American novel. It gave an account of how a patient had been saved by a therapist who took the sins of the patients on her and became a miserable sinner. This had struck Ruth Strauss as most significant and interesting. She compared the process with the change from white to black – that is the therapist, previously white, became black and the patient, previously black, became white. Nobody else seemed interested and thought such things as that it was the usual scapegoat mechanism. Gordon Prince found difficulty in bringing black and white into relation with sin and guilt. He evidently thought it far fetched and we wanted to put the discussion on a semantic level. Fred Plaut laid emphasis on the inconspicuousness of the patient and thought that this linked up with Ruth Strauss's white as innocent and emotionally cut off. He drew attention to the relation between the black and the passions of the people.

He thought the inconspicuousness of the patient – that is of her ego – was illustrated by the dream content which stated that she should keep in the background because there were so many eminent people about. Michael Fordham tried to point out that we were talking about dream transference phenomena that did not happen in the analytic hour, but happened when the patient was in bed. He tried to say something by calling it a dream transference; further he wanted to say there were other kinds of transference which occupied the interview, and gave examples. He thought this created bad feeling in the group. Did it?

TRANSFERENCE GROUP MEETING, 1 DECEMBER 1953

Present: All members except Dr Prince.

The meeting started by taking up the question mark with which M.F.'s report had ended. Members seemed to agree that it was not the proposed division into patients with dreams and those with behaviour-transferences that had had a disquieting effect during our previous meeting. At the same time R.S. felt unhappy as she thought she had not conveyed to the group the marked change which had taken place in her patient, a change which had been going hand in hand with developments in the transference.

This gambit gave F.P. his opportunity to deliver himself of a schema designed to illustrate the difficulty of finding a method of study for transference phenomena. The group had been struggling with this difficulty from the beginning, as was reflected by vacillations between intimate personal data, broad generalisations and diagrams and also an individual case study. To-day's diagram formed the pivot of our discussion. It is reproduced here (see p. 203) with acknowledgements to M.F. and R.S. (the solid dot representing the shadow behind the analyst and the patient).

The immediate result of this demonstration was that members gave again more personal details about transference situations. The outcome seemed to be a more precise formulation of two major questions, i.e. 'What determines the analyst's ability to accept or tolerate his patient's transference?' 'What happens if he fails to accept it?'. Acceptance meant that he would not insist on declaring the content of a transference to be the patient's projection. On the other hand, it was agreed that at the beginning of analysis interpretations of projected material were often required in order to get the patient into the analytical situation. Toleration implied that the analyst was prepared to discover new realities about himself.

The answer to the second question, mainly given by M.F., was that an enlargement of the patient's shadow occurred within the analytical situation which, in turn, resulted in an increase of the analyst's shadow and so on, necessitating in the end rather discreditable methods to deal with the resultant difficulty. Before an answer to the first question could be attempted, it was first necessary to face another problem: when does the analyst delay and when does he give transference interpretations? In this context certain 'dangers' were mentioned by members, e.g. H.A. said that unless a positive transference had been established, she found it too dangerous to explain the situation between her and a certain male patient beset with a negative mother archetype. R.S. did not agree with this and said that she, on the contrary, often found it necessary to analyse the negative transference early on. She, R.S. on the other hand, had had difficulty with an intellectual man who was not interested in anything and thought that the world owed him a living because of his un-recognised genius. She feared that a vigorous attack on his unrelatedness would be dangerous. M.S. seemed to support his notion with a case of hers, a schizoid woman who had a breakdown in terms of a physical illness, just when she became aware that her phantasies might be applicable to the relationship with her analyst. Previously M.S. had made futile attempts for 9 months to make the patient aware of the absence of relationship.

M.F. was stung into action by H.A.'s use of the word 'explanation'. Whether by association or otherwise, he mentioned the case of a teacher, a woman who had been in analysis with someone else. The other analyst had been in the habit of letting the patient use active imagination in order to deal with a certain negative imago which they had called 'a part of myself' but which was related to the patient's experience with her own mother who had expected lady-like behaviour of her daughter. Active imagination in this case did not really constitute more than what the patient might just as well have consciously thought and had helped to avoid active transference.

H.A. mentioned her experiences with Mrs Jung, who had rejected her transference by saying "but I am not like that", with the result of that H.A. felt as if she had been pushed out of an aeroplane.

R.S. stated under what circumstances she would delay transference interpretation and M.F. took this up by recounting a recent session in which a woman patient had upbraided him for calling destructive sexual desires "Lust". He did not refer back to the original situation under which the term had been coined, not at least for the time being, and this delay produced increased tension and more relevant material and emotion emerged in consequence.

The combination of R.S. and M.F.'s apparently rationally considered approach proved too much for the present writer, who challenged by saying that one's decision about transference interpretations was not arrived at in this fashion as a general rule. M.F. agreed and came clean about the occasion which he had mentioned: he had felt tired and so, instead of giving an answer to the patient, he had silently sighed to himself: 'Oh God, here we go again!' In this mood he had kept quiet for the moment. He added that two wave-like movements seemed to go out from both patient and analyst during a session and where the two lines met a valid transference interpretation could lead to the area of mutual agreement (see diagram). Yet, F.P. said, these waves were not quite random either. What was it that influenced their course, as it was certainly not just the analyst's conscious decision? How could this puzzling phenomenon be investigated? Then, like the old Roman senator with his tedious 'ceterum censeo', he repeated that a comparative study of a case in which two analysts had treated the same patient was likely to be helpful. Nobody else seemed interested. He therefore gave vent to his frustration by stating that it was virtually impossible to do damage where one was conscious that an utterance might be 'dangerous' to the transference situation, as R.S. had implied earlier on.

M.F. contradicted, referring to a patient whose request for more sessions he had refused in a hasty manner and to two other patients who mentioned some stored up grievances only at the time when they were considering terminating their analyses. None of the three actually did stop and using this criterion, F.P. said that his point about dangerous talk or actions had been proved, i.e. that this idea had more to do with the analyst's own anxiety than with the patient's transference.

This received support from M.S., who mentioned that patients somehow managed to get themselves into situations which were relevant to their problems and therefore to the transference. She recalled how frequently she had had to clear weeping hysterics out of the lavatories at the Tavvi (Tavistock Centre). These patients had been given wrong appointments or their appointments had been refused or mixed up (M.S. left it to our imagination whether she had acted out of sympathy or whether more pressing selfish motives had been at work).

The present writer's refusal to take notes had been falsely diagnosed as an attack of hubris. When the meeting broke up at 10.25, R.S. threatened to send her super-intellectual patient to him, presumably as a therapeutic measure.

Legend to Diagram: The irregularly shaped area on the left represents

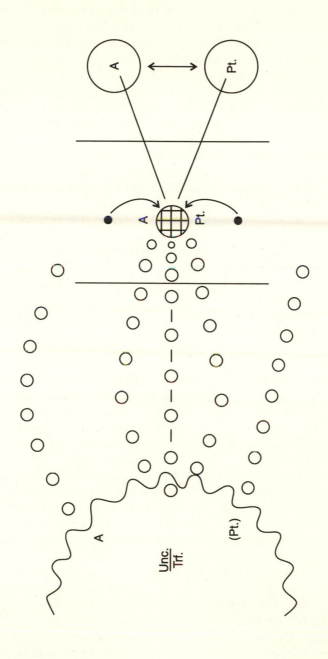

what the group previously called the Unconscious Transference. From it phenomena arise, such as dreams and behaviour, some of which are caught by the screen or filter which demarcates the analytical hour.

As the result of analysing these phenomena, an agreed area of mutual recognition is built up between patient and analyst – the squared circle in the diagram, and it is from this area that the relatively integrated personalities of patient and A on the right hand side of the picture emerge. These can then be said to be in relationship to each other with relatively little interference from transference phenomena.

Among the finer points was the fact that the Unc. Trf. (Unconscious Transference) contains the patient's image of the analyst A, which is therefore an ingredient of the transference phenomena which arise from this dark area like bubbles of gas. (The same applies to a lesser degree to the analyst's picture of the patient.) Sometimes a chain of these bubbles strikes the filter in rapid succession. No sooner is one analysed than the next one arises. Sometimes a particularly large one refuses to go through the filter and cannot be drawn into the area of mutual recog- nition and then a blockage is felt to have occurred. Behind the analyst and the patient there stands the shadow which needs to be recognized by both.

(Reported by Fred Plaut)

TRANSFERENCE GROUP MEETING, 8 DECEMBER 1953

All members of the group were present and the proceedings started with a reading of his report by Fred Plaut. It appeared that at the last meeting he had determined not to lose his notes and had therefore abstained from taking any! In spite of this he produced a summary that appeared to the scribe (who had missed the meeting concerned) to be a full, dynamic and entertaining summary.

On the basis of the minutes of the previous meeting a lively discussion arose upon the topic of the relationship between transference analysis and Active Imagination. Michael Fordham postulated that Active Imagination was used by some analysts, or rather that its use by the analysand was encouraged, as a substitute for the living out of transference material in frequent personal interviews. Fred Plaut wondered how Jung could do it – he implied could get away with it, and suggested that the answer lay in the strength of his Mana. Hella Adler felt rather that Jung's ability to keep the patient at bay, so to speak, depended rather upon his being so much in touch with the patient's Unconscious.

Gordon Prince, although aware of the apparent sacrilege, asked whether it could not be done by any analyst, since there was a tendency among many patients to be only too ready to keep their transference experience outside the personal relationship with the analyst. Michael Fordham seemed to agree with this and thought it an important point that the patient might dissolve all personal relationships in Active Imagination.

Ruth Strauss and Gordon Prince between them produced the rather obvious dictum that any 'technique', such as Active Imagination or Free Association, could be used as a defence and not surprisingly the rest of the group agreed.

Michael Fordham pointed out that Active Imagination has to do with the Individuation case, where the personal transference is not of such importance. Gordon Prince admitted doubts of his own ability to differentiate the individuation case from others but Michael Fordham said that he had no such difficulty, using as criterion the fact that the patient was an individual who no longer projected himself into some collective vehicle such as a political creed but showed clearly his need to orientate himself by some individual philosophy of life.

Discussion on Individuation was stimulated. Ruth Strauss asked why this process had to happen within analysis at all. Fred Plaut denied this necessity, saying the Individuation occurred in Alchemy and mentioned the mystics and the Gnostics. Michael Fordham denied that what happened in these systems was Individuation and a certain amount of rather wild argument ensued which included questions difficult to answer, such as whether or not Leonardo and Goethe were individuated in terms of their time.

Reverting to the question of why analysis was a necessary condition of individuation, Michael Fordham suggested that analysis was needed because of the persistence in the individual of infantile remnants. Ruth Strauss and Gordon Prince disagreed and Prince went on to express the opinion that whether an analysis focussed more on reductive or individuation material was determined to some extent upon the interests of the analyst. Encouraged by some support from Fred Plaut, he went on to express again his doubts about the recognition of the individuation case.

Michael Fordham amplified on what constituted an individuation case and Ruth Strauss said that it depends upon the relationship of the patient's ego to his collective material. Fred Plaut asked why the individuation patient needed to go on analysing and Michael Fordham said it was because of a need to constellate the Puer Aeternus by means of the relationship to the analyst as psychopompos; also because individuation is a new thing and needs to be experienced in relationship with someone with a knowledge of living psychology.

Gordon Prince suggested that the Self and the infantile contents of the psyche are always constellated together and there was some measure of agreement about this. Prince quoted two adjacent dreams of a middle-aged woman, one concerned with a Golden, God-like Child and its successor with a clinging, whining child. Emboldened by these symbols, Prince further declared that the symbol of the Child implied that dependence was always present in the idea of individuation but this was attacked by Fred Plaut and Michael Fordham, the latter pointing out that the Divine Child was omnipotent and carried the world upon his shoulders.

Prince retreated to brood inwardly, with the vague idea that there was something clever about his suggestion that had not been completely disposed of by its opponents.

Michael Fordham returned to the transference in individuation with the useful statement that you need an analyst to individuate because you need a person, as opposed to something like Matter, into which the process can be projected. By doing it with a person the process can be kept a psychological one and in the end the Man becomes his own redeemer. All this was maintained against a running fire from Fred Plaut and others and talk about the Alchemists resulted in some discussion about the Secret. Fordham said that the alchemists had a secret because they did not know and this was supported by Prince against the general feeling of the group.

Discussion became lively and rather undirected when the arrival of Mrs Fordham destroyed any idea of the omnipotence of her husband and the group disbanded.

(Reported by Gordon Prince)

TRANSFERENCE GROUP MEETING, 15 DECEMBER 1953

Present: Dr Michael Fordham, Dr Fred Plaut, Mrs Mary Williams, Dr Prince was on holiday. Apologies for absence were received from Mrs Adler (with excuses) and from Mrs Strauss (without).

Fred Plaut commented on the emotional nature of the discussion last time and wondered if the main subject accounted for any of the absences. Michael Fordham considered this and said that talking of symbols is a way of creating unconsciousness or madness, particularly symbols of the self, but we did not express our phantasies as to the possible state of the absentees, nor of our own as the 'tough' survivors.

Discussion of the individuation case continued. Fred Plaut thought that such people needed to bring their individuation symbols to a person so that they did not go mad. The ego needed reinforcement when the Self was manifesting itself. Mary Williams suggested that the analyst was a mediator, rather like a priest, but Michael Fordham announced that the analyst *was* God. This startled M.W., as she felt the danger of identifying with the patients' projection. M.F. then elaborated on his bombshell and said the analyst had to take such projections without blinking. One must remember one's frame of reference, that is that psychologically God is the Self. The analyst should not be afraid to be his Self, as that helped to start the process of individuation in the patient. F.P. pointed out that one had to be sure that the patient had a strong enough ego to relate to a symbol, for if he sees it as a concrete fact he is mad. He instanced a case of a brutish man who had amassed a large fortune through black marketeering. He insisted on seeing the analyst as a saint and felt that if only he could do something for him, save his life or something, he would be redeemed. F.P. couldn't stand this projection indefinitely and destroyed it by saying he would like to learn how to be a successful smuggler. The patient couldn't take this and went away. M.W. wondered why so many experienced analysts couldn't bear to be regarded as healers. M.F. thought it was important not to be a healer and F.P. spoke of the danger of losing one's ego in the projected archetype. M.F. said we didn't know what healing was anyway and F.P. said we did know what it was to act as though we were healers. He disliked his role as a consultant because of this projection, particularly as he felt that the consultant did nothing.

Returning to the problem of the patient with an obstinate 'God' projection, M.F. said the analyst had to live it through indefinitely, without aiming at a change. M.W. supposed that the opposite would come up sometime and M.F. said that in his experience no interpretation gets you out of it: you have to take it, having faith that there will be a change. M.W. said she found the interminable negative transferences were the most trying, not the dramatic ones, but those where she was constantly seen as the preventing person who just makes everything impossible. F.P. found the God projection most trying and M.F. those patients who isolate themselves with their material and give him no chance for transference interpretations, except of the isolation, as nothing else shows. M.W. wondered whether interpretations on the lines of what the patient is doing to the analyst might help in such a case but F.P. thought that there was a danger that one only taught the patient transference interpretation tricks by such methods, tricks which would help them to hide deeper feelings.

F.P. then returned to his attitude to saviour transferences and wondered whether it had anything to do with his Jewish origin. The Saviour had not yet come. He might be Him. M.W. said she thought this was an implicit hope in every male Orthodox Jew but F.P. said he felt they viewed the Saviour as a sort of Prime Minister, a political figure, not as a God. (There seems some muddle here.). F.P. turned the attention away from himself to M.F. who had previously said that his reactions to Self transferences had to do with his origin. He then explained that this was the earth. His people thought that nature was supreme and were unable to take any interest in psychic matters. M.W. failed to follow this reasoning, so could not make further notes on it.

M.F. went on to say that the analyst's role was both saving and preventing, punishing and rewarding. F.P. asked if the patients' ego became stronger if the analyst could accept his projections and M.F. said that if the analyst handed a projection back, he put too heavy a burden on the patient. M.W. cited a case of a schizoid obsessional who often remarked: 'If you can stand it, perhaps I can.'

F.P. went back to M.F.'s diagram and said he thought the idea of the ego as the centre of the Self disturbed people. M.F. instanced evidence for this in children's dreams and drawings. F. preferred to say that the ego was the centre of consciousness and M.F. added that consciousness was the centre of the Self. It was the god of the moment. F.P. didn't like this. A centre meant to him the essence of what surrounds it and he didn't think that was a description of the ego. M.F. insisted that the ego is the god of childhood, the central numinous thing. We then realised that the diagram refers to children. The relation of the ego to the Self changes in different phases of life. M.F. finished up by saying that people with weak egos make the analyst God and this is an anticipation of the ego coming into being through the Self as in childhood.

(Reported by Mary Williams)

TRANSFERENCE GROUP MEETING, 5 JANUARY 1954

(Apologies for incomplete notes, partly on account of having shown material.)

All members of the group were present and Mary Stein began with reading her report on the preceding meeting. It may have been tempting for some members to go further into the discussion of the 'tough survivors' and their opposites of the previous meeting but members refrained from doing so and tried to stick to the main object of the transference between patient and analyst.

Ruth Strauss, referring to Michael Fordham's remark on 'those patients who isolate themselves with their material', asked for an example. M.F. mentioned two patients, one of whom ended analysis after six months; the other after two years. The main feature in both analyses was that the patient would go on producing phantasies and dreams without reacting to the analyst's interpretation, except by going into a sort of trance, thereby 'castrating' the analyst.

The question arose: what is lacking in patients like these? M.F. referred to Fairbairn who had been dealing at length with this problem. R.S. then suggested 'luring the patient out' of his isolation. She gave as examples two patients to whom she had shown that she herself had been through similar experiences but had been able to deal with the situation nevertheless. This would produce a special means of identification of the patient with the analyst, thereby helping the patient to make the first step out of his isolation.

Fred Plaut thought it was apparently a personal matter of how the analyst related himself to the patient. Whereas M.F. held that, if that stage could be reached, the patient had already got over the difficulty in question. F.P. suggested that the difference between M.F.'s and R.S.'s patients was that the former were psychotic, while the latter were neurotic. This, however, was not entirely convincing to R.S., who had been thinking of her patients far more as being borderline psychotics than neurotics.

M.F. put forward the idea of comparing notes on transference in different clinical situations. M.S. mentioned that in other groups the mixing up of projection and transference had been discussed.

F.P. encouraged further critical questions on the previous report, particularly from the three absentees. He also thought it might be helpful to review the minutes of the ten previous meetings at this juncture. M.F. suggested that F.P. should undertake this.

R.S. then said she would like to show two more paintings of the patient whose material had been discussed previously. The chief reason why she wanted to do this was that she thought the paintings would reveal the development which had taken place, far more convincingly than she had been able to put it over by her own words.

Picture 1 shows in the centre a tower, on whose top a large black bird is standing. The patient, a nude figure, kneels down, leaning her forehead against the tower to hide her face for fear of the two fire spitting dragons that are on either side of the bird. The dragons' bodies are green on top and yellow underneath. The background of the picture is of a darkish grey.

Picture 2 shows the same tower with the bird but now the patient is standing up, her face uplifted and her arms raised towards the tips of the bird's wings. The wings have spread and a golden yellow flow pours down from the bird's body. In the place of the dragons are two trees with green leaves. The dragons themselves can be seen inside the patient in the middle of her back.

When bringing the pictures, the patient explained that the images had turned up spontaneously after her analyst had gone on a holiday. The bird stood for her analyst, of whom she had long been thinking as a dark bird belonging to the night. This bird had existed before creation and was therefore also responsible for the presence of the two dragons. The patient had felt that she had to touch the wings of the bird to overcome the fear of the dragons. By doing so the change of the situation had come about.

F.P. remarked that the image of the black bird seemed to him particularly fitting for R.S.'s personality and there seemed to be general agreement on this.

M.F., however, pointed out that R.S. was not a black bird, after all, and that, to him, the alchemical symbolism of these pictures was most striking: the black bird, the prima materia, with the dragons and the fire developing into the being that poured out the yellow flow – the light. He agreed with R.S. that the paintings were the result of true Active Imagination, i.e. caused by the transference situation.

F.P. pointed out that the ego was subsequently developing out of the Self. R.S. added that the patient had remarkably changed when she brought the pictures, in that she behaved far more directly and warmly than ever before. M.F. thought that this confirmed the immediate effect of active imagination on the development of the ego.

Gordon Prince asked whether these images would also have occurred if the analysis had not been interrupted. R.S. thought that the process might have been delayed without her absence. G.P. felt, however, more inclined to think that the strong love feeling of the patient to the analyst had been produced by the analyst's absence.

M.F. supported this by putting forward his theory of 'the analyst as scapegoat', i.e. through the analyst's absence positive contents can come to the fore.

On this point the discussion ended somewhat abruptly, since time was already advanced.

(Reported by Ruth Strauss)

TRANSFERENCE GROUP MEETING, 12 JANUARY 1954

Hella Adler was not present owing to domestic affairs; all other members were there.

The first part of the discussion was stimulated by Gordon Prince, who asked a large number of questions centering round problems of transference interpretation. He said that these were stimulated by his supervisor's interest in the transference and his analyst's comparative lack of interest in it. He wanted to know whether interpretation should be given early or late, whether the type of patient was important, whether interpretations were essential and necessary. Many of these questions were taken up and answered by implication later on, when members gave examples of different kinds of transference and different kinds of procedure in relation to it. Fred Plaut, for example, instanced two types of transference, one in which no interpretation was needed for a long time. This he believed to be due to a positive figure, which he represented well enough for the patient's analysis to develop without the patient's transference. He compared this with another obsessional who had had numerous previous psychiatric treatments: the patient badgered him with questions and comments and thus active transference interpretations were called for. This transference he thought was based on a negative mother fixation and on the previous treatments she received, which she felt did not give any space for her to say what she wanted, and what she felt. Ruth Strauss instanced two further transference situations at the beginning of analysis. In one there was a dream during the first week in which she was replaced by a very disagreeable sister. This brought out the shadow. In another dreamed before the patient came the interview was filled with the 'members of the family' who had to be got out of the room before the interview could proceed. Everybody agreed that the second case was common and everybody showed interest in it, but the discussion continued to separate out different classes of transference without developing any single one. There was a measure of agreement that some kinds of transference did not need interpretation over long periods. It was considered that transference interpretations were called for when the patient's behaviour threatened the relationship between patient and analyst. It was further agreed that anxiety was an important indication. These considerations sprang out of another question from Gordon Prince who asked: why do we make interpretations at all? In a further answer to this question, Fred Plaut gave the example of a man whose interview was determined by a spoilt boy attitude. The patient seems to have asked the same kind of question of Fred Plaut that Gordon Prince wanted to ask, for he said: why do you regard it as incumbent upon you to tell me about this? Fred Plaut made a blundering reply.

There continues a tendency to be surprised that patients know things about analysts. This was voiced by Mary Stein who gave examples of patients who behaved differently according to how she felt. Michael Fordham asked her why she was surprised. The discussion then moved towards the question of types. Michael Fordham said Fred Plaut's first case seemed to be an extroverted feeling type, and there was a discussion of this phenomenon. It seemed that feeling types had good relation to the object, knew how to manage it and in consequence the same sort of thing happened in the relation between the patient and analyst. However, Fred Plaut pointed out that the real transference expressed itself through the inferior function. Gordon Prince discussed an observation that sensation types tend to express their feeling through their bodies, in their clothes and the way they are dressed. He had one patient whose mood could be told from the dress she had on. It was pointed out that the patient was reflecting her conscious mood in this way and that the physical manifestations would be more inclined to manifest themselves in intuitive types. Fred Plaut went on to ask our view about a positive and a negative transference and whether it was necessary to work through both these as a routine. Reference was made to Jung's view that love and hate were not opposites but love and hate were balanced by fear. Somewhere enantiodromia was brought in as being the counterpart to ambivalence. The discussion then turned on indifference as opposite to love and hate. Michael Fordham took up his case of a man who tended to get isolated in his material and so appeared indifferent to his analyst. He thought that this indifference was illusory and defensive and covered a fear of the analyst cluttering the patient with his 'correct interpretations'. This fear had been voiced by the patient. The indifference was an attempt to make out that the patient was uninfluenced, whereas exactly the reverse was the case.

This led on to the importance of partial interpretations and leaving room to the patient to give their own interpretations. Again it became apparent that all sorts of different procedures were required in different cases. Michael Fordham then said an example of where he had interpreted everything that the patient said in the first part of the interview owing to the patient's anxiety and that only in the second half could she begin to express her own feelings directly.

In conclusion Fred Plaut asked whether the meeting would not agree that we should separate out the different transference phenomena since a more differentiated frame of reference seemed required. It was clear that attempts had been made in this interview to find a classification and that we could now proceed by taking one of the categories discussed. Gordon Prince agreed to produce a case he had mentioned.

It had been an easy going discussion, unusually so; there seemed to be fewer 'hobby horses' about.

TRANSFERENCE GROUP MEETING, 19 JANUARY 1954

'Family Favourites' or 'The Archetypes at Home'

(A Play in many Acts)
E.S. – Dr Plaut
Y.S. – Dr Prince
Y.D. – Mary Williams
E.D. – Ruth Strauss
Master – Dr Fordham

Present: DRAMATIS PERSONAE, with the exception of the middle daughter (who is away on holiday).

The scene opens on a large Regency drawing room, with much empty floor space. The furniture is an incongruous hotch-potch: stacks of green steel-and-canvas chairs, reminiscent of a seaside pavilion out of season; two armchairs of indefinable age but undeniable decrepitude, as well as an imperious couch which had seen better days (and probably nights!) are drawn around a friendly gas fire. The fire is joined by an aroma of coffee in a pitched battle against the sobriety of utility lampshades and a severe blackboard. From the mantelpiece the patriarch's photograph looks into the middle distance.

As the curtain rises, the Younger Sister and the Elder Son are settled with their coffee cups on the said couch. The Younger Son, carrying sheaves of paper and his cup, is just moving towards one of the armchairs (the less uncomfortable one).

E.S.: You can't sit there, it's the Master's chair.
Y.S.: The throne you hope to inherit? I'll certainly sit in it!

They are interrupted by the entry of the Master, closely followed by the Elder Sister, who is attired as 'Bird of the Night'. There is silence as the Master distributes papers to everyone and proceeds to read last week's lesson in a lighthearted, routine manner. Occasionally there is a slight stumble in the otherwise even canter of his voice as he frowns mildly at the indifferent English his Secretary has put into the typescript but the family group eagerly come to the rescue and a few corrections are made on the spot. So he reaches the end, still lighthearted and obviously not expecting any contradictions concerning the factual details of his text but no sooner has he finished, expecting at least the usual grunts of approval, than the Younger Son pipes up:

Y.S.:   Pater, with all due respect to your superior wisdom and authority, allow me to point out an error made, no doubt by your secretary. The Pretender, that exhibitionistic memory trickster, the one I must needs acknowledge as my elder brother, he did NOT give a neat reply! And with his usual modesty I am sure he would be the first one to admit that, on his own evidence, he was stymied by his patient's wit! In the name of scientific truth and for the sake of future generations . . .

E.S.   (glad of the opportunity to make a conciliatory gesture so early on in the proceedings): I am glad that this was pointed out; my reply was blundering, no doubt.

They all put 'blundering' into their Minutes. Having scored the first point, the Y.S. starts with a brief preamble, modestly referring to his limitations and relative inexperience, not omitting to pay tribute to the Master who nevertheless saw fit to send him a patient. He then recites his case in great detail, while the Master doodles gently. When he reaches an incontrovertible point he appeals to the Master for confirmation. The latter complies with a nod or a 'Yes'.

After the first 15 minutes of the recital the Elder Son begins to doodle in the forlorn hope that his Younger Brother will be deceived into thinking that the mass of detailed information has forced the elder one to take notes in writing instead of merely memorizing. Alas, another conciliatory gesture has been wasted! After a further 10 minutes of uninterrupted case recital, the Elder Son can bear it no longer. He addresses himself mainly to his sisters, as he feels that the Master does not wish to be drawn into any wrangling.

E.S.:   I thought we were going to discuss transference interpretations made during the first two sessions in the case of an obsessional patient.

A general skirmish follows this remark. No matter what E.S. says now, Y.S. counters with barely veiled hostility, introducing his blows with phrases like: 'I wonder whether one can say that', or 'I should hesitate to be certain about this; I don't think that is what the Master meant'; or 'Can one divorce the patient from all the circumstances?' The main point of the argument, in which both sisters join, appears to be that the Y.S. jumped to a conclusion when he interpreted the patient's 'Have you treated many cases like me?' as meaning that she suffered from having been referred by the Master to a disciple, to wit the Y.S. After every shot he fires at his sibling, Y.S. looks at the Master to spot the direction of the prevailing wind but the Master doodles on.

Y.S.:   No matter what you say, my patient relaxed at once and on subsequent occasions found it necessary to tell me that I had been wrong. What better proof could there be for the correctness of my interpretation, I pray thee?

Y.D.   (who has had second thoughts about the burden of the argument now addresses herself coyly to the Master, who begins to look up):

I am, so to speak, brand new,
But so much, I know, is true:
The strongest analytic phallus
Have you and only you!

Master   (now fully awake):   The obsessional patient harbours primitive sex magic and tries to manoeuvre the analyst into a position where he would become a moral code behind which the patient could feel safe.

E.D.   (taking her cue from the Master, explains to E.B., who is not very well versed in sex magic):   You must side with the patient; say 'There it is, we both have to face it, for better or worse.'

E.S.   expresses some astonishment.

Master   (corrects his E.D.):   Enter into it, not become identified with it. (Here he winks at his E.S., whose self confessed lapses are known to the whole family.)

E.D.:   Enter into it.

Master   (with emphasis):   Yes, certainly, language never was my strong point but my patients' pictures speak for themselves.

The E.S. persuades the Master to tell more about the entry into the patient's sex magic at the earliest opportunity. While they go into a huddle, the lights begin to dim and the rest of the family prepares for bed.

Just as the curtain is about to fall, an Archetype enters the room and declaims:

If we shadows have offended,
Think but this and all is mended:
That while you were talking here,
Transferences began to appear.*

---

* With apologies to W. Shakespeare.

He vanishes before anyone can reply, or even be sure of his existence.

CURTAIN

(Adapted for the stage by A. Plaut)

TRANSFERENCE GROUP MEETING, SESSION 14

The first phase of this session provided scintillating entertainment for the group and gratuitous psychotherapy for Gordon Prince. At the beginning of the Thirteenth Session, G.P. had chosen to sit in a particular chair. This apparently incensed Fred Plaut, who appeared to consider this chair the 'Throne' and himself the 'heir apparent'.

The poverty of Gordon Prince's case presentation thereafter left the field clear for Fred Plaut's active imagination and at the current session he was able to produce a dramatic opus of some magnitude on a familiar theme. To Gordon Prince (admittedly not unbiased), this sounded like something by Eliot out of Ibsen, adapted for pantomime by Tennessee Williams for presentation by Jacy Hylton on ice. It was none the less entertaining and seemed to capture the content and feeling of the relevant session to the satisfaction of the group. Gordon Prince was tempted to respond by embedding these minutes in a poem of some length and had got as far as opening with the lines:

> Do not badger, bigger brother,
> Be benign or else be off.

However, he lacked the motivation and inspiration to continue and, contenting himself with the thought of the well-known eventual triumph of the younger son of the fairy tales, turned to Michael Fordham's presentation of the main business.

This concerned the treatment of a woman in her early forties and was designed to illustrate his handling of a transference centred around the magical sexual fantasies of the patient: this type of transference had been mentioned at the previous meeting as characteristic of the obsessional but the patient under consideration was not submitted as a classical obsessional sufferer.

She had come to M.F. for analysis, having heard him speak at a meeting, because of difficulties in sexual relationships. At the time of entering analysis she had a boy friend and she confronted M.F. with the quasi-Kleinian interpretations that this man had been in the habit of making about her behaviour. She plunged straight into infantile material but M.F. felt that nothing she said could be relied upon, it had no body in it. This description could hardly be applied to the patient herself. In this first stage of the therapy M.F. accepted the implied challenge and offered 'better' interpretations than the boy friend.

The second stage of the analysis found the patient showing signs of wanting to masturbate in the interview and gradually revealing a sex-magic masturbatory system, stimulated by Fordham's deliberate usage of sexually cathected words. This system included the idea of her taking in all M.F.'s secretions and excretions, good objects, to counteract her internalised bad ones. She felt that the analyst, being a Jungian, was shocked and there was some discussion of the handling of this.

Ruth Strauss here suggested that the patient needed the idea of Jungian order to control her own chaos. Fred Plaut wanted to know from where the patient got the idea that M.F. was, on one occasion, pale with shock. It was agreed that she had seized upon an incidental fluctuation of complexion and incorporated it into her fantasies about the analyst. At this stage of the analysis, M.F. insisted upon increasing the frequency of interviews from two to four per week, telling the patient that this was necessary to obtain continuity for both their sakes. This was felt by the group to speak of M.F.'s countertransference. The patient accepted the change gladly but soon produced violent resistances based on money. She insisted that M.F. had no sense of reality about money but in fact she would have spasms of excessive spending upon clothes etc., a pattern that had to do with the contrast between her father's careful and her mother's erratic attitude towards money. Ruth Strauss felt that this resistance was due to the patient's fear of the strength of the transference/countertransference. The increase in interviews made her feel accepted but this made her anxious: she would rather keep the analyst at arm's length.

M.F. described the fluctuating and violent emotional relationship that ensued as the hard core of the transference in which the analyst is deeply involved and which has to be lived through. He described how the patient got to the stage of saying he was God – which he accepted. This acceptance was challenged by Fred Plaut and led to a discussion of getting into or caught by the patient's magic. Fred Plaut and Gordon Prince seemed to agree that with obsessionals particularly active manoeuvres were sometimes needed to overcome early transference resistance and gave examples; but M.F. considered that these only dealt with superficialities and did not touch the core of the transference. He denied that he was using magic when stimulating the patient with cathected words. He compared the manoeuvre to giving a child a toy which he could use to express his magic.

A crisis arose in this analysis, when the patient found she had an early carcinoma of the breast. M.F. accepted this as a synchronicity. He refused to visit the patient in hospital, where she had an acute anxiety when she experienced the presence of God and the grace of God. This carried her through the stress of the necessary operation.

When able to resume the analysis she asserted that the analysis had caused the carcinoma (the excessive excitement of her breasts, which was not relieved). M.F. did not take this up. As the analysis proceeded, she was able to separate two kinds of sexual excitement: (1) Loving, in which there was no breast feeling and which led to sleep; (2) Lust, which she felt to be destructive. Michael Fordham was able to relate this dichotomy to the whole pattern of her infantile and later actual sexual experience.

Ruth Strauss observed that M.F. had analysed this transference reductively and the group ended the session in agreement that its members often did this but seldom discussed it at 25, Park Crescent.

(Recorded by GSP)

TRANSFERENCE GROUP MEETING, 9 FEBRUARY 1954

Hella was still away and Gordon was absent owing to illness in the family. The Self hid behind Michael and popped up from time to time to put out its tongue at Fred (Dr Plaut).

MICHAEL   (referring to Mary's interpretations of his case):   I sympathise with them but I can't get at them. They might work well if Mary gave them.

FRED   (triumphantly):   Then it does depend on who gives them!

MICHAEL: No it doesn't. It's because it's something which has come out of her and is integrated. The personality of the analyst is only significant in superficial ways.

RUTH: Yet the personality tends to constellate certain projections.

MARY: Is it true that different analysts may constellate different things and that other things may get left out?

FRED   (harking back to something he feels Michael has wriggled out of):   What do you mean by 'work': it might work if somebody else said it?

MICHAEL   (keeping up a patter while he changes the rabbit to a more convenient pocket):   This kind of transference goes on whatever you do or say, as long as you don't do anything outrageous and don't make too many irrelevant interpretations. It just works itself through. The form would be different with a woman but not the essential process. That's why it takes years.

FRED: But surely we all know of patients who go to another analyst after many years and then get at something which has never been touched.

MICHAEL: It may seem so at first, that is the honeymoon stage. Then you get back to the same old thing. It seems to me that what happens is that the patient gets stuck at a resistance, then the analyst feels guilty because he can't get through it and he gives the patient an opportunity to go off. I don't.

RUTH: But there are always resistances. Wouldn't that mean an eternal analysis?

MICHAEL: No. A number of analyses come to a termination.

FRED (foiled, retreats to ground held in second meeting): I can't help feeling there's a theoretical plan in Michael's diagram. It presupposes a perfectly integrated analyst, that all the archetypes are in harmony in the analyst.

MICHAEL: I left a space for the mutual chaos.

FRED: But you've got the analyst in a circle with all the archetypes inside. That makes the analyst God.

MICHAEL (blandly): Yes.

RUTH: Might I introduce a modification? It depends on whether the analyst is capable of carrying the archetypal projections.

FRED: It's theoretical! It's impossible!

MICHAEL: If the Self is constellated, the analyst has to work with such projections.

FRED: The Father and I are one. I don't believe it!

RUTH: You *do* carry the Self but you hope for a relationship later.

MICHAEL: I can think of one patient with whom I felt I was analysing out of the Self. I was prepared to let anything happen and feel integrated about it.

FRED: How can you tell you are integrated?

MICHAEL: What you can't tell is irrelevant. You just are the Self for long periods.

FRED: That's bad! How will the patient find the human being behind it?

MICHAEL: The Ego is part of the Self.

FRED: I don't believe that either.

MICHAEL: I'm often accused of being inhuman. I have a stock of replies to this: 'it's not my business to be human; otherwise I shan't be doing my analytical job'.

FRED: You separate yourself from the job. You say: 'I'm the Self
             in my job but not outside – there I'm human'.

MICHAEL   (charmingly):   I don't believe what you say matters really.
             The patient brings the Self to you as a problem and you
             become it. It is not a voluntary process. What you are makes
             a difference as the analysis progresses – not in the Self
             projection stage. (Ruth gives an example.) There is no
             possible thing you can't be.

FRED: But certain roles you are more frequently.

MICHAEL: I agree, one gets certain roles at certain times in one's work.
             Some analysts have bees in their bonnets. That's bad!

FRED   (seeing Michael through aroma of bees):   Stock replies are
             that. They make me squirm! (He tries to manoeuvre Michael
             into contradicting himself and fails. Mary gives an example
             of a Self projection to liven things up again.) Do *you* say
             you're God?

MARY: No, I don't *say* it.

MICHAEL   (brightly):   I do!

MARY: That seems to me like using magic. (Michael agrees.)

FRED   (wringing his hands):   What happens to analysts who are
             God? It terrifies me!

RUTH: It does something to analysts but does it have an effect on
             the whole personality?

MICHAEL   (to Fred):   Does a Self projection call out everything
             you've got?

FRED: I don't trust myself to have enough consciousness to know
             but it hasn't in recent years. It did when I started.

RUTH: Was that regrettable? Did you want to get over it?

MICHAEL: The effect of the Self is evident in analysts. Very few don't
             think they're the only ones who are any good.

FRED: Jung told me that. Then you can't even talk to any other
             analyst as you are the only God!

MARY   (innocently):   Michael is rather like God: inscrutable,
             detached and good-looking – which helps a lot.

MICHAEL   (looks pleased but can't quite take it):   I think Fred answers
             that description!

MARY: Except he is not detached.

FRED: Now we're talking about personalities.

MICHAEL: No. We're talking about the damage analysis does to
             analysts. I have a perfect analyst in the corner of the room

(points to the ceiling). He makes comments. Sometimes he disappears; then I know he's got into me.

FRED: When I'm depressed, seeing patients helps. I think it's a bad sign. It argues in favour of inflation from the patients' projections. The supposedly contained archetypes contain the analyst.

RUTH: You could arrive at a more positive conclusion. If you couldn't get out of the depression you would have no contact with the patient. As this doesn't happen, something in you has been activated which gets you out of it.

MARY: Once when I was most depressed and humiliated, I found myself analysing brilliantly with no trouble at all.

FRED   (seeing light):   You stopped being clever!

MICHAEL   (musing):   This God inflation business doesn't seem to happen to the younger analysts.

MARY: I think it's something to do with training in groups. You can't get far with an inflation in a group!

(Enter Fred – Exit Self)

(Reported by Mary Williams)

Glossary

Active imagination: active imagination was described by Jung as 'a sequence of fantasies produced by deliberate concentration' (*CW* 9, i, para. 101); within analysis it 'is a method of introspection for observing the stream of interior images' (ibid., para. 319). This involved the analyst's and patient's contemplation of the impersonal archetypal features of the dreams and images the patient produced. During the sessions the imagery produced by the patients was related to historical, alchemical and mythological parallels, but not to personal history and experience. The purpose was to integrate the images into the self. It treated the material as symbolic rather than concrete and its perspective was teleological. It saw the archetype as something which could not be reduced and the analytic task as finding a new route out of an old impasse.

Actions of the self: the most frequently described actions of the self are those covered by the dynamic activity of *deintegration* and *reintegration*. However, those behaviours and actions which can be described by Jung's phrase as an 'irrational fact' and which retrospectively are shown to be significant in the life of the individual are also actions of the self. Thus Fordham in his memoir reflects on the apparent irrationality of not accepting a consultant's post when he was a far from secure young doctor, and considers that his behaviour was evidence of an action of the self since it led him to concentrate his energies on building up the Society of Analytical Psychology and the development of Jung's ideas in clinical practice. Jung in his autobiography described how after his break-up with Freud and following the turmoil of his breakdown, he found in the drawing of mandalas a new peacefulness. A state of inner calm came over him which he felt was especially significant. He described the non-linear approach to the self (for him playing and drawing) as a circumambulation with an overall directional aim towards a centre

(Jung 1963, p. 196). The making of these drawings was an action of the self. The centre for him was in the mandala and it was this that Fordham imaginatively took hold of and postulated could be the core in infancy out of which, by deintegration and reintegration, the infant came into relation with the environment. For Jung this mandala imagery gave him stability; he wrote: 'I knew that in finding the mandala as an experience of the self I had attained what for me was the ultimate' (ibid.). It was an experience of the self which transcended the limitations of the ego's consciousness and took Jung forward out of the impasse he felt stuck in. Since all actions of the self potentially contribute to individuation, another way of describing what happened to Jung might be as the realization of the self. Retrospectively this could look like the development of one's self after one's own image.

Alpha function: a term proposed by the psychoanalyst W. Bion. Alpha function refers to the unknown process of making meaning out of sensations, to the conversion of sensations or sense data into mental contents. See also *beta element*. (Hinshelwood [1991] has made a clear summary of Bion's theory of thinking.)

Analysis as a dialectical procedure: 'Analysis as a dialectical procedure is based on processes which neither I nor my patient can control consciously, and that analysis depends on the relatively greater experience of the analyst in *deintegrating* so as to meet the patient's *disintegration*' (Fordham 1957a, p. 97, my italics).

Analytical psychology: this is the term used by Jung after 1913 to refer to his psychology. 'Analytical psychology is daily concerned, in the normal and sick alike, with disturbances of conscious apprehension caused by the admixture of archetypal images' (*CW* 8, para. 279). Jung distinguished analytical psychology from psychoanalysis and from Adler's individual psychology. He refers to the analytical as deriving 'from the fact that this branch of psychology developed out of the original Freudian psychoanalysis. Freud identified psychoanalysis with his theory of sex and repression, and thereby riveted it to a doctrinaire framework. For this reason I avoid the expression "psychoanalysis" when I am discussing other than merely technical matters' (para. 701). He continues with a description of psychoanalysis as a 'therapeutic method' (para. 702) with a 'rationalistic conception of the unconscious' (para. 708). He describes the difference in emphasis he brings to his psychology which conceives of the unconscious, not as the repository only of what has been repressed from consciousness, but as creating new contents and the source of much positive activity, creativity and undirected thoughts. He thought of analytical psychology as complementary to psychoanalysis.

An analytical psychologist is someone trained by a recognized institute in Jung's archetypal psychology.

Anima and animus: the anima is the contra-sexual archetypal image in man, the animus in woman. The anima is the imaginative and inspirational aspect of male psychology, which often takes the form of an alluring and potentially dangerous female figure. The animus is the discriminating, conceptualizing, classifying and meaning-enhancing element in female psychic life. Jung wrote that behind the animus was 'the archetype of meaning: just as the anima is the archetype of life itself' (*CW* 9, i, para. 66). The danger in the anima and animus is to be found in the way a one-sided involvement with this aspect of the archetype can lead to upheaval, turmoil and change, especially if the person is in the grip of the image. This can occur when the image and an actual person become confused. They are examples of opposites within the psyche (see *theory of opposites*). For men and women integration of this psychic principle is one of the tasks of life, usually expressed in intimate relationships.

Archetype: Jung's discovery of archetypes and archetypal imagery was one of his most significant contributions to knowledge. One way he described archetypes was: 'Archetypes are typical modes of apprehension, and wherever we meet with uniform and regularly recurring modes of apprehension we are dealing with an archetype, no matter whether its mythological character is recognised or not' (*CW* 8, para. 280). Gordon in her glossary has defined archetype as:

> A metapsychological, a conceptual, model to account for the recurrence and apparent universality in man in different cultures and in different epochs of certain experiences and images, the archetypal images. [See *collective unconscious*.] The activation of archetypal contents – whether personages, themes or sensuous patterns – is usually accompanied by strong affect and powerful fantasies. Jung has described the archetype as a psychosomatic entity, whose physical expression takes the form of instinctive activity and its mental expression the form of images. He has also compared them to the invisible presence of the crystal lattice in a saturated solution. The archetypes, so Jung makes clear, are devoid of content to begin with until personal experience renders them visible and hence potentially conscious. They may also be thought of as psychic 'programmers'.
>
> (Gordon 1978)

Fordham used Jung's term, archetype, 'a dynamic structure closely related to instinct' (Fordham 1976a, pp. 5–6), to refer to the expression in children and adults of impulses 'originating in neurophysiological structures and biochemical changes'. What this meant was that Jung's description of the bi-polarity of the archetypes – that they comprised a spiritual and an instinctual pole – could now be thought of as bringing together in infancy and childhood the body and the psyche. The spiritual pole of the archetype would give rise to fantasies and the instinctual to impulses.

Archetypal images: 'The form through which archetypal processes can become visible, conscious and hence experienced. According to Jung, archetypal images represent the goals of the instincts (Gordon 1978) (see *collective unconscious*). When these archetypal images appear in a person's life they combine aspects of the unconscious and momentary elements of their conscious situation. An archetypal image refers both to the inner world of unconsciousness and to the aspect of the inner world which is externally in consciousness, as if the person who experiences the image has one eye looking inwards and one eye looking outwards. This does not mean that the images themselves are innate or inherited. Archetypal images arise from processes which are initially impersonal, but which become more and more personal. Archetypal images refer to relationships to significant objects. While their origin may be impersonal, archetypal images in their impact and intensity express what is most personal and primitive in the relationship referred to by the images. Their universality is in their form. It sometimes happens that an analyst accepts a projection from a patient 'in a whole-hearted manner making no direct attempt to help the patient to sort out what belongs to him, what to the analyst, and what to neither as well as both. On the contrary they will allow themselves to become this image bodily, to "incarnate" it bodily for the patient' (Plaut 1956, p. 15). This gave rise to the term to 'incarnate an archetypal image', which is, of course, literally impossible.

Archetypal personages: 'Personages experienced either in phantasy or through projection onto an external person, characterised by the fact that they appear in different cultures, at different times and often feature in myths, fairy tales, art and literature; e. g. the great mother, the phallic mother, the eternal youth, the trickster, the witch, the magician, the wise old man, the divine child, etc' (Gordon 1978).

Autism: a mental state where the sufferer lives without reference to the environment in a state of mind in which trust and normal communication is often absent. In its extreme form it has similarities to mental deficiency and psychosis. Some classification systems distinguish this extreme form of autism from secondary autism where the sufferer has no mental deficiency. Autism according to Fordham's research is a disorder

of the self arising from failures in deintegration and needs to be considered
on a spectrum, thereby allowing different syndromes to combine to give
an individual pattern to the disorder. Compare the case of Alan with
James (Chapter 7).

Beta element: a term proposed by the psychoanalyst Wilfred Bion. Beta
elements can be raw sense data or other accumulations of experience
which are not, and cannot be, thought about, but which have to be
evacuated. The evacuation of beta elements into another person is a
pathological form of projective identification. For a beta element to be
converted into an alpha element it has to go through a process which
converts it into a mental content which has meaning. Bion called this
process 'alpha function'.

Collective unconscious: 'This is a concept developed by Jung. It refers
to that part of the mind that contains impulses, drives and fantasies that
have never yet been conscious but are characteristic of humans in
general. In other words, in the collective unconscious lies the communal
and collective heritage of the species, man. The degree of unconsciousness is likely to be greater in the collective unconscious than in the
personal unconscious' (Gordon 1978). Jung described a three-layered
hypothetical internal structure consisting of consciousness, personal
unconsciousness and a deeper level of impersonal unconsciousness. In a
geographical image he described consciousness as the island in the
ocean, the personal unconscious as the area just below the water level,
consisting of repressed experiences of which we are only partly aware,
such as forgotten memories or infantile impulses; while deep down
connecting us to the earth and the millennia of human and animal
experience lay the collective unconscious.

Employing a comparative method, Jung described the universality of
certain uniform and regular unconscious behaviours across all peoples
and races. These instinctual and spiritual behaviours had universal characteristics, implying that there was a strong pull within man to experience
life along historical lines. The presence of a religious function within
man, for instance, can be traced through the ages in its changing
manifestations. So too can myths, which have impersonal as well as
personal content.

In the deeper layers of the unconscious Jung imagined nodal points
around which experience and emotion gathered, such that they acquired
characteristics which he described in terms of the images that these
nodal points gave rise to. He called those structures 'archetypes' and the
images 'archetypal images'. The images are not inherited but Jung
postulated that there was an inherited predisposition to form images. A

contemporary analogy which has some similar features would be to say that research into language acquisition indicates that, universally, up to puberty human beings are 'hardwired' to produce syntactic structures, but each person learns their own language. Mary Williams pointed out using clinical examples that the personal and the collective unconscious could be separated for the purposes of exposition but that it was undesirable to separate them in practice. She encapsulated this in an influential formulation: '(1) that nothing in the personal experience needs to be repressed unless the ego feels threatened by its archetypal power; and (2) that the archetypal activity which forms the individual's myth is dependent on material supplied by the personal unconscious' (Williams 1963, p. 49).

Compensation: a term used by Jung to describe

> an inherent self-regulation of the psychic apparatus. In this sense, I regard the activity of the *unconscious* as a balancing of the one-sidedness of the general *attitude* produced by the function of *consciousness*. . . . The activity of consciousness is *selective*. Selection means *direction*. But direction requires the *exclusion of everything irrelevant*. This is bound to make the conscious *orientation* one-sided. The contents that are excluded and inhibited by the chosen direction sink into the unconscious, where they form a counterweight to the conscious orientation. The strengthening of this counter position keeps pace with the increase of conscious one-sidedness until finally a noticeable tension is produced . . . in the end the tension becomes so acute that the repressed unconscious contents break through. . . . As a rule, the unconscious compensation does not run counter to consciousness, but is rather a balancing or supplementing of the conscious orientation.
>
> (Jung, *CW* 6, para. 694)

Containment: this term was used by Jung in his description of the marriage relationship, where personalities which are often very different are contained psychologically one by the other (*CW* 17). The term has subsequently (and without attribution) been made use of by psychoanalysts, especially Bion, to refer to a theory of development in which the infant through a process of projective identification puts into the mother experiences which it cannot make sense of and which the mother through her reverie does make sense of and returns to the infant in an emotionally digestible form. By extension this has come to describe patient–analyst contact. A vast literature has emerged in psychoanalysis on containment, including the examination of language – e.g. does language contain the feeling or feeling the language or both at different times? Meltzer distinguished container/contained from projective identification by highlighting Bion's use of the term container to refer to a place, with a boundary that was safe, private and within which thinking could occur. Its opposite was a claustrum. Projective identification he distinguished from intrusive identification, the former being concerned with communicating, the latter with omnipotent phantasy and action such as control of the other person from the inside (Meltzer 1986b). In Fordham's theory the mother who receives her infant's deintegrative experiences makes sense of them and in so doing helps the infant reintegrate is a containing mother. Containment is now recognized to be essential for healthy development. (See *mandala symbolism*.)

Countertransference: originally this referred to the analyst's response to his patient, arising from what was projected into him by the patient. It came to be used as information about the patient (see *syntonic transference/countertransference*). Fordham argued for a more accurate usage:

> apart from an analyst's appropriate reactions, his transitory projections and displacements cease to be called countertransference since they represent the analyst acting on and reacting to his patient . . . . It is when the interacting systems become obstructed that a special label is needed and, to my mind, it is then that the term *countertransference* is appropriate.
>
> (Fordham 1979c)

Delusional transference: the characteristic of a delusional transference is that the patient develops a fixed idea about the therapist which is not influenceable by reason or evidence. Further investigation of this in very disturbed patients can often reveal the sense in the delusion, namely how it has arisen.

Deintegrate: 'That which differentiates out of the matrix of the self through the process of deintegration. Like the ethologists' "innate release mechanism", the deintegrate potentiates a "readiness for experience, a readiness to perceive and act" even though there is as yet "not an actual perception or action"' (Fordham 1957a, p. 127; Gordon 1978). Fordham says of a deintegrate that it is 'endowed with and is continuous with the self' (Fordham 1985a, p. 54). A deintegrate of the self would retain characteristics of wholeness. A deintegrate could be an instinctual act, such as the hungry baby's cry, i.e. it would be contributing to the organism's biological adaptation, or it could be the creation of an image with potentially symbolic meaning. In the former example the deintegrate is manifesting itself objectively; in the latter it is subjective. The most significant deintegrate of the self is the ego.

Deintegration: 'The spontaneous division of the self into parts – a manifest necessity if consciousness is ever to arise. . . . It is the spontaneous property of the self behind ego formation' (Fordham 1957a, p. 117).

> In essence, deintegration and reintegration describe a fluctuating state of learning in which the infant opens itself to new experiences and then withdraws in order to reintegrate and consolidate those experiences. During a deintegrative activity, the infant maintains continuity with the main body of the self (or its centre), while venturing into the external world to accumulate experience in motor action and sensory stimulation. . . . Such a concept of the self brings a new dimension to both depth psychology and developmental psychology, for it is now conceived to be a dynamic structure through whose activity the infant's emotional and ego growth takes place.
>
> (Fordham 1988f, p. 64)

Depressive position: in the British psychoanalytic object-relations school, evidence has been put forward for the child's wish cannibalistically to attack the breast, the hypothesized sequel to which is the child becoming anxious and concerned about the damage he's done (depressed but not clinically so) and his trying to make reparation. Ruthlessness and concern come together, and with this a considerable expansion of consciousness. This is a simplified description of the depressive position and the way opposites can combine, i.e. of individuation processes in childhood.

Ego: 'The ego grows out of the interaction between deintegrates and the environmental mother, and her extensions. The interaction produces many self representations, the most stable and prominent of which is the ego' (Fordham 1987b, p. 362). 'It is the self which integrates the ego fragments and so produces the ego centre'; and later Fordham wrote: 'Structuring of the personality comes about as the result of the rhythm of integration and deintegration of the self, for it creates an ego nucleus' (Fordham 1957a, pp. 126–8). The purpose of the ego is to maintain consciousness and within it are contained feelings of personal identity. It is the reality-testing organ of the mind, the centre of consciousness. Jung described the ego as the exponent in consciousness of the self. 'The ego stands to the self as the moved to the mover. . . . The self, like the unconscious, is an *a priori* existent out of which the ego evolves. It is an unconscious prefiguration of the ego. It is not I who create myself, rather I happen to myself' (*CW* 11, para. 391). This description of the ego works well enough until unconscious contents of the ego are considered, especially those which have never been conscious, i.e. that have not been subject to repression, such as the ego defences. This suggests that there must be unconscious features of the ego and these have come to be thought of as located in the shadow.

Ego-dystonic: something which is unacceptable to or incompatible with a person's idea of himself.

Fantasy material in analysis: analytical psychologists treat the fantasy material in analysis ontogenetically as *reactivations* of past fixations, and think of the material as a purposeful attempt to resolve the conflict which exists in the present in the consulting room.

Fusion: there is an early stage in human development when subject and object are less distinct, when the experience of the baby is mainly pleasurable, which can be thought of as a blissful fused state, fusion. This state is, according to Fordham, transitory and probably connected partly to the absence of a developed perceptual apparatus and partly to the avoidance of the pain of consciousness. It is also often described as the blissful goal of regression. Infant observations have revealed, however, that the idea that infants are part of their parent's unconscious – i.e. that there is a primary state of fusion between mother and infant – is not correct. This idea also would be incompatible with the infant's having an original self in the way Fordham has described. This do not mean that episodic experiences of feeling as if a fused state of mind has occurred cannot and do not happen. Rather Fordham is pointing to a change in the Jungian model of development, from an initial state of *participation mystique* to one where the infant has an original separate self.

Identification: 'A process by which a person fuses or confuses his own identity with someone else's' (Gordon 1978). Jung called it a form of 'unconscious imitation'. He also described it as a process which can be applied to parts of oneself so that it can occur that a person identifies with an attribute of theirs and thinks that this is what they are really like. In psychoanalysis, however, identification is thought of as an important process in the development of personality.

Identity: Jung uses the term to denote 'a psychological conformity' which is unconscious and which precedes identification. This conformity signified the absence of conscious differentiation between subject and object, and in that sense refers to a primitive form of projection. Identity he thought characterized early states of mind in infancy and the unconscious of adults 'which, in so far as it has not become a content of consciousness, remains in a permanent state of identity with objects' (*CW* 6, para. 741). In Jung's conception of identity the infant did not have a primary self. Fordham's work has substantially revised this way of thinking about infancy, since he has shown that actions of the self are on a continuum, beginning with the first deintegrative and reintegrative sequences. In contrast, Jung's ideas are linked to his idea of the unconscious of the infant being close to the collective unconscious and the unconscious of his parents. Identity also refers to the sense of oneself existing over time.

Individuation: 'The process by which individual beings are formed and differentiated. In particular, it is the development of the psychological individual as being distinct from the general, collective psychology. Individuation therefore is a process of differentiation having as its goal the development of the individual personality' (Jung, *CW* 6, para. 757). 'Individuation is practically the same as the development of consciousness out of the original state of identity' (ibid., para. 762). 'What therefore is the essence of individuation? It is surely the progressive realisation of our own worth, both positive and negative, in relation to the realities of spiritual and instinctual life, i.e. the contents of the inner world, and the outer world comprising people and the society in which we live' (Fordham 1973e, p. 108). For Jung individuation was a process of the self whereby the individual gradually became free from the opposites by a symbolical solution ('a suspension of the will') which allowed them to have complete equality. The opposites in this instance were the self and the ego.

> When there is full parity of the opposites, attested by the ego's absolute participation in both, this necessarily leads to a suspension of the will, for the will can no longer operate when every motive has an equally strong counter motive. Since life cannot tolerate a standstill, a damming up of vital energy results, and this would lead to an insupportable condition did not the tension of the opposites produce a new, uniting function that transcends them.
>
> (Jung, *CW* 6, para. 824)

Infant observation: the systematic study of an infant from birth until two years. The observer, usually a person undergoing training in analytical psychotherapy, visits a baby and its caretakers in their family setting weekly for one hour. Notes are written up of the observation with attention being paid to the emotional states of the infant and the mother/ principal caretaker. These notes are then discussed in a seminar led by someone experienced in infant–mother observation.

Inner world: 'All that I experience is psychic. Even physical pain is a psychic image which I experience; my sense impressions – for all that they force upon me a world of impenetrable objects occupying space – are psychic images, and these alone constitute my immediate experience, for they alone are the immediate objects of my consciousness' (Jung, *CW* 8, para. 680). The inner world does not have to feel inner to the person whose world it is (see the case of Alan, ch. 7).

Introjection: the process by which the qualities or functions of an object or a person external to the individual are incorporated, absorbed and so put inside him and then experienced as an inner, personal possession (Gordon 1978).

Libido: Jung uses the concept 'libido' as synonymous with 'psychic energy', irrespective of the particular area or channel into which it happens to have been drawn. This contrasts with Freud's use of the term libido. In his first formulation he thought of libido as the energy attached specifically to the sexual instincts; in his second formulation he distinguished ego-libido from object-libido; and in his third formulation he defined libido as the energy of Eros or the life instinct, while another form of energy was thought to be attached to Thanatos, the death instinct (Gordon 1978).

Mandala symbolism: Jung discovered that mandalas were 'cryptograms concerning the state of the self'. The discovery was gradual. It began with him sketching in a notebook. He noticed the form of his drawings, which were circles, with a centre, framed by a square and with the whole area loosely divided into four. He saw that the variations in these drawings corresponded to the state of his self: 'In them I saw the self – that is my whole being actively at work' (Jung 1963, p. 187). At first Jung did not know what to make of that and felt isolated. Then he was sent Richard Wilhelm's manuscript of *The Secret of the Golden Flower* and saw that the mandala was an important Taoist symbol of wholeness. Combining these experiences with his work with patients, who in dreams produced a series of mandalas, he began to work out their significance, not just as a symbol of the self, but also as a way of understanding how his fragmented patients sought and found containment. In Jung's examinations of mandala symbolism he described the relationship between the centre, the space around the centre and the circumference. The centre, the contents which surrounded it and the boundary circumference represented the self, which Jung differentiated from the ego. Fordham has compared the impact of the early feeds on the baby's mind to Jung's work on mandala symbolism: 'The whole object might then be compared with a mandala that has a nipple at the centre and various objects placed within the magic circle' (Fordham 1988f, p. 65). For Fordham to liken the breast to a mandala was to root his studies of infancy in the symbolism of the self and the way it unfolded through interaction. This was because mandala symbolism had been such a significant factor in Jung's theory of the self: 'they [mandala symbols] signify nothing less than a psychic centre of the personality not to be identified with the ego' (*CW* 12, para. 126).

Mysticism: mystical experiences when applied to psychology frequently denote mystification, rather than a distinct experience with recognizable qualities. The first thing to be said about mystical experiences is that they are a form of consciousness which have a quality of reconciliation about them. All descriptions of mystical experiences contain a description of the impact of the experience, its clarity and importance, yet at the same time retain something inexpressible about them. William James (1902) has identified four characteristics of these experiences: ineffability; a noetic quality; transience; and passivity. Ineffability, in itself a negative characteristic, is the first and is more a state of feeling than a state of the intellect; its quality has to be experienced. As to the noetic quality, these experiences are accompanied by the feeling of having understood something, a revelation, an insight, a new truth. The third, transience, acknowledges that the state rarely lasts for long, although its recurrence is not without development. Finally, passivity is the feature which accompanies the feeling of having been in the grip of a superior power. Mystical states are often recorded by poets, scientists and imaginative people and are experienced by them as an irrational form of consciousness, usually with a revelatory content. Christian mysticism is a special version of mysticism which has within it an idea that the devout person by vocation, training and application of a rigorous regime of denial can overcome the physical limitations of his body and step by step approach nearer to God. As a historical phenomenon it flourished in Europe during medieval times. The church had considerable difficulty assimilating mystics and the penalties for unorthodoxy were severe.

Numinous experience: this refers to experience which has a particular significance for the individual, is impressive, awesome and involuntary in its occurrence. There is a visible and invisible quality of people and objects which can be numinous. Another feature often written about in connection with religious experience is the transcendent quality to the deep experience of the numinous. Jung wrote: 'The numinosum . . . is a dynamic agency or effect not caused by an arbitrary act of will. On the contrary, it seizes and controls the human subject, who is always rather its victim than its creator. . . . The numinosum is either a quality belonging to a visible object or the influence of an invisible presence that causes a peculiar alteration of consciousness' (*CW* 11, para. 6).

Oedipus complex: originally described by Freud as unconscious feelings centring on the wish to possess the parent of the opposite sex and eliminate the parent of the same sex. Its successful resolution he thought was through positive identification with the parent of the same sex. Kleinians have continued Freud's work on the centrality of the Oedipus complex by adding the dimension of phantasy which has revealed the importance of pre-genital components (oral and anal) in early development. Klein's work on those led on to her theory of the depressive position. Jung differed from Freud in his attitude to the Oedipus complex in that Jung thought its significance was not in its actual wishes but more in its symbolic content. Therapeutically he placed more emphasis on the fact that it gave evidence of the reactivation of regressive wishes and therefore required attention to be paid to what was happening in the present which was blocking the person's adaptation (*CW* 4, para. 570). Jung thought that 'the Freudian school got stuck at the Oedipus motif, i.e. the archetype of incest. . . . They failed to recognise that . . . sexuality is not the only possible dominant in the psychic process' (*CW* 10, para. 659). Jung described the regressive features of the Oedipus complex as retreating back to the 'presexual stage of earliest infancy', where 'Fear of incest turns into fear of being devoured by the mother' (*CW* 5, para. 654). By doing this he was pointing to the primitive, archetypal, non-sexual (in the sense of pregenital) features of the Oedipus complex. The 'famous incest tendency', he wrote, has changed at this level to a 'Jonah-and-the-whale-complex', with variants such as 'the witch who eats children' (*CW* 5, para. 654). (In my view Klein's work on the importance of the phantasy content (pre-genital) of the Oedipus complex is a clinical development compatible with Jung's ideas about the archetypal nature and symbolic content of these feelings.)

Original self: this is the term used to describe the original state of integration of the infant. Later, through the deintegrative and reintegrative process, this original self will come into relation to the environment, consciousness will arise and experiences of inner and outer reality begin to take·shape in the mind.

Part-object: an object in analytic language is 'that towards which action or desire is directed; that which the subject requires in order to achieve instinctual satisfaction; that to which the subject relates himself. In psychoanalytical writings, objects are nearly always persons, parts of persons, or symbols of one or the other' (Rycroft 1968). A part-object can therefore be part of a person, and thus the relationship to it can be partial in meaning. The term also applies to hypothetical stages of development, where part-object relating refers to using people or parts of them for one's own gratification, and whole-object relating to the recognition of the needs and feelings of the object being related to. The psychology of part-objects has been studied in great detail by Kleinians (see Hinshelwood 1991, p. 378).

Participation mystique: a term borrowed by Jung from the writings of the anthropologist Lévy-Bruhl, which denotes 'a peculiar kind of psychological connection with objects, and consists in the fact that the subject cannot clearly distinguish himself from the object but is bound to it by a direct relationship which amounts to partial *identity*. This identity results from an *a priori* oneness of subject and object' (Jung, *CW* 6, para. 781).

Personal unconscious: that part of the unconscious described by Jung as containing personal experiences, feelings, wishes, impulses and memories which have been repressed because they are painful, ethically unacceptable or ego-dystonic for some other reason.

Primal scene: 'The primal scene is the patient's (child's) conception of his parents having intercourse regarded as an idea around which phantasy has been woven rather than as a recollection of something actually perceived' (Rycroft 1968).

Projection: 'The expulsion of a subjective content into an object; it is the opposite of *introjection*.' This was how Jung described it (*CW* 6, para. 783). It is an unconscious process and while it often operates as a means of ridding the psyche of uncomfortable experience it can also be a way of getting rid of a 'good' part of oneself such as in self-depreciation.

Projective identification: a term first used by Klein to describe the way in which part of the ego is unconsciously pushed into another person or part of them for aggressive and controlling purposes. Subsequently it has been described as a normal way in which an infant communicates with his mother by conveying to her his state of mind by inducing in her feelings which he is having. The difference between these two forms of projective identification is that the former is motivated by the desire to evacuate something unpleasant and the latter by the desire to communicate a state of mind.

Psyche, Jung's model of: Jung's model of the psyche is of a dynamic self-regulating system with its own energy, which he called libido. This energy is neutral, it is not a force, and it flows between two opposing poles rather like electricity. These poles Jung called the opposites and the more tension there was between them the more energy was generated. Some examples of opposites are consciousness and unconsciousness, progression and regression, extroversion and introversion. Opposites could also be between functions, such as thinking and feeling, or within a function, such as positive and negative feelings. The principle which governed Jung's conception of psychic energy was enantiodromia, which he described as 'sooner or later everything runs into its opposite' (*CW* 7, para. 111), or becomes its opposite. And Jung, being a psychologist, thought that 'Everything is relative, because everything rests on an inner polarity; for everything is a phenomenon of energy' (*CW* 7, para. 115). Part of the economics of this model of the psyche is compensation: for instance unconscious attitudes compensating for conscious ones, especially the idea that what is repressed from consciousness will find expression through the unconscious.

Psychoanalysis: a method of treatment for the neuroses invented by Freud, and a theory of the development of the personality. The method requires of the patient that they should freely associate, that is report without inhibition or preparedness whatever comes into their mind during the session time. A key concept is transference, which is the emotional state of mind the patient brings to the analyst, frequently containing feelings associated with important figures in their personal history. The response of the analyst may consist of clarification, elucidation or interpretation, the latter bringing together conscious and unconscious content and process. Key concepts for the theory are: the existence of the unconscious as a repository for repressed affects, impulses, instinctual longings and thoughts; and defences against experiencing what is unconscious. The analysis of dreams is an important part of the process. Later, and with accelerated momentum in the 1950s and 1960s, psychoanalysts have investigated psychotic areas of the personality. A psychoanalyst is someone trained by a recognized institute in this method.

Reductive method of analysis: reductive analysis within the transference is 'the elucidation of complex structures and the resolution of them into their simpler components' (Fordham 1967b, p. 54). This approach involves the analysing of childhood as part of the transference. It reduces only the complexity of the unconscious structures (not the patient from an adult to a child). Jung recognized the importance of this method and identified it primarily with psychoanalysis and the doctrine of analysing repression. He was critical of this method mainly for its 'nothing but' approach and the tendency of Freudians to be dogmatic about the sexual theory, as if that were the whole story. He recognized its place in the early periods of all analysis but felt it could be destructive if continued too long. He was more interested in the inner world as a phenomenon deriving from what he called 'affectivity'. He thought that the complexes he had discovered in his patients through his association experiments were linked by emotion – that feelings were the currency of the mind, and fantasy its material form. Because he thought of libido as a neutral energy he did not subscribe to the Freudian theory of sublimation as the displacement of sexual energy into a desexualized form. He compared this idea to the 'alchemist's trick of turning the base into the noble' (*CW* 15, para. 53). Nor did he think that the unconscious consisted of only personal repressed material. For him 'the true reason for a neurosis always lies in the present' (*CW* 10, para. 363), and while detours into the past of the patient may be of interest to him, the search for explanatory causes was not, in his view, primary in psychotherapeutic 'cure'. Realization of the self, referred to as individuation by Jung, as a later stage of the analytic process, was brought forward by Fordham to include the early reductive periods of analysis. Theoretically the implication of this was that something more to do with the wholeness of the person than with their consciousness alone was activated in the analytic process, even when it was the analysis of childhood.

Reintegration: Fordham called the dynamic of the self deintegration and reintegration since the self was an integrate. Deintegration was the term used when referring to the energy going outwards towards objects and reintegration when the energy was returning to the self.

Self: Jung described the self as 'the subject of my total psyche, which also includes the unconscious' (*CW* 6, para. 706). He continues, 'In so far as psychic totality, consisting of both conscious and unconscious contents, is a postulate, it is a *transcendental* concept, for it presupposes the existence of unconscious factors on empirical grounds and thus characterises an entity that can be described only in part but, for the other part, remains at present unknowable and illimitable' (ibid., para. 789). The symbols of the self 'possess a distinct *numinosity*'. Fordham has suggested that it is not so much unknowable as inexperienceable. He has further pointed out that throughout Jung's writings are statements which indicate that 'the self is not the whole psyche-soma since the ego is no part of it' (Fordham 1985a, p. 23). Jung in his writings makes it clear that one of the main functions of the self within the psyche is integration. The self brings together all the elements and functions of the personality. In Fordham's work there is an original or primal self which is his way of describing the original integrate, the psychosomatic unity of the infant. This primary integrate is a phenomenonless state which develops by a process of deintegration and reintegration, with each reintegration forming a new dynamic equilibrium within the infant. The self as Fordham described it was the instigator as much as the receptor of infant experience. This biological idea, based on adaptation (almost a niche model of survival, where the niche adapts too), has become the most radical of all Fordham's discoveries. It has given rise to a model of ego development which is particularly Jungian (see Chapter 5). An adequate definition of the self is not, however, possible since the language used by Jung to describe it is abstract, metaphorical and without explanatory power. Fordham's understanding of the self as manifest in experience is that while its long-term aim is integrative 'it appears to be exceedingly disruptive while the individuation process is proceeding' (Fordham 1987b, p. 354). Both Jung and Fordham describe the self at times as an archetype. Fordham's latest position is that its significant feature is its dynamic quality. When the self is considered in relation to the ego it would seem, however, that the connection between the self and ego is archetypal in quality (see *ego*).

Self-object: 'When the object is mainly a record of reality, it may be called a reality object; when it is mainly constructed by the self and so records states of the self, made out of exteroceptive and introceptive sense data, then it may be called a self object. . . . It appears that self objects increase in affectively charged states, whilst in quiet contemplative exploring activities real objects predominate' (Fordham 1985a, p. 56). Experiences that are suffused with qualities of the infant's self are initially those that Jung referred to when describing 'identity'. 'Identity' is the precursor to states of identification and 'on it also depends the possibility of projection and introjection' (Jung, *CW* 6, para. 741). Fordham's thinking is based on observation of the infant's emerging capacity to refine its discriminations: 'According to self theory the self has boundaries by the time birth takes place as infant observations indicate; it also has potential for developing structures, but I assume they would require self objects finding representation in the ego. These objects would develop through deintegrative/integrative sequences' (Fordham 1985a, p. 56).

Shadow: the Jungian concept of the shadow ('the thing a person has no wish to be' (Jung, *CW* 16, para. 470) is the term used to describe those aspects of one's personality (usually repressed) which are embarrassing, awkward, shameful, aggressive, ungenerous and unlovable. In society it is the antisocial people and the outcasts who make up its shadow. For those who have not had any reductive analysis much of the shadow consists of infantile feelings, and the assimilation of these aspects of the shadow of the personality cannot be accomplished without analysing the infantile transference. A shadow unattended to increases in potency until it becomes unmanageable. The integration of the shadow is the route which leads to the self, since it is conceived that the uniting functions of the self enable whole reactions to occur, making it possible for us to react as individuals to experiences. As part of this integration of the shadow, Fordham thought, the Freudian fixation points could be usefully understood as 'centres of developing consciousness round which archetypal motifs, as deintegrates of the self, centre in alluring profusion' (Fordham 1957a, p. 83). This was important as it allowed the Jungians to use a more embodied language to describe their patient's conflicts.

Symbol: Jung distinguished symbols from signs. Signs stand for known things; symbols, on the other hand, he defined as: 'the best possible description or formulation of a relatively unknown fact, which is none the less known to exist or is postulated as existing' (*CW* 6, para. 814). By examining a symbol fully what is revealed is that it 'is a living thing, it is an expression for something that cannot be characterised in any other or better way. The symbol is alive only so long as it is pregnant with meaning' (*CW* 6, para. 816). It combines personal and impersonal elements, rational and irrational, is essentially paradoxical and is not indicative of a symptom, as is sometimes the case in psychoanalytic theory. Here a symbol is often taken to mean representing in consciousness an un- conscious idea, conflict or wish, which is a semiotic interpretation. Appreciation of the symbolic attitude in Jungian psychology therefore necessarily brings with it understanding of the way in which opposing elements within the psyche co-exist creatively, which is a hermeneutic approach. In any thorough-going analysis perhaps one of the most potent symbols which arises in some shape or form is that of the parental couple and the creativity of their intercourse, with all the concomitant conflicts that this gives rise to.

Synchronicity: 'The coincidence of a psychic state in the observer with a simultaneous objective, external event that corresponds to the psychic state or content where there is no evidence of a causal connection between the psychic state and the external event and where such a connection is not even conceivable' (Jung, *CW* 8, para. 984). The special phenomenon of synchronicity as opposed to synchronous events is that there is a lowering of ego consciousness allowing unconsciousness to flow into the space created by this *abaissement du niveau mental* with a concomitant experience of a meaningful kind. Having fish for lunch on Friday, 1 April, thinking of making an April Fish of someone (April Fool), noticing an inscription with the word fish on it, being shown a piece of embroidery with a fish on it and being told a dream by a patient in which a large fish swam towards her and landed at her feet – all happened to Jung on the same day but this was emphatically not an experience of synchronicity but of synchronous events. He said of it: 'There is no possible justification for seeing in this anything but a chance grouping. Runs or series which are composed of quite ordinary occurrences must for the present be regarded as fortuitous' (*CW* 8, para. 826). 'Synchronicity therefore consists of two factors. (a) An unconscious image comes into consciousness either directly (i.e. literally) or indirectly (symbolised or suggested) in the form of a dream, idea or premonition. (b) An objective situation coincides with this content' (*CW* 8, para. 858).

Synthetic method of analysis: this combined amplification of the archetypal images with active imagination and was also called prospective. Amplification involved the elaboration of the impersonal associations of the image, for instance by reference to literature or myth. It was as if Jung, the hermeneut, steered the patient out of the anchorage of his memories into the channel of the next period of his life. This method, he thought, was not suitable for people who were young or who had not integrated their childhood experiences. Fordham's influence at the SAP led to the dichotomy synthetic and reductive being viewed more as historical and to do with Freud and Jung's differences. Reductive analysis came to be understood as synthetic. (See also the relation of the personal to the collective unconscious.)

Syntonic transference/countertransference: the term syntonic transference/countertransference referred to the analyst's experience of parts of the patient which had been projected into him, and which were treated as information about the patient's state of mind. 'In analysis there are reactions on the part of the analyst which are syntonic and can make the patient more conscious, but these are different from the countertransference illusion, where the increase in consciousness will come about only if the analyst himself examines his own reaction' (Fordham 1957a, p. 91). Later Fordham was to review this concept and link it more to projective identification:

> I have come to think that the clinical experiences subsumed under this heading seem better considered in terms of an introject that has failed to become reprojected. The two unconscious processes, projection and introjection, are thus considered valuable processes, and together with information gained by listening and observing, form the basis on which technique rests. A syntonic countertransference is thus part of a more complex situation. Because the introject is of little

use at the time, it becomes negative, since it deflects the analyst from his aim of working at the level the patient has reached. It is relevant only to what is right under the surface and well defended by the patient. Conceiving analysis as including not only the unconscious content being resisted but also the resistances themselves, it can be asked why does the analyst have the experience? If through introjection an analyst gets indirect experience he often cannot understand, could it not be that he defends himself against the patient's own defences by knowing beforehand? Since he has no evidence of the source of his experiences, the conclusion I would draw is that he has ceased to listen to what his patient has been saying, because of his unconscious hostility to the defences that the patient seeks to communicate to him. In other words he treats the patient as if his defences do not exist. This illusion can lead to brilliant 'intuition', and the like that sometimes produce exciting results. It does not belong to analysis of the patient because the defences are ignored.

(Fordham 1974k, p. 276)

Theory of opposites: Jung thought that the complementary nature of opposites, that each required the other, was expressed within the psyche by an energy pattern, which he called 'enantiodromia', which meant 'a drive into its opposite'. Because of this idea the bringing together of the opposites can only ever be temporary. The theory of opposition is essential to Jung's model of the psyche. Energy, he thought, required two poles to run between, to create a tension that in its oscillations gave rise to consciousness and vitality. The dynamism created by the flow between the opposite poles is evidence of psychic health; being stuck at one end or the other, all good or all bad, or all intellect no body, of psychic disequilibrium and neurosis. He linked his theory to the idea of *compensation* (q.v.). Essentially if there was too great a flow of libido in one direction then it would be likely to reverse. So, for instance, a 'perfect mother' is likely to become a 'bad' mother at some point and the purpose of this is to allow the aggression within the child to find expression in a necessary way.

Theory of types: habitual ways of responding denote personality types. Jung organized his delineation of the characteristics of types (a) by attitude, whether they were more introverted or extroverted; and (b) by function, whether they favoured thinking or sensation, feeling or intuition. The possible combinations of functions and types, which contain opposites, further elaborated his model of psychic functioning. Thinking, by which Jung meant the use of those processes which gave meaning and understanding to experience, is the opposite of feeling, which gives value and weighs experience. These two are considered rational. Sensation consists of perceptions made through the senses; and intuition is the word Jung used to describe perception via the unconscious. These two are irrational. Combinations of these functions and attitude preferences give rise to personality types which have dominant and inferior functions and attitudes. Jung stressed the importance of paying attention to the inferior functions and attitude preferences within the psyche when related to the compensatory nature of intra-psychic regulation. If unattached to aspects of the personality and pushed into unconsciousness they can acquire great destructive potency.

Transcendent or symbolic function: 'refers to that process which links the conscious to the unconscious and the strange to the familiar; its form is intimately relevant to its content. It is characterised by the "as-if" attitude and so facilitates the experience of representation, not identification; consequently it involves the recognition of similarities in objects that are, at the same time, known to be separate and distinct. This then enables men to relate to unobservable realities in terms of observable phenomena and so mediate the experience of the world as having meaning and significance' (Gordon 1978). Jung described it as follows: 'When there is full parity of the opposites, attested by the ego's absolute participation in both, this necessarily leads to a suspension of the will, for the will can no longer operate when every motive has an equally strong counter motive. Since life cannot tolerate a standstill, a damming up of vital energy results, and this would lead to an insupportable condition did not the tension of the opposites produce a new, uniting function that transcends them' (*CW* 6, para. 824).

Transference: is that relationship in which the perception and the experience one person has of another is determined primarily, not by the reality and characteristics of that other person, but by the inner situation of the percipient – by his experiences, expectations, complexes, fantasies, feelings, etc. Transference is the result of the projection of unintegrated parts; since projection is an unconscious process these parts are on the whole unconscious, repressed or split off from consciousness. 'The transference phenomenon is an inevitable feature of every thorough analysis, for it is imperative that the doctor should get into the closest possible touch with the patient's line of psychological development' (Jung, quoted in Gordon 1978).

Vertex: this term entered the analytic literature through the writings of the psychoanalyst W. Bion (see Hinshelwood [1991] for a summary of his achievements). Bion described the different points of view of thinkers about, critics of, and contributors to psychoanalysis as having their own particular vertices. A vertex might be sociological, religious, mythological, developmental and so on, and the purpose of describing a person's point of view, or angle of approach, in this way was to facilitate communication such that he hoped that the different points of view might be able to be reconciled.

Chronology

Michael Scott Montague Fordham

1905:   Born 4 August at 1 Tor Gardens, London W8; father Montague
           Edward, mother Sara Gertrude. Youngest of three children;
           brother, Christopher, born 1899, sister, Thea, born 1897.

1909:   Moved to Limpsfield, Surrey, then to Berryfield Cottage on
           the South Downs.

1910:   Moved to Hillcroft Steep, Hampshire.

1916–19:   Emsworth Preparatory School. During the First World War
           his father worked for the Ministry of Labour and the family
           moved back into London.

1919:   Passed the interview for Royal Navy Officer Cadet training
           at Osborn, one of 30 out of 300 applicants. Failed written
           examination.

1919:   Family bought 40 Well Walk, Hampstead.

1919–24:   Greshams.

1920:   Mother died from an asthma attack on a family holiday in
           Brittany.

1924:   Trinity College, Cambridge. Having passed his first MB at
           school he studied for the first part of the natural sciences Tripos
           and second MB. Once there he won a senior exhibition.

1926:   After only two years got a 2:1 degree in the first part of the
           natural sciences Tripos and took his second MB.

1927–31:   St Bartholomew's Hospital Medical School. Awarded the
           Schuter scholarship in Physiology and Anatomy with a mark
           of 98/100 in the physiology examination.

1928:   Married Molly Swabey.

1931–2:   Bch, MB, MRCP. House Physician

1932–3:   Junior House Officer, Longrove Mental Hospital, Epsom,
           Surrey.

1933:   Meeting with Dr Godwin Baynes in Zurich. Beginning of interest in Jung's work. First analysis with Dr Baynes (duration seven months). Birth of Max, Fordham's son, in June.

1934:   Fellowship in Child Psychiatry at London Child Guidance Clinic, later part of the Tavistock Centre. Met Frieda Hoyle. First meeting with Jung in Zurich.

1935:   Made Chairman of the Analytical Psychology Club.

1935–6:   Second short period of analysis with Dr Baynes (duration four months).

1936:   Jung supports his change of analyst to Hilde Kirsch.

1936–9:   Commuting between London and Nottingham, working as a psychiatrist in child guidance in Nottingham, where Frieda Hoyle (later Fordham) worked as a social worker, and in London at Dr Strauss's Department at St Batholomew's Hospital.

1939:   Hilde Kirsch emigrates to USA. End of his analysis.

1940:   Divorce from Molly. Marriage to Frieda. Max and Molly to Jamaica to stay with Molly's brother to avoid the bombing of London.

1941:   Appointed Consultant, Nottingham, Sheffield and Chester-field Child Guidance Clinics.

1942:   Consultant psychiatrist for evacuee children in the Midlands. Death of Molly. Her ship was torpedoed returning to England.

1943:   Invited to come to London to help found what was to become the Society of Analytical Psychology.

1944:   Moved to 1 St Katherine's Precinct. *The Life of Childhood* published.

1945:   Beginning of his involvement with the Medical Section of the British Psychological Society. Friendship with the psychoanalyst John Rickman and the start of discussions between psychoanalysts and analytical psychologists in the forum of the British Psychological Society Medical Section.

1946:   Society of Analytical Psychology started. Appointed Consultant to the child guidance clinic of the West End Hospital for Nervous Diseases. Starts private practice and developing the training at the Society.

1947:   Jung asked Herbert Read to ask Fordham if he would agree to be the co-editor, with Read, of his *Collected Works*. Editing the *Collected Works*. Awarded an MD for *The Life of Childhood*.

1948:   Death of Montague Fordham.

1952:   First visit to America to meet William McGuire, executive editor of the *Collected Works* of C.G. Jung.

1955:   Beginning of *Journal of Analytical Psychology*.

1956:   First signs of dissent within the SAP between the Zurich-orientated analysts and the analysts whose loyalty was to the SAP training and practising methods.

1957:   *New Directions in Analytical Psychology* published.

1958:   *The Objective Psyche* published.

1961:   Death of Jung.

1962–3: Elected Chairman of the Psychotherapy Section of the Royal Medico Psychological Association, which later became the Royal College of Psychiatrists.

1969:   *Children as Individuals* (a substantially revised version of *The Life of Childhood*) published.

1971:   Founder FRCPsych.

1974:   Hon. Fellow of the British Psychological Society.

1976:   Zurich analysts form their own Society led by Gerhard Adler. *The Self and Autism* published. Start of infant obser- vation seminars at the SAP.

1981:   Major illness, nearly dies.

1984:   Visit to America. Move from St Katherine's Precinct.

1985:   *Explorations into the Self* published.

1986:   *Journal of Analytical Psychology* devoted to the contribution of Michael Fordham.

1988:   Death of Frieda.

1993:   Publication of memoir, *The Making of an Analyst*.

1994:   *Children as Individuals* reissued with revisions. *The Fenceless Field*, collection of papers edited by R. Hobdell, published.

1995:   *Analyst–Patient Interaction*, edited by S. Shamdasani, published.

Bibliography of the work
of Michael Fordham

(Compiled by Roger Hobdell)

1932

'Lumbar Puncture and the Subarachnoid Haemorrhage', *St Bartholomew's Hospital Journal*, December.

1937

(a) 'The Psychological Approach to Functional Disorders of Childhood', *St Bartholomew's Hospital Journal*, vol. XLIV, no. 5.
(b) 'What Parent and Teacher Expect of the Child Guidance Clinic', *The New Era*, vol. 18, no. 8.
(c) 'Are Parents or Children to Blame?', *The Psychologist*, August.
(d) 'How Children Learn to Grow Up', *The Psychologist*, September.
(e) 'Psychological Types in Children', *The Psychologist*, October.

1938

'Children and Fairy Stories', *The Psychologist*, January.

1939

'The Analysis of Children', Guild Lecture no. 4. London, Guild of Pastoral Psychology.

1942

(a) 'Jung's Psychology', letter to the *British Medical Journal*, 29 August.
(b) 'The Meaning of Children's Pictures', *Apropos*, no. 2.

1943

(a) 'Psychiatry of Children', letter to the Medical Officer.
(b) Contribution to the Proceedings of the Child Guidance Interclinic Conference, October. Published by the Provisional National Council for Mental Health.

1944

The Life of Childhood: A Contribution to Analytical Psychology, London, Kegan, Paul, Trench, Trubner. (Revised as *Children as Individuals*, 1969.)

1945

(a) 'The Analytical Approach to Mysticism', *Revue Suisse de Psychologie et de Psychologie appliquée*, vol. 4, nos 3–4. Reprinted as 'The Dark Night of the Soul', in *The Objective Psyche*, 1958.
(b) 'Discoverer of the Complex', *The Leader*.
(c) 'Professor C.G. Jung' (written in honour of his seventieth birthday), *British Journal of Medical Psychology*, vol. 20, no. 3. Revised and expanded as 'The Development and Status of Jung's Researches', in *The Objective Psyche*, 1958.

1946

(a) 'Psychology in the Child's Education', letters to the *British Medical Journal*, 13 and 27 July.
(b) 'A Comparative Study between the Effects of Analysis and Electrical Convulsive Therapy in a Case of Schizophrenia', *British Journal of Medical Psychology*, vol. 20.
(c) 'Analytical Psychology Applied to Children', *The Nervous Child*, vol. 5, no. 2. Revised and expanded as 'Child Analysis', in *New Developments in Analytical Psychology*, 1957.

1947

(a) 'Integration, Disintegration and Early Ego Development', *The Nervous Child*, vol. 6, no. 3. Incorporated into 'Some Observations of the Self and Ego in Childhood', in *New Developments in Analytical Psychology*, 1957.
(b) 'Physical Therapy of Mental Disorders', *British Medical Journal*, vol. 2, no. 72.
(c) 'Analytical Psychology and Religious Experience', Guild Lecture, no. 46, London Guild of Pastoral Psychology. Revised as 'Analytical Psychology and Religious Experience', in *The Objective Psyche*, 1958.
(d) 'Psychological Methods of Treatment', *The Medical Press*, vol. 217, no. 5634.
(e) 'The Modern Treatment of Behaviour Disorders in Childhood', *The Medical Press*, vol. 218, no. 5669.

1948

(a) 'Vom Seelenleben des Kindes', translation by H. Basch-Leichts of *The Life of Childhood*, Zurich, Rascher.
(b) 'C.G. Jung'. Observer Profiles, *Observer*.
(c) 'The Individual and Collective Psychology', *British Journal of Medical Psychology*, vol. 21, no. 2.

1949

(a) 'The Contribution of Analytical Psychology to Psychotherapy', contribution to a symposium on mental health, *British Medical Bulletin*, vol. 6, nos 1–2. Revised as 'Analytical Psychology and Psychotherapy', in *The Objective Psyche*, 1958.
(b) 'On the Reality of the Archetypes', contribution to a 'Discussion on Archetypes and Internal Objects', *British Journal of Medical Psychology*, vol. 22, nos 1 and 2. Developed into 'Biological Theory and the Concept of Archetypes', in *New Developments in Analytical Psychology*, 1957.

1951

(a) 'The Concept of the Objective Psyche', *British Journal of Medical Psychology*, vol. 14, no. 4. Reprinted in *The Objective Psyche*, 1958.

(b) 'Some Observations on the Self in Childhood', *British Journal of Medical Psychology*, vol. 24, no. 2. Material incorporated into chapter of the same name in *New Developments in Analytical Psychology*, 1957.

(c) Review of E. Ziman, *Jealousy in Children: A Guide for Parents*, *The Listener*, 29 March 1952.

1952

(a) 'Psychotherapy in Schizophrenia', *The Medical Press*, vol. 228, no. 26.

(b) 'Reflections on the Control and Discipline of Children', paper read to the Analytical Psychology Club of Los Angeles, 16 May (unpublished).

1953

(a) 'A Child Guidance Approach to Marriage', contribution to Clinical Studies in Marriage and the Family: A Symposium on Methods, *British Journal of Medical Psychology*, vol. 26, nos 3 and 4.

(b) Critical notice of Victor White, *God and the Unconscious*, and Pere Bruno (ed.), *Conflict and Light*, *British Journal of Medical Psychology*, vol. 26, nos 3 and 4.

1954

Review of L. Jackson, *Aggression and its Interpretation*, *The New Era*, vol. 35, no. 8.

1955

(a) 'Editorial Note', *Journal of Analytical Psychology*, vol. 1, no. 1.

(b) 'On Jung's Contribution to Social Psychiatry', *International Journal of Social Psychiatry*, vol. 1, no. 1.

(c) 'An Appreciation of "Answer to Job"', *British Journal of Medical Psychology*, vol. 28, no. 4.

(d) 'The Origins of the Ego in Childhood', in *Studien zur analytischen Psychologie C.G. Jung*, Zurich, Rascher. Translated by Bader and Hastern as 'Über die Entwicklung des Ichs in der Kindheit', in *Zeitschrift für analytische Psychologie*, vol. 2, no. 4, 1971. Reprinted in *New Developments in Analytical Psychology*, 1957.

(e) 'A Note on the Significance of Archetypes for the Transference in Childhood', *Acta Psychotherapeutica*, Supplementary volume 3, Basel and New York.

(f) 'Reflections on the Archetypes and Synchronicity', *Harvest*, no. 2.

1956

(a) 'Active Imagination and Imaginative Activity', *Journal of Analytical Psychology*, vol. 1, no. 2.

(b) Review of J. Goldbrunner, *Individuation: A Study of the Depth Psychology of C.G. Jung*, *Mental Health*, vol. 25, no. 3.

(c) 'The Evolution of Jung's Researches', *British Journal of Medical Psychology*, vol. 29, no. 1. Read to the British Psychological Society, 26 October, Jung's 80th birthday, as part of a symposium on Jung's contribution to analytical thought and practice.

(d) Obituary: Emma Jung. *Journal of Analytical Psychology*, vol. 1, no. 2.

1957

(a) *New Developments in Analytical Psychology*, foreword by C.G. Jung, London, Routledge & Kegan Paul.
(b) 'Reflections on Image and Symbol', *Journal of Analytical Psychology*, vol. 2, no. 1.
(c) Critical notice of M. Klein, P. Heimann, R. Money Kyrle (eds), *New Directions in Psycho-Analysis*, *Journal of Analytical Psychology*, vol. 2, no. 2.

1958

(a) *The Objective Psyche*, London, Routledge & Kegan Paul.
(b) Review of C.G. Jung, *The Transcendent Function*, *Journal of Analytical Psychology*, vol. 3, no. 1.
(c) Review of D. Richter (ed.), *Schizophrenia: Somatic Aspects*, *Journal of Analytical Psychology*, vol. 3, no. 1.
(d) 'Individuation and Ego Development', *Journal of Analytical Psychology*, vol. 3, no. 2.
(e) Critical notice of M. Klein, *Envy and Gratitude: A Study of Unconscious Sources*, *Journal of Analytical Psychology*, vol. 3, no. 2.

1959

(a) Critical notice of C.G. Jung, *The Undiscovered Self*, *Journal of Analytical Psychology*, vol. 4, no. 1.
(b) 'Dynamic Psychology and the Care of Patients', *The Medical Press*, vol. 242, no. 26.
(c) Review of E. Bertine, *Human Relationships*, *Journal of Analytical Psychology*, vol. 4, no. 2.

1960

(a) 'Countertransference', *British Journal of Medical Psychology*, vol. 33, no. 1. Reprinted in *Technique in Jungian Analysis*, Library of Analytical Psychology, vol. 2, 1974.
(b) 'A Case for the Razor', *Times Literary Supplement*, 12 February.
(c) Review of J. Jacobi, *Complex, Archetype and Symbol in the Psychology of C.G. Jung*, *Journal of Analytical Psychology*, vol. 5, no. 1.
(d) Review of L. Stein, *Loathsome Women*, *Journal of Analytical Psychology*, vol. 5, no. 1.
(e) Review of H.B. and A.C. English (eds), *A Comprehensive Dictionary of Psychological and Psychoanalytical Terms*, *Journal of Analytical Psychology*, vol. 5, no. 1.
(f) 'The Development of Analytical Psychology in Great Britain', *Harvest*, no. 6.
(g) 'Ego, Self and Mental Health', *British Journal of Medical Psychology*, vol. 33, no. 249.
(h) 'The Emergence of a Symbol in a Five Year Old Child', *Journal of Analytical Psychology*, vol. 5, no. 1.
(i) 'The Relevance of Analytical Theory to Alchemy, Mysticism, and Theology', *Journal of Analytical Psychology*, vol. 5, no. 2.

(j) Critical notice of D. Cox, *Jung and St Paul*, *Journal of Analytical Psychology*, vol. 5, no. 2.

1961

(a) 'Comment on the Theory of the Original Self', *Journal of Analytical Psychology*, vol. 6, no. 1.
(b) Obituary: Eva Metman, *Journal of Analytical Psychology*, vol. 6, no. 1.
(c) 'Psychotherapy and the Care of Patients: Out Patient Psychotherapy', symposium report, Department of Psychological Medicine, University of Edinburgh.
(d) Obituary: C.G Jung, *British Journal of Medical Psychology*, vol. 34, nos 3 and 4.
(e) 'Symposium on Training – Editorial Introduction', *Journal of Analytical Psychology*, vol. 6, no. 2.
(f) Review of J.M. Turner and Barbel Inhelder (eds), *Discussion on Child Development*, vol. 4, *Journal of Analytical Psychology*, vol. 6, no. 2.
(g) Review of W.M. Watt, *The Cure for Human Troubles*, *Journal of Analytical Psychology*, vol. 6, no. 2.
(h) Review of M. Capes (ed.), *Communication or Conflict*, *Journal of Analytical Psychology*, vol. 6, no. 2.
(i) 'Suggestions towards a Theory of Supervision', in a 'Symposium on Training' and a 'Reply to Dr Edinger', *Journal of Analytical Psychology*, vol. 6, no. 2.
(j) Obituary: M. Rosenthall, *Journal of Analytical Psychology*, vol. 6, no. 2.
(k) 'Analytic Observations on Patients Using Hallucinogenic Drugs', Proceedings of the quarterly meeting of the Royal Medico-Psychological Association.

1962

(a) 'The Self in Jung's Writings', Guild Lecture 117, Guild of Pastoral Psychology.
(b) 'An Evaluation of Jung's Work', Guild Lecture 119, Guild of Pastoral Psychology.
(c) 'The Theory of Archetypes as Applied to Child Development with Particular Reference to the Self', in G. Adler (ed.), *The Archetype* (Proceedings of the Second International Congress of Analytical Psychology), Basel and New York, Karger.
(d) 'Comment on James Hillman's Paper in the Symposium on Training', *Journal of Analytical Psychology*, vol. 7, no. 1.
(e) 'An Interpretation of Jung's Thesis about Synchronicity', *British Journal of Medical Psychology*, vol. 35, no. 3. Reprinted as ch. 9 of *Explorations into the Self*, Library of Analytical Psychology, vol. 7, London, Academic Press, 1985.
(f) Review of K.R. Eissler, *Leonardo da Vinci*, *Journal of Analytical Psychology*, vol. 7, no. 2.
(g) Obituary: F.M. Greenbaum, *Journal of Analytical Psychology*, vol. 7, no. 2.

1963

(a) 'The Empirical Foundation and Theories of the Self in Jung's Works', *Journal of Analytical Psychology*, vol. 8, no. 1. Reprinted in *Analytical Psychology: A Modern Science*, Library of Analytical Psychology, vol. 1, 1974.

(b) 'Editorial' for M. Fordham (ed.), *Contact with Jung*, London, Tavistock.
(c) 'Notes on the Transference and its Management in a Schizoid Child', *Journal of Child Psychotherapy*, vol. 1, no. 1.
(d) Review of A. des Lauriers, *The Experience of Reality in Childhood Schizophrenia*, *Journal of Analytical Psychology*, vol. 8, no. 2.
(e) Review of E. Lewis, *Children and their Religion*, *Journal of Analytical Psychology*, vol. 8, no. 2.
(f) 'Myths, Archetypes and Patterns of Childhood', *Harvest*, no. 9.

1964

(a) 'Psychology and the Supernatural', *New Society*, 75, 5 March.
(b) 'The Relation of the Ego to the Self', *British Journal of Medical Psychology*, vol. 37.
(c) 'The Ego and Self in Analytic Practice', *Journal of Psychology*, vol. 1, no. 1, Lahore, India, Government House.
(d) 'Note on Mr O'Regan's Poem from the Point of View of Analytical Psychology', in 'Visions: A Symposium', *Broadway*, vol. 19, no. 16 (*Westminster Hospital Gazette*).
(e) 'Well-motivated Parents: The Importance of the Environment in the Therapy of a Schizophrenic Child', *Journal of Analytical Psychology*, vol. 9, no. 2.
(f) Review of J.L. Henderson and M. Oakes, *The Wisdom of the Serpent*, *Journal of Analytical Psychology*, vol. 9, no. 2.
(g) Review of D.H. Malan, *A Study of Brief Psychotherapy*, *Journal of Analytical Psychology*, vol. 9, no. 2.

1965

(a) 'Editorial Note', *Journal of Analytical Psychology*, vol. 10, no. 1.
(b) 'The Self in Childhood' (Sixth International Congress of Psychotherapy 1964), *Psychotherapy and Psychosomatic Medicine*, vol. 13.
(c) 'Contribution à une théorie de l'autisme infantile', in *Psychiatrie de l'Enfant*, Paris, PUF. Revised for ch. 7 of *The Self and Autism*, 1976.
(d) Review of E. Jacobson, *The Self and Object World*, *International Journal of Psycho-Analysis*, vol. 46, no. 4.
(e) 'The Importance of Analysing Childhood for Assimilation of the Shadow', *Journal of Analytical Psychology*, vol. 10, no. 1. Reprinted in *Analytical Psychology: A Modern Science*, Library of Analytical Psychology, vol. 1, 1973.
(f) Review of D. Rosenthal (ed.), *The Genain Quadruplets: R.D. Laing, and A. Esterson, Sanity, Madness, and the Family*, vol. 1, *M. Rokeach, Three Christ's of Ypsilanti*, *Journal of Analytical Psychology*, vol. 10, no. 2.

1966

(a) 'Notes on the Psychotherapy of Infantile Autism', *British Journal of Medical Psychology*, vol. 39, no. 4.
(b) 'The Social and Psychological Relevance of Myths', *Clare Market Review*, London School of Economics.
(c) 'A Comment on "In Pursuit of First Principles" by L. Stein', *Journal of Analytical Psychology*, vol. 11, no. 1.
(d) Review of E.M. Harding, *The Parental Image: Its Injury and Reconstruction*, *Journal of Analytical Psychology*, vol. 11, no. 1.

(e) Review of J. Arlow and C. Brenner, *Psychoanalytic Concepts and the Structural Theory*, *Journal of Analytical Psychology*, vol. 11, no. 1.
(f) 'Is God Supernatural?', *Theology*, vol. 69, no. 555. Reprinted and amended in *Explorations into the Self*, Library of Analytical Psychology, vol. 7, London, Academic Press.

1967

(a) 'Editorial' (on experimental studies), *Journal of Analytical Psychology*, vol. 12, no. 1.
(b) 'Active Imagination – Deintegration or Disintegration?', *Journal of Analytical Psychology*, vol. 12, no. 1. Incorporated into ch. 14, *Jungian Psychotherapy*, 1978.
(c) Review of R. Litman (ed.), *Psychoanalysis in the Americas*, *Journal of Analytical Psychology*, vol. 12, no. 2.
(d) Review of W. Muensterberger and S. Axelrad, *The Psychoanalytic Study of Society 111*, *Journal of Analytical Psychology*, vol. 12, no. 1.
(e) Review of A.U. Vasavada, *Tripura-Rahasaya (Jnanakhanda)* (translated and with a study of the process of individuation), *Journal of Analytical Psychology*, vol. 12, no. 1.
(f) Review of E.H. Erickson, *Insight and Responsibility*, *Theology*, vol. 70, no. 561.
(g) Review of H. Kimball-Jones, *Towards a Christian Understanding of the Homosexual*, *Theology*, vol. 70, no. 570.

1968

(a) 'Psychiatry: Its Definition and its Practice', Guild Lecture 140, London Guild of Pastoral Psychology.
(b) 'Reflections on Training Analysis', in J.B. Wheelwright (ed.), *The Analytic Process: Aims, Analysis, Training*, New York, Putnam. Reprinted in the *Journal of Analytical Psychology*, vol. 15, no. 1.
(c) Review of D. Wyss, *Depth Psychology: A Critical History*, *British Journal of Social and Clinical Psychology*, February.
(d) Review of D. Morris, *The Naked Ape, and Primate Ethology*, *British Journal of Psychiatry*, vol. 114.
(e) Review of D. Meltzer, *The Psychoanalytic Process*, *Journal of Analytical Psychology*, vol. 13, no. 2.
(f) Review of B. Wolstein, *Theory of Psychoanalytic Therapy*, *Journal of Analytical Psychology*, vol. 13, no. 2.
(g) Review of J.L. Henderson, *Thresholds of Initiation*, *Journal of Analytical Psychology*, vol. 13, no. 2.
(h) Review of E. Bertine, *Jung's Contribution to our Time*, *Guardian*, 6 September.
(i) Obituary: Culver M. Barker, *Journal of Analytical Psychology*, vol. 13, no. 2.
(j) 'Individuation in Childhood', in J.B. Wheelwright (ed.), *The Reality of the Psyche*, New York, Putnam. Revised for ch. 4, *The Self and Autism*, 1976.

1969

(a) *Children as Individuals*, London, Hodder & Stoughton. Second, revised edn of *The Life of Childhood*, 1944.
(b) 'Theorie und Praxis der Kinderanalyse aus der Sicht der analytischen

Psychologie C.G. Jung', in G. Biermann (ed.), *Handbuch der Kinderpsychotherapie*, Munich and Basle, Reinhart.

(c) Obituary: Frances E. Smart, *Journal of Analytical Psychology*, vol. 14, no. 1.

(d) 'Technique and Counter-transference', *Journal of Analytical Psychology*, vol. 14, no. 2.

(e) Review of H. Racker, *Transference and Counter-transference*, *Journal of Analytical Psychology*, vol. 14, no. 2. Revised version published in *Technique in Jungian Analysis*, Library of Analytical Psychology, vol. 2.

(f) Review of B. Bettelheim, *The Empty Fortress*, *Journal of Analytical Psychology*, vol. 14, no. 2.

(g) Review of P. Roazen, *Freud: Political and Social Thought*, *Journal of Analytical Psychology*, vol. 14, no. 2.

1970

(a) 'Reflections on Training Analysis', *Journal of Analytical Psychology*, vol. 15, no. 1.

(b) Review of I. Maybaum, *Creation and Guilt*, *Theology*, vol. 73, no. 599.

(c) 'Note sul transfert', *Rivista di psicologia analitica*, vol. 1, no. 1. Ch. 4, *New Developments in Analytical Psychology*, trans. Aldo Carotenuto, 1957.

(d) 'Reply to Plaut's Comment', *Journal of Analytical Psychology*, vol. 15, no. 2.

(e) Review of C.A. Meier, *Ancient Incubation and Modern Psychotherapy*, *Journal of Analytical Psychology*, vol. 15, no. 2.

(f) Review of J. Hillman (ed.), *Timeless Documents of the Soul*, *Journal of Analytical Psychology*, vol. 15, no. 2.

(g) Review of J.M. Tanner and B. Inhelder (eds), *Discussions on Child Development*, *British Journal of Psychiatry*, vol. 117.

1971

(a) 'Editorial Notice', *Journal of Analytical Psychology*, vol. 16, no. 1.

(b) Review of A. Freud, H. Hartman *et al.*, *The Psycho-analytic Study of the Child*, vol. XXIV, *Journal of Analytical Psychology*, vol. 16, no. 1.

(c) 'Primary Self, Primary Narcissism, and Related Concepts', *Journal of Analytical Psychology*, vol. 16, no. 2. Published in translation in *Zeitschrift für analytische Psychologie*, vol. 3, no. 4, and revised for ch. 5, *The Self and Autism*, 1976.

(d) 'Reply to Comments' (on the above paper), *Journal of Analytical Psychology*, vol. 16, no. 2.

(e) 'Religious Experience in Childhood', in H. Kirsch (ed.), *The Well-tended Tree: Essays into the Spirit of our Time*, New York, Putnam. Revised for ch. 3, *The Self and Autism*, 1976.

1972

(a) Review of E. James (ed.), *The Child in his Family*, *British Journal of Psychiatry*, vol. 120.

(b) 'Il successo ed il fallimento della psicoterapia visto attraverso la sua falsa conclusiva', *Rivista di psicologia analitica*, vol. 3, no. 1.

(c) Critical notice of M.M. Mahler, *On Human Symbiosis and the Vicissitudes of Individuation*, vol. 1, *Infantile Psychosis*, *Journal of Analytical Psychology*, vol. 17, no. 2.

(d) 'Notes on Psychological Types', *Journal of Analytical Psychology*, vol. 17, no. 2.
(e) 'Tribute to D.W. Winnicott', *Scientific Bulletin of the British Psycho-analytical Society and Institute of Psycho-Analysis*, no. 57.
(f) 'The Interrelation between Patient and Therapist', *Journal of Analytical Psychology*, vol. 17, no. 2.
(g) 'A Theory of Maturation', in B.B. Woolman (ed.), *Handbook of Psychoanalysis*, New York, Van Nostrand Reinhold.

1973
(a) 'Rifflessioni sull'analisi infantile', *Rivista di psicologia analitica*, vol. 4, no. 2. Delivered at the Rome conference, 'Jung e la cultura Europea'. Also in *Enciclopedia*, 1974, Instituto della Enciclopedia Italiana. Both translations from the English original, 'Reflections on Child Analysis', revised for ch. 8, *The Self and Autism*, 1976.
(b) 'Editorial preface' to C.G. Jung, *Synchronicity*, Bollingen pbk edn.
(c) 'Maturation of the Self in Infancy', in *Analytical Psychology: A Modern Science*, Library of Analytical Psychology, vol. 1, 1974.
(d) Review of P. Lomas, *True and False Experience*, British Journal of Psychiatry, vol. 123.
(e) *Analytical Psychology: a Modern Science*, by M. Fordham, R. Gozdon, J. Hubback, K. Lambert and M. Williams (eds), London, Heineman Medical Books.

1974
(a) 'Jung's Conception of Transference', *Journal of Analytical Psychology*, vol. 19, no. 1.
(b) 'Family Interviews in a Child Guidance Setting', an abstract in the *Bulletin of the British Psychological Society*, vol. 27.
(c) 'Jungian Views of the Body–Mind Relationship', *Spring*. Reprinted in *Explorations into the Self*, Library of Analytical Psychology, vol. 7, Academic Press, 1985.
(d) 'Simbolismo nella prima e seconda infanzia', *Rivista de psicologia analitica*, vol. 5, no. 2.
(e) *Das Kind wie Individuum*, Munich and Basle, Ernst. Translation of *Children as Individuals*.
(f) 'Defences of the Self', *Journal of Analytical Psychology*, vol. 19, no. 2.
(g) Review of D. Meltzer, *Sexual States of Mind*, *Journal of Analytical Psychology*, vol. 19, no. 2.
(h) 'On Terminating Analysis', in *Technique in Jungian Analysis*, Library of Analytical Psychology, vol. 2, 1974.
(i) 'Notes on the Transference', in *Technique in Jungian Analysis*, Library of Analytical Psychology, vol. 2, 1974. First published in *New Developments in Analytical Psychology*, 1957.
(j) 'Ending Phase as an Indicator of the Success or Failure of Psychotherapy', in G. Adler (ed.), *Success and Failure in Analysis*, New York, Putnam for the C.G. Jung Foundation.
(k) 'Technique and Countertransference', in *Technique in Jungian Analysis*, Library of Analytical Psychology, vol. 2.

1975

(a) Review of W. McGuire (ed.), *The Freud–Jung Letters: The Correspondence between Sigmund Freud and C.G. Jung*, *Journal of Analytical Psychology*, vol. 20, no. 1.

(b) Letter to the Editor in reply to N.A. Trahms, *Journal of Analytical Psychology*, vol. 20, no. 1.

(c) 'On Interpretation', *Zeitschrift für analytische Psychologie*, vol. 7. Revised for ch. 12, *Jungian Psychotherapy*, 1978.

(d) 'Memories and Thoughts about C.G. Jung', *Journal of Analytical Psychology*, vol. 20, no. 2.

(e) Obituary: John Layard, *Journal of Analytical Psychology*, vol. 20, no. 2.

1976

(a) *The Self and Autism*, Library of Analytical Psychology, vol. 3, London, Academic Press.

(b) Obituary: R.F.C. Hull, *Journal of Analytical Psychology*, vol. 21, no.1.

(c) 'Discussion of T.B. Kirsch's "The Practice of Multiple Analysis in Analytical Psychology"', *Contemporary Psychoanalysis*, vol. 12, no. 2.

(d) 'Analytical Psychology', in Stephen Krauss (ed.), *Encyclopedic Handbook of Medical Psychology*, London, Butterworth.

1977

(a) Review of M. Mahler, F. Pine and A. Bergman, *The Psychological Birth of the Human Infant*, *Journal of Analytical Psychology*, vol. 22, no. 1.

(b) Obituary: E.A. Bennett, *The Lancet*, 2 April.

(c) 'Maturation of a Child within the Family', *Journal of Analytical Psychology*, vol. 22, no. 2.

(d) Letter to the Editor (on directed and undirected thinking, and the editing of the *Collected Works* of C.G. Jung), *Journal of Analytical Psychology*, vol. 22, no. 2.

(e) Review of D. Meltzer *et al.*, *Explorations in Autism – a Psychoanalytic Study*, *Journal of Analytical Psychology*, vol. 22, no. 2.

(f) 'A Possible Root of Active Imagination', *Journal of Analytical Psychology*, vol. 22, no. 4. Incorporated in ch. 14, *Jungian Psychotherapy*, 1978.

(g) 'Die analytische (komplex) Psychologie in England', in *Die Psychologie des 20. Jahrhunderts*, Zurich, Kinder Verlag. English translation in *Journal of Analytical Psychology*, vol. 24, no. 4.

1978

(a) *Jungian Psychotherapy: A Study in Analytical Psychology*, Chichester, John Wiley.

(b) 'Some Idiosyncratic Behaviour of Therapists', *Journal of Analytical Psychology*, vol. 23, no. 2. Incorporated as ch. 11, *Jungian Psychotherapy*.

(c) 'A Discursive Review' of R. Langs, *The Therapeutic Interaction*, *Journal of Analytical Psychology*, vol. 23, no. 2.

(d) 'Carl Gustav Jung', in *Enciclopedia*, Milan, Unedi.

(e) 'Comment on Clifford Scott's Paper', *Journal of Analytical Psychology*, vol. 23, no. 4.

(f) Review of D.W. Winnicott, *The Piggle*, *Journal of Analytical Psychology*, vol. 23, no. 4.

(g) 'Principia della psicoterapia analitica infantile', *Rivista di psicologia analitica*, vol. 9.

1979

(a) 'The Self as an Imaginative Construct', *Journal of Analytical Psychology*, vol. 24, no. 1.
(b) 'Analytical Psychology in England', *Journal of Analytical Psychology*, vol. 24, no. 4.
(c) 'Analytical Psychology and Counter-transference', *Contemporary Psychoanalysis*, vol. 15, no. 4. Also in L. Epstein and A.H. Feiner (eds), *Counter-transference: The Therapist's Contribution to Treatment*, New York, Jason Aronson.

1980

(a) Letter to the Editor (replying to G. Adler), *Journal of Analytical Psychology*, vol. 25, no. 2.
(b) Critical notice of D. Meltzer, *The Kleinian Development*, *Journal of Analytical Psychology*, vol. 25, no. 2.
(c) Review of W. McGuire, V. Kirsch *et al.* (eds), *The Shaman from Elko* (papers in honour of Joseph Henderson's 75th birthday), *Journal of Analytical Psychology*, vol. 25, no. 2.
(d) Review of J. Lacan, *The Four Fundamental Concepts of Psychoanalysis*, *British Journal of Psychiatry*, vol. 136.
(e) 'The Emergence of Child Analysis', *Journal of Analytical Psychology*, vol. 25, no. 4.
(f) 'Principles of Analytic Psychotherapy in Childhood', in I.F. Baker (ed.), *Methods of Treatment in Analytical Psychology*, Verlag Adolf Bonz GMBH, D-Fellbach.

1981

(a) 'Neumann and Childhood', *Journal of Analytical Psychology*, vol. 26, no. 2.
(b) 'Reply to Comment by K. Newton', *Journal of Analytical Psychology*, vol. 26, no. 2.
(c) Obituary: Jess C. Guthrie, *Journal of Analytical Psychology*, vol. 26, no. 2.

1982

(a) Contribution to a symposium, 'How Do I Assess Progress in Supervision?', *Journal of Analytical Psychology*, vol. 27, no. 2.
(b) Review of J.-B. Pontalis, *Frontiers in Psychoanalysis: Between the Dream and Psychic Pain*, *Journal of Analytical Psychology*, vol. 27, no. 2.
(c) Obituary: Bernice Rothwell, *Journal of Analytical Psychology*, vol. 27, no. 2.
(d) Obituary: John D Barrett, *Journal of Analytical Psychology*, vol. 27, no. 2.

1983

Letter to the Editor (on ego–self terminology), *Journal of Analytical Psychology*, vol. 28, no. 4.

1984

(a) Review of J. Klauber, *Difficulties in the Analytic Encounter*, *Journal of Analytical Psychology*, vol. 29, no. 1.

(b) Review of D. Meltzer, *Dream-Life: A Re-examination of Psychoanalytic Theory and Technique*, *Journal of Analytical Psychology*, vol. 29, no. 4.

1985

(a) *Explorations into the Self*, Library of Analytical Psychology, vol. 7, London, Academic Press.

(b) 'Abandonment in Infancy', *Chiron*, vol. 2, no. 1.

1987

(a) Obituary: Kenneth Lambert, *Journal of Analytical Psychology*, vol. 32, no. 2.

(b) 'Actions of the Self', in P. Young-Eisendrath and J. Hall (eds), *The Book of the Self*, New York University Press.

1988

(a) 'The Androgyne: Some Inconclusive Reflections on Sexual Perversions', *Journal of Analytical Psychology*, vol. 33, no. 3.

(b) 'Principles of Child Analysis', in M. Sidoli and M. Davies (eds), *Jungian Child Psychotherapy*, London, Karnac.

(c) 'Acting Out', in M. Sidoli and M. Davies (eds), *Jungian Child Psychotherapy*, London, Karnac.

(d) 'How I Do Analysis', in M.J. Spiegelman (ed.), *How I Do Analysis*, Phoenix, AZ, Falcon Press.

(e) 'In Discussion with Karl Figlio', *Free Associations*, vol. 12.

(f) 'The Infant's Reach', *Psychological Perspectives*, vol. 21.

(g) Review of C. Socarides, *The Pre-oedipal Origin and Psychoanalytic Therapy of Sexual Perversions*, *Journal of Analytical Psychology*, vol. 34, no. 2.

(h) 'Some Historical Reflections', *Journal of Analytical Psychology*, vol. 34, no. 3.

(i) Review of D. Meltzer, *The Apprehension of Beauty*, *Journal of Analytical Psychology*, vol. 34, no. 3.

1990

(a) 'Riflessioni sull maturazione nell'eta del lattante e nella prima infanzia', *Analisi: Rivista Internationale di Psicoterapia Clinica*, vol. 1, no. 2.

1991

(a) 'The Supposed Limits of Interpretation', *Journal of Analytical Psychology*, vol. 36, no. 2.

(b) 'Rejoinder to Nathan Schwartz Salant on "Vision, Interpretation, and the Interactive field"', *Journal of Analytical Psychology*, vol. 36, no. 3.

(c) 'Identification', unpublished. Revised version in 1994b.

1992

(a) 'Riflessioni personali sul observazione infantile', in *Obsservare il bambino: Revista di Psicologia Analitica*, no. 45.

1993

(a) 'Notes for the Formation of a Model of Infant Development', *Journal of Analytical Psychology*, vol. 38, no. 1.

(b) 'On Not Knowing Beforehand', *Journal of Analytical Psychology*, vol. 38, no. 2.
(c) Review of D. Meltzer, *The Claustrum: An Investigation of Claustrophobic Phenomena, Journal of Analytical Psychology*, vol. 38, no. 4.
(d) 'The Jung–Klein Hybrid', *Free Associations*, vol. 3, pt 4, no. 28.
(e) *The Making of an Analyst: A Memoir*, London, Free Association Books.

1994

(a) 'Ending Psychotherapy', *Group Analysis*, vol. 27.
(b) *Freud, Jung, Klein – The Fenceless Field: Essays on Psychoanalysis and Analytical Psychology* (ed. R. Hobdell), London, Routledge.
(c) *Children as Individuals*, 3rd edn, London, Free Association Books.

1995

Collected Papers on Technique, edited and introduced by S. Shamdasani, London, Routledge, in press.

General bibliography

Alvarez, A. (1992) *Live Company: Psychoanalytic Psychotherapy with Autistic, Borderline, Deprived and Abused Children*, London, Tavistock/Routledge.
Astor, J. (1990) 'The Emergence of Fordham's Model of Development', *Journal of Analytical Psychology (JAP)*, vol. 35, no. 3.
Bender, L. (1953) 'Childhood Schizophrenia', *Psychiatric Quarterly*, vol. 27.
Bettelheim, B. (1967) *The Empty Fortress*, New York, Free Press.
Bick, E. (1968) 'The Experience of the Skin in Early Object Relations', *International Journal of Psycho-Analysis (IJPA)*, vol. 49.
Bion, W. (1959) 'Attacks on Linking', *IJPA*, vol. 40.
—— (1962a) 'A Theory of Thinking', *IJPA*, vol. 43.
—— (1962b) *Learning from Experience*, London, Heinemann.
—— (1967) *Second Thoughts*, New York, Aronson.
—— (1970) *Attention and Interpretation*, London, Tavistock.
Buber, M. (1957) *Eclipse of God*, New York, Harper.
Call, J.D. (1964) 'New-born Approach Behaviour and Early Ego Development', *IJPA*, vol. 45.
Edelman, G. (1987) *Neural Darwinism: The Theory of Neuronal Group Selection*, New York, Basic Books.
Figlio, K. (1988) 'Michael Fordham in Discussion with Karl Figlio', *Free Associations*, vol. 12.
Freud, S. (1910) *Leonardo da Vinci, and a Memory of his Childhood*, in James Strachey (ed.) *The Standard Edition of the Complete Psychological Works of Sigmund Freud*, 24 vols, London, Hogarth 1953–73, vol. 11.
—— (1914) *On the History of the Psycho-Analytic Movement*, Standard Edition, vol. 14.
—— (1917) *Mourning and Melancholia*, Standard Edition, vol. 14.
—— (1921) *Group Psychology and the Analysis of the Ego*, Standard Edition, vol. 18.
The Freud–Jung Letters (1974) *The Correspondence between Sigmund Freud and C.G. Jung*, ed. William McGuire, London, Hogarth Press.
Gallard, M. (1994) 'Jung's Attitude during the Second World War in the Light of the Historical and Professional Context', *JAP*, vol. 39, no. 2.
Gordon, R. (1965) 'The Concept of Projective Identification', *JAP*, vol. 10, no. 2.

—— (1978) *Dying and Creating*, Library of Analytical Psychology, vol. 4.

—— (1985) 'Big Self and Little Self, Some Reflections', *JAP*, vol. 30, no. 3.

—— (1986) 'Individuation in the Developmental Process', *JAP*, vol. 31, no. 3.

Gregory, R.L. (1963) *Eye and Brain*, London and New York, Weidenfeld & Nicholson for World University Library.

Head, H. and Holmes, G. (1911) 'Sensory Disturbances from Cerebral Lesions', *Brain*, no. 34.

Henderson, J. (1975) 'C.G. Jung: A Reminiscent Picture of his Method', *JAP*, vol. 20, no. 2.

Hinshelwood, R. (1991) *A Dictionary of Kleinian Thought*, London, Free Association Books.

Hobdell, R. (ed.) (1995) *Freud, Jung, Klein – the Fenceless Field: Essays on Psychoanalysis and Analytical Psychology by Michael Fordham*, London, Routledge.

Hubback, J. (1986a) 'Fordham the Clinician as Seen in his Writings', *JAP*, vol. 31, no. 3.

—— (1986b) 'Frieda Fordham's Influence on Michael', *JAP*, vol. 31, no. 3.

James, W. (1902) *Varieties of Religious Experience*, London, Collins.

Joseph, B. (1989) *Psychic Equilibrium and Psychic Change*, London, Routledge.

Jung, C.G. (1957–79) *Collected Works* (*CW*), London, Routledge & Kegan Paul.

Volume 1, *Psychiatric Studies*.

Volume 2, *Experimental Researches*.

Volume 3, *The Psychogenesis of Mental Disease*.

Volume 4, *Freud and Psychoanalysis*.

Volume 5, *Symbols of Transformation*.

Volume 6, *Psychological Types*.

Volume 7, *Two Essays on Analytical Psychology*.

Volume 8, *The Structure and Dynamics of the Psyche*.

Volume 9, i, *The Archetypes and the Collective Unconscious*; ii, *Aion*.

Volume 10, *Civilization in Transition*.

Volume 11, *Psychology and Religion: East and West*.

Volume 12, *Psychology and Alchemy*.

Volume 13, *Alchemical Studies*.

Volume 14, *Mysterium Conjunctionis*.

Volume 15, *The Spirit in Man, Art and Literature*.

Volume 16, *The Practice of Psychotherapy*.

Volume 17, *The Development of Personality*.

Volume 18, *The Symbolic Life*.

Volume 19, *General Bibliography*.

Volume 20, *General Index*.

Supplementary Volume A, *The Zofinga Lectures*.

Seminar Papers, vol. 1, *Dream Analysis*.

—— (1963) *Memories, Dreams and Reflections*, London, Collins and Routledge Kegan.

—— (1973–6) *C.G. Jung Letters*, 2 vols, ed. G. Adler, London, Routledge.

—— (1978) *C.G. Jung Speaking, Interviews and Encounters*, ed. W. McGuire and R.F.C. Hull, London, Thames & Hudson.

Kanner, L. (1948) *Child Psychiatry*, Oxford, Blackwell.
Kant, I. (1934) *The Critique of Pure Reason*, London, Everyman.
Kellogg, R. (1969) *Analysing Children's Art*, Palo Alto, Mayfield.
Kerr, J. (1994) *A Most Dangerous Method: The Story of Jung, Freud, and Sabina Spielrein*, London, Sinclair Stevenson.
Kohut, H. (1977) *The Restoration of the Self*, New York, International Universities Press.
Klein, M. (1932) *The Psycho-Analysis of Children*, London, Hogarth.
—— (1946) 'Notes on Some Schizoid Mechanisms', in P. Heimann, S. Isaacs and J. Riviere (eds), *Developments in Psycho-Analysis*, London, Hogarth, 1952.
Laplanche, J. and Pontalis, J.-B. (1973) *The Language of Psychoanalysis*, London, Hogarth.
Little, M. (1957) 'R: The Analyst's Total Response', *IJPA*, vol. 38.
Lorenz, K. (1952) *King Solomon's Ring*, London, Methuen.
Meltzer, D. (1986a) 'The Analytical World: Institutions and Limitations', *JAP*, vol. 31, no. 3.
—— (1986b) 'The Conceptual Distinction between Projective Identification (Klein) and Container–Contained (Bion)', in *Studies in Extended Metapsychology*, Strath Tay, Clunie Press.
—— (1992) *The Claustrum*, Strath Tay, Clunie Press.
Meltzer, D., Bremner, J., Hoxter, S., Weddell, D. and Wittenberg, I. (1975) *Explorations in Autism*, Strath Tay, Clunie Press.
Naifeh, S. (1993) 'Experiencing the Self', review of M. Fordham, *Explorations into the Self*, *San Francisco Jung Institute Library Journal*, vol. 12, no. 1.
Neumann, E. (1973) *The Child*, London, Hodder & Stoughton.
Pauli, W. (1955) 'The Influence of Archetypal Ideas on the Scientific Theories of Kepler', in *The Interpretation of Nature and the Psyche*, London and New York, Bollinger Series LI.
Piaget, J. (1953) *The Origins of Intelligence in the Child*, London, International University Press.
Piontelli, Alessandra (1992) *From Fetus to Child: An Observational and Psychoanalytic Study*, London, Routledge, New Library of Psychoanalysis, vol. 15.
Plaut, A. (1956) *British Journal of Medical Psychology*, vol. 29.
Plotkin, H. (1991) 'The Testing of Evolutionary Epistemology', review of G. Edelman, *Neural Darwinism*, *Biology and Philosophy*, vol. 6.
Rosenfeld, H. (1983) 'Primitive Object Relations and Mechanisms', *IJPA*, vol. 64.
—— (1987) *Impasse and Interpretation*, London, Tavistock.
Rycroft, C. (1968) *A Critical Dictionary of Psychoanalysis*, London, Nelson.
St John of the Cross (1953) *Complete Works of St John of the Cross*, trans. E. Allison Peers, London, Watkins.
Samuels, A. (1985) *Jung and the Post-Jungians*, London, Routledge.
—— (1994) 'The Professionalization of Carl G. Jung's Analytical Psychology Clubs', *Journal of the History of the Behavioural Sciences*, vol. 30, no. 2.
Satinover, J. (1985) 'At the Mercy of Another: Abandonment and Restitution in Psychoses and Psychotic Character', *Chiron*.

Scott, R. D. (1956) 'Notes on the Body Image and Schema', *JAP*, vol. 1, no. 2.

Segal, H. (1983) 'Some Clinical Implications of Melanie Klein's Work', *IJPA*, vol. 64.

Shamdasani, S. (1995) Introduction to *Collected Papers on Technique*, by M. Fordham, London, Routledge.

Spiegelman, J. (1988) *Jungian Analysts: Their Visions and Vulnerabilities*, Phoenix, AZ, Falcon Press.

Steiner, J. (1993) *Psychic Retreats: Pathological Organizations in Psychotic, Neurotic, and Borderline Patients*, London, Routledge, New Library of Psychoanalysis, vol. 19.

Stern, D.S. (1985) *The Interpersonal World of the Infant*, New York, Basic Books.

Tustin, F. (1972) *Autism and Childhood Psychoses*, London, Hogarth.

—— (1994) 'The Perpetuation of an Error', *Journal of Child Psychotherapy*, vol. 20, no. 1.

Urban, E. (1994) Review of A. Alvarez, *Live Company: Psychoanalytic Psychotherapy with Autistic, Borderline, Deprived and Abused Children*, *JAP*, vol. 39, no. 2.

White, V. (1960) *Soul and Psyche: An Enquiry into the Relationship of Psychology and Religion*, London, Collins.

Williams, M. (1963) 'The Indivisibility of the Personal and the Collective Unconscious', *JAP*, vol. 8, no. 1.

Winnicott, D.W. (1964) Review of C.G. Jung, *Memories, Dreams and Reflections*, *IJPA*, vol. 45.

—— (1965) *The Maturational Processes and the Facilitating Environment*, London, Hogarth.

Zinkin, L. (1991) 'The Klein Connection in the London School: The Search for Origins', *JAP*, vol. 36, no. 1.

Index